# OUR LAND
### AND
# LAND POLICY

CALIFORNIA

SHOWING RAILROADS AND

RAILROAD LAND GRANTS

Scale of Miles.

# OUR LAND
## AND
# LAND POLICY

## SPEECHES, LECTURES, AND MISCELLANEOUS WRITINGS

By

Henry George

Edited by Kenneth C. Wenzer

Michigan State University Press

East Lansing

∞ The paper used in this publication meets the minimum requirements of
ANSI/NISO Z39.48–1992 (R 1997) (Permanence of Paper).

Michigan State University Press
East Lansing, Michigan 48823-5202

Printed and bound in the United States of America

04 03 02 01 00 99   1 2 3 4 5 6 7 8 9

Library of Congress Cataloging-in-Publication Data


George, Henry, 1839-1897.
    Our Land and Land Policy / by Henry George; edited by Kenneth C.
Wenzer.
        p. cm.
    Originally published: San Francisco : White & Bauer, 1871.
    Includes bibliographical references.
    ISBN 0-87013-522-8 (alk. paper)
    1. Public lands–United States. 2. Public lands–California. 3. Land tenure–
United States. I. Wenzer, Kenneth C., 1950–    II. Title

HD197 1871c 1999
333.1'0973–dc21

                                                                    99-049018


Book design by Michael J. Brooks
Cover design by Heidi Dailey

Visit Michigan State University Press on the World-Wide Web at:
www.msu.edu/unit/msupress

For

Evan and Jada

# CONTENTS

CONTENTS

# PREFATORY NOTE

This volume is made up of selections from the miscellaneous written and spoken utterances of Henry George not otherwise appearing in book form. It does not purport to contain all of this class of his productions. To make such a publication would require several volumes like this. The present volume is intended to contain only such speeches, lectures, sermons, essays and other writings as serve to exhibit Mr. George's varied powers of tongue and pen and set forth in many of its phases his philosophy of the natural order.

The most important matter in this collection is that with which it opens–"Our Land and Land Policy"–given to the public for the first time since its original limited publication in 1871, when its author was only locally known in San Francisco as a newspaper writer. It engaged, with other work, four months in the writing, and was Mr. George's first attempt to set forth the essentials of his philosophy. Of it he said long afterwards: "Something like a thousand copies were sold, but I saw that to command attention the work must be done more thoroughly." The work was done more thoroughly in "Progress and Poverty" eight years later. To that celebrated book "Our Land and Land Policy" bears the relation of acorn to oak. Mr. George towards the end of his life contemplated republishing the little work, believing that it might interest many whom the larger book would not at first reach. Death intervened between the plan and its carrying out. Mr. George thought of making such changes in "Our Land and Land Policy" as in his opinion would fit it more nearly to the present times, but as his was the only hand that could properly do this, it is here presented precisely as he published it in 1871.

Henry George, Jr.
New York, December, 1900.

Leo Nikolaevich Tolstoy and Henry George, Jr. at Yasnaya Polyana on June 5, 1909. Courtesy of Michael Curtis (Director, Henry George School, Philadelphia extension). Photography by David Wolfson, Tokoma Park, Md.

# PREFACE
## 1999 Edition

The untimely death of Henry George shocked his family. Correspondence from all corners of the globe expressed not only the predictable grief and commiseration, but also evinced a strong determination to continue the struggle for social justice by breaking up land and corporate monopolies. These monopolies strangled the better instincts of people, denied them opportunity for an equality ordained by natural laws, and mocked democracy. Henry George, Jr. (1862–1916), became his father's heir-apparent to the single-tax cause. Working under the strains of a personal loss and cherishing the memory of a loving parent, he carried on the fight, in part, by publishing his father's writings. The unfinished *The Science of Political Economy* of 1898 was the son's first tribute. The second was the biography *Henry George* two years later.

The third is this collection of essays and speeches collectively titled *Our Land and Land Policy* after its first piece. It was gathered together three years after his father's death and initially made its appearance in 1901, and then as part of George's collected works by Doubleday Page and Company in the first decade of the twentieth century. It has precipitously evaporated into virtual nonexistence: volumes are indeed a rare commodity.

The material in this book nearly spans the elder George's writing career and adds quite nicely to his published works extant. The speeches and articles merit consideration, for they reflect different aspects of this man's thinking for over two decades. *Our Land and Land Policy* was first put out in 1871 by White and Bauer of San Francisco. It should be carefully read, for it contains George's first known mention of what has come down as the single tax.[1] It is also his initial broadside against land monopolization and speculation as the sources of America's evils. *Our Land and Land Policy* is therefore a historically important document. At the time of the writing of this book, George was an apprentice economist. At this stage he accepted private property in land (in *Progress and Poverty* it is regarded as a common heritage) and taxes on luxury items. This first major endeavor bespeaks of an understanding of Nature, a desire for the betterment of people, and a concern for future generations. It is the fruit of "one of those experiences that make those who have had them feel thereafter that they can vaguely appreciate what mystics and poets have called the 'ecstatic vision.'"[2] George would remember that after a long horse ride, he stopped for a breath and had

> asked a passing teamster, for want of something better to say, what land was worth there. He pointed to some cows grazing off so far that they looked like mice and said: "I don't know exactly, but there is a man over there who will sell some land for a thousand dollars an acre." Like a flash it came upon me that here was the reason of advancing poverty with advancing wealth. With the growth of population, land grows in value, and the men who work it must pay more for the privilege. I turned back, amidst quiet thought, to the perception that then came to me and has been with me ever since.[3]

The younger George, describing this incident thirty years later, wrote in his own words:

> Yet there have arisen those in the history of the world who dreamed of a reign of justice and of the prolonged, if not indeed continuous life of the community. Such a dreamer was this Californian–this small, erect young man; with full, sandy beard; fresh, alert face; shining blue eyes; who, careless of dress, and wrapped in thought, rode a mustang pony about San Francisco. In the streets of the great Eastern city [New York] he had seen the want and suffering that accompany civilization. It had made him who came "from the open West sick at heart." He knew nothing of the schools, but this that he saw he could not believe was the natural order. What was that order? He vowed that he would find it. And afterwards as he rode in the Oakland foothills came the flash-like revelation–the monopoly of the land, the locking up of the storehouse of nature! There was the seat of the evil. He asked no one if he was right: he *knew* he was right. . . . He did not need to go to books or to consult the sages. There the thing lay plainly to view for any who would see.[4]

The son's reprinting of this first lengthy essay and the ten others that span the years 1871 to 1894 had given him the mandate of preserving his father's writing without alteration. The new edition presented here has continued this tradition. The notation by the two Georges appears at the end of each selection, and annotation for the present edition has been included at the end of the book.

No historian works in isolation, and a number of colleagues and close friends have been supportive. At the Henry George Foundation of America: Sharon Feinman. At the Robert Schalkenbach Foundation: Ted Gwartney, Nan Braman, Sonny Rivera, and Mark Sullivan. Besides their fine help, a timely grant from this organization enabled the completion of this work. Funding from the Lincoln Institute of Land Policy has also been of great assistance and so has Joan Youngman of this institution. Both Annette Tanner and Martha Bates of Michigan State University Press have been congenial coworkers. At McKeldin Library (University of Maryland, College Park): the two indispensable librarians Lily Griner and Patricia Heron. Dr. Thomas West of the history department of the Catholic University of America and Lorin Evans of Washington Apple Pi have also been helpful. My family, Oliver and Raisonique (my two cats), and Clio (my dog) cannot be done justice in type for their constant presence and love.

Neither can adequate words be expressed for the unceasing activity of Henry George, Jr. In June 1909 he set out for the Old World. A major object of his visit was to meet the greatest disciple of his father, Leo Nikolaevich Tolstoy, the famed Russian novelist. While on a train headed west across Russia the younger George was surprised to learn that soon after he sent a telegram to Tolstoy expressing his wish to see him, the news had flashed through every car and everyone started to treat him with deference.[5] A simple response to a request for a visit, sent by wire to his beloved teacher's son, reads: "I will be very glad to see you, I am waiting."[6] So glad was Tolstoy at this prospect that very day he penned an article titled "Concerning the Arrival of Henry George's Son" which appeared in Russian newspapers. On June 5 the younger George did spend a memorable day at Yasnaya Polyana. His article, "Tolstoy in the Twilight" recalls the visit.[7] Tolstoy

sat there in the chair, age seemed to have placed its hand heavily upon him; yet he appeared not so feeble as delicate. But the eyes revealed the keen, buoyant, spirit within. It was a life joyously spending itself to the very end, undaunted by the approach of death.

Before he spoke, Tolstoy gave me a deliberate, searching gaze, mixed with a peculiarly kind expression; and then, as if not displeased, offered a very cordial and personal welcome, during which I noticed my father's portrait holding a post of honour on the wall.

"Your father was my friend," he said with a singular sweetness and simplicity. . . .

I said I had heard that there was another book under way. Did it deal with political economy?

"No," he answered; "this is not on political economy. It treats of moral questions, which your father put first."

This led him to refer to an article on my father's teachings, for which my visit had served as text and which he had just sent off to a St. Petersburg newspaper. "Perhaps the paper will fear to print it, for we have little freedom here, and there is little discussion. But if that paper will not print it, then I hope to get it into another."

He handed me a copy of the article. It was in the Slavonic language [Russian]. When translated, I found the following passages which throw a strong light upon social, governmental, and revolutionary conditions in Russia today, as well as showing the vigour and hope of this wonderful old man's mind:

[I have just received a telegram from the son of Henry George expressing a desire to visit me. The thought of meeting the son of one of the most remarkable men of the 19th century keenly reminded me of everything done by him. But also of the stagnation which exists, not only in our Russian government but in every government of the so-called civilised world, in regard to the radical solution of all economic questions and which was already set forth so many years ago with such irresistible clearness and conviction by that great man.]

The land question revolves around the deliverance of mankind from slavery produced by its private ownership, which to my mind, is now in the same situation in which the questions of serfdom in Russia and slavery in America were in the days of my youth. The difference is only that while the injustice of private landownership is quite as flagrant as that of slave ownership, it is much more widely and deeply connected with all human relations. It extends to all parts of the world (slavery existed only in America and Russia) and is much more tormenting to the land slave than personal slavery. How strange, one might say how ridiculous, were they not so cruel, and did they not involve the suffering of the majority of the toiling masses, are those attempts at the reconstruction of society proposed and undertaken by the two inimical camps–the state and revolutionary.[8] Both do so through all kinds of measures, with the exception of that one which alone can destroy that crying injustice from which the overwhelming majority of the people suffer, which when driven inwards is still more dangerous than when it outwardly appears. All these efforts for the solution of political questions by new enactments without the destruction of private landownership, reminds one of the splendid comparison by Henry George, of all such enactments to the action of the fool, who having placed the whole of the burden on one of the two baskets that hung upon the donkey's back, filled the other with an equal weight of stones. . . .

I rejoice at the thought that, no matter how far may be the governmental and revolutionary workers from the reasonable solution of the land question, it nevertheless will be (and very soon) solved especially in Russia. It will not be done by those strange, groundless, arbitrary, unfeasible and, above all, unjust theories of expropriation, and the still more foolish state measures for the destruction of village communes and the establishment of small landownerships, that is, the strengthening and confirming of that system against which the struggle is to be directed.[9] But it will and must be solved in one way alone–by the recognition of the equal right of every man to live upon and be nourished by the land on which he was born–that same principle which is so invincibly proved by all the teachings of Henry George. I think thus, because the thought of the equal right of all men to the soil, notwithstanding all the efforts of "educated" people to drive that thought by all kinds of schemes of expropriation and the destruction of the village communes from the minds of the Russian people, nevertheless lives in the minds of the Russian people of today, and sooner or later–and I believe sooner–will be fully realised. . . .

In connection with this unqualified espousal of what he was pleased to call the "teachings of Henry George," my host directed that the translations of the George books into the Slavonic tongue be brought to him. They proved to be all of the principal books except "The Open Letter to the Pope" (obviously inappropriate for Russia where the Greek Church holds sway),[10] and the unfinished "Science of Political Economy." He also showed me a large number of the translated pamphlets and lectures–all in cheap form for popular circulation. The translator and populariser of the works is his intimate friend and neighbour, Sergei D. Nikolaev, who, he said, would come to the house in the evening.[11]

Tolstoy talked with the utmost fervour and enthusiasm of the truth of these books as if the matter was impersonal to me, and he suddenly tossed the rug off his feet and got out of his chair to go over to a table and write his name in some of the copies. . . .

While we stood there in his workroom I asked him for a portrait of himself, with his autograph. He immediately produced a picture from a cupboard, and sat down at a table to write on it.

"Would it be good English to say, 'With best love?'" he asked.

"It would be the English that honours most," I replied.

"I loved your father," he rejoined simply. And then, after a pause, during which he wrote his name on the picture, he said: "They arrest men here in Russia for circulating my books. I have written them asking why they arrest such men, who are blameless. Why not arrest the man who wrote the books? But they did not reply, and they do not arrest me."

Then he said, rising: "If you will not stay and sleep with us, I must urge you to go at once to catch your train."

And at the head of the stairway he stopped and took my hand, saying simply, "This is the last time I shall meet you. I shall see your father soon. Is there any commission you would have me take to him?"

For a moment I was lost in wonder at his meaning. But his eyes were quietly waiting for an answer.

"Tell him the work is going on," I replied.

# Our Land and Land Policy

## I. The Lands of the United States

### Extent of the Public Domain

According to the latest report of the Commissioner of the General Land Office, the public domain not yet disposed of amounted on the 30th of June, 1870, to 1,387,732,209 acres.[1]

These figures are truly enormous, and paraded as they always are whenever land enough for a small empire is asked for by some new railroad company, or it is proposed to vote away a few million acres to encourage steamship building, it is no wonder that they have a dazzling effect, and that our public lands should really seem "practically inexhaustible." For this vast area is more than eleven times as large as the great State of California; more than six times as large as the united area of the thirteen original States; three times as large as all Europe outside of Russia. Thirteen hundred and eighty-seven millions of acres! Room for thirteen million good-sized American farms; for two hundred million such farms as the peasants of France and Belgium consider themselves rich to own; or for four hundred million such tracts as constituted the patrimony of an ancient Roman! Yet when we come to look closely at the homestead possibilities expressed by these figures, their grandeur begins to melt away. In the first place, in these 1,387,732,209 acres are included the lands which have been granted, but not yet patented, to railroad and other corporations, which, counting the grants made at the last session, amount to about 200,000,000 acres in round numbers; in the next place, we must deduct the 369,000,000 acres of Alaska, for in all human probability it will be some hundreds if not some thousands of years before that Territory will be of much avail for agricultural purposes; in the third place, we must deduct the water surface of all the land States and Territories (exclusive of Alaska), which, taking as a basis the 5,000,000 acres of water surface contained in California, cannot be less than 80,000,000 acres, and probably largely exceeds that amount. Still further, we must deduct the amount which will be given under existing laws to the States yet to be erected, and which has been granted, or reserved for other purposes, which in the aggregate cannot fall short of 100,000,000 acres; leaving a net area of 650,000,000 acres–less than half the gross amount of public land as given by the Commissioner.

When we come to consider what this land is, the magnificence of our first conception is subject to still further curtailment. For it includes that portion of the United States which is of the least value for agricultural purposes. It includes the three greatest mountain chains of the continent, the dry elevated plains of the eastern slope of the Rocky Mountains and the arid alkali-cursed stretches of the great interior basin; and it includes, too, a great deal of land in the older land States which has been passed by the settler as worthless. Colorado, Wyoming, Utah, Nevada, Idaho, Montana, New Mexico, and Arizona, though having an abundance of natural wealth of another kind, probably contain less good land in proportion to their area than any other States or Territories of the Union, excepting Alaska.[2] They contain numerous valleys which with irrigation will produce heavy crops, and vast areas of good grazing lands which will make this section the great stock range of the Union; but the proportion of available agricultural land which they contain is very small.

Taking everything into consideration, and remembering that by the necessities of their construction the railroads follow the water courses and pass through the lowest valleys, and therefore get the best land, and that it is fair to presume that other grants also take the best, it is not too high an estimate to assume that, out of the 650,000,000 acres which we have seen are left to the United States, there are at least 200,000,000 acres which for agricultural or even for grazing purposes are absolutely worthless, and which if ever reclaimed will not be reclaimed until the pressure of population upon our lands is greater than is the present pressure of population upon the lands of Great Britain.

And, thus, the 1,387,732,209 acres which make such a showing in the Land Office Reports come down in round numbers to but 450,000,000 acres out of which farms can be carved, and even of this a great proportion consists of land which can be cultivated only by means of irrigation, and of land which is only useful for grazing.

This estimate is a high one. Mr. E. T. Peters, of the Statistical Bureau, estimates the absolutely worthless land at 241,000,000 acres.[3] Senator Stewart, in a recent speech, puts the land fit for homes at one third of the whole—332,000,000 acres by his figuring, as he makes no deductions except for Alaska and the Texas Pacific grant. Assuming his proportion to be correct, and admitting that the railroads, etc., take their proportion of the bad as well as of the good land, we would have, after making the proper deductions, but 216,000,000 acres of arable land yet left to the United States.

But taking it at 450,000,000 acres, our present population is in round numbers 40,000,000, and thus our "limitless domain," of which Congressmen talk so much when about to vote a few million acres of it away, after all amounts to but twelve acres per head of our present population.

## OUR COMING POPULATION

But let us look at those who are coming. The amount of our public land is but one factor; the number of those for whose use it will be needed is the other. Our population, as shown by the census of last year, is 38,307,399. In 1860 it was 31,443,321, giving an increase for the decade of 6,864,078, or of a fraction less than twenty-two per cent. Previous to this, each decade had shown a steady increase at the rate of thirty-five per cent., and this may be considered the rate of our normal growth. The war, with its losses and burdens, and the political, financial and industrial perturbations to which it gave rise, checked our growth during the last decade, but in that on which we have now entered, there is little doubt that the growth of the nation will resume its normal rate, to go on without retardation, unless by some such disturbing influence as that of our great Civil War, until the pressure of population begins to approximate to the pressure of population in the older countries.

Taking, then, this normal rate as the basis of our calculation, let us see what the increase of our population for the next fifty years will be:

| Our population will be in: | An increase in that decade of: |
|---|---|
| 1880 . . . . . . . . . . . . 51,714,989 | . . . . . . . . . . . . . . . . . . . . . 13,407,590 |
| 1890 . . . . . . . . . . . . 69,815,235 | . . . . . . . . . . . . . . . . . . . . . 18,100,246 |
| 1900 . . . . . . . . . . . . 94,250,567 | . . . . . . . . . . . . . . . . . . . . . 24,435,332 |
| 1910 . . . . . . . . . . . 127,238,267 | . . . . . . . . . . . . . . . . . . . . . 32,987,700 |
| 1920 . . . . . . . . . . 171,771,610 | . . . . . . . . . . . . . . . . . . . . . 44,533,593 |

This estimate is a low one. The best estimates heretofore made give us a population of from 100,000,000 to 115,000,000 in 1900, and from 185,000,000 to 200,000,000 in 1920, and there is little doubt that the Census of 1870, on which the calculation is based, does not show the true numbers of our people.[4] But it is best to be on the safe side, and the figures given are sufficiently imposing. In truth, it is difficult to appreciate, certainly impossible to overestimate, the tremendous significance of these figures when applied to the matter we are considering.

By 1880, the end of the present decade, our population will be thirteen millions and a half more than in 1870–that is to say, we shall have an addition to our population of more than twice as many people as are now living in all the States and Territories west of the Mississippi (including the whole of Louisiana), an addition in ten years of as many people as there were in the whole of the United States in 1832.

By 1890 we shall have added to our present population thirty-one and a half millions, an addition equal to the present population of the whole of Great Britain.

By the year 1900–twenty-nine years off–we shall have an addition of fifty-six millions of people; that is, we shall have doubled, and have increased eighteen millions beside.

By 1910, the end of the fourth decade, our increase over the population of 1870 will be *eighty-nine millions,* and by 1920 the increase will be nearly *one hundred and thirty-four millions;* that is to say, at the end of a half century from 1870 we shall have multiplied four and a half times, and the United States will then contain their present population plus another population half as large as the present population of the whole of Europe.

What becomes of our accustomed idea of the immensity of our public domain in the light of these sober facts? Does our 450,000,000 acres of available public land seem "practically inexhaustible" when we turn our faces towards the future, and hear in imagination, in the years that are almost on us, the steady tramp of the tens of millions, and of the hundreds of millions, who are coming?

Vast as this area is, it amounts to but thirty-three acres per head to the increased population which we will gain in the present decade; to but fourteen acres per head to the new population which we will have in twenty years; to but four acres per head of the additional population which we will have by the close of the century!

We need not carry the calculation any further. Our public domain will not last so long. In fact, if we go ahead, disposing of it at the rate we are now doing, it will not begin to last so long, and we may even count upon our ten fingers the years beyond which our public lands will be hardly worth speaking of.

Between the years 1800 and 1870 our population increased about thirty-three millions. During this increase of population, besides the disposal of vast tracts of wild lands held by the original States, the Government has disposed of some 650,000,000 acres of the public domain.[5] We have now some 450,000,000 acres of available land left, which, in the aggregate, is not of near as good a quality as that previously disposed of. The increase of population will amount to thirty-two millions in the next twenty years! Evidently, if we get rid of our remaining public land at the rate which we have been getting rid of it since the organisation of the General Land Office, it will be all gone some time before the year 1890, and no child born this year or last year, or even three years before that, can possibly get himself a homestead out of Uncle Sam's farm, unless he is willing to take a mountain-top or alkali patch, or to emigrate to Alaska.

But the rate at which we are disposing of our public lands is increasing more rapidly than the rate at which our population grows. Over 200,000,000 acres have been granted during the last ten years to railroads alone, while bills are now pending in Congress which call for about all there is left. And as our population increases, the public domain becomes less and less, and the prospective value of land greater and greater, so will the desire of speculators to get hold of land increase, and unless there is a radical change in our land policy, we may expect to see the public domain passing into private hands at a constantly increasing rate. When a thing is plenty, nobody wants it; when it begins to get scarce, there is a general rush for it.

It will be said: Even if the public domain does pass into private hands, there will be as much unoccupied land as there otherwise would be, and let our population increase as rapidly as it may, it will be a long time before there can be any real scarcity of land in the United States. This is very true. Before we become as populous as France or England, we must have a population, not of one hundred millions or two hundred millions, or even five hundred millions; but of *one thousand millions,* and even then, if it is properly divided and properly cultivated, we shall not have reached the limit of our land to support population. That limit is far, far off–so far in fact that we need give ourselves no more trouble about it than about the exhaustion of our coal measures. The danger that we have to fear, is not the overcrowding, but the monopolisation of our land–not that there will not be land enough to support all, but that land will be so high that the poor man cannot buy it. That time is not very far distant.

## THE PROSPECTIVE VALUE OF LAND

Some years ago an Ohio Senator* asserted that by the close of the century there would not be an acre of average land in the United States that would not be worth fifty dollars in gold.

Supposing that our present land policy is to be continued, if he was mistaken at all, it was in setting the time too far off.

Between the years 1810 and 1870, the increase in the population of the United States was no greater than it will be between the years 1870 and 1890. Coincident with this increase of population we have seen the value of land go up from nothing to from $20 to $150 per acre over a much larger area than our public domain now includes of good agricultural land.

And as soon as the public domain becomes nearly monopolised, land will go up with a rush. The Government, with its millions of acres of public land, has been the great bear in the land market. When it withdraws, the bulls will have it their own way. That there is land to be had for $2.50 per acre in Dakota lessens the value of New York farms. Because there is yet cheap land to be had in some parts of the State, land in the Santa Clara and Alameda [V]alleys is not worth as much.[6]

And in considering the prospective value of land in the United States, there are two other things to be kept in mind: First, that with our shiftless farming we are exhausting our land. That is, that year by year we require not only more land for an increased population, but more land for the same population. And, second, that the tendency of cheapened processes of manufacture is to increase the value of land.

---

* Benjamin F. Wade (1800–78) was a senator from Ohio who was a radical advocate of Reconstruction and the coauthor of the Wade-Davis Bill (containing harsh conditions relating to the postwar South), which was vetoed by Lincoln in 1864.

## LAND POLICY OF THE UNITED STATES

The best commentary upon our national land policy is the fact, stated by Senator Stewart, that of the 447,000,000 acres disposed of by the Government, not 100,000,000 have passed directly into the hands of cultivators. If we add to this amount the lands which have been granted, but not delivered, we have an aggregate of 650,000,000 acres disposed of to but 100,000,000 acres directly to cultivators–that is to say, six sevenths of the land have been put into the hands of people who did not want to use it themselves, but to make a profit (that is, to exact a tax) from those who do use it.

A generation hence our children will look with astonishment at the recklessness with which the public domain has been squandered. It will seem to them that we must have been mad. For certainly our whole land policy, with here and there a gleam of common sense shooting through it, seems to have been dictated by the desire to get rid of our lands as fast as possible. As the Commissioner of the General Land Office puts it, seemingly without consciousness of the sarcasm involved, "It has ever been the anxious desire of the Government to transmute its title to the soil into private ownership by the most speedy processes that could be devised."

In one sense our land dealings have been liberal enough. The Government has made nothing to speak of from its lands, for the receipts from sales have been not much more than sufficient to pay the cost of acquisition or extinguishment of Indian title, and the expenses of surveying and of the land office. But our liberality has been that of a prince who gives away a dukedom to gratify a whim, or lets at a nominal rent to a favoured Farmer-General the collection of taxes for a province.[7] We have been liberal, very liberal, to everybody but those who have a right to our liberality, and to every importunate beggar to whom we would have refused money we have given land–that is, we have given to him or to them the privilege of taxing the people who alone would put this land to any use.

So far as the Indians, on the one hand, and the English proprietaries of Crown grants, on the other, were concerned, the founders of the American Republic were clearly of the opinion that the land belongs to him who will use it; but farther than this they did not seem to inquire. In the early days of the Government the sale of wild lands was looked upon as a source from which abundant revenue might be drawn. Sales were at first made in tracts of not less than a quarter township, or nine square miles, to the highest bidder, at a minimum of $2 per acre, on long credits. It was not until 1820 that the minimum price was reduced to $1.25 cash, and the Government condescended to retail in tracts of 160 acres. And it was not until 1841, sixty-five years after the Declaration of Independence, that the right of pre-emption was given to settlers upon surveyed land. In 1862 this right was extended to unsurveyed land. And in the same year, 1862, the right of every citizen to land, upon the sole condition of cultivating it, was first recognised by the passage of the Homestead law, which gives to the settler, after five years' occupancy and the payment of $22 in fees, 160 acres of minimum ($1.25) or 80 acres of double-minimum ($2.50) land.[8]

Still further in the right direction did the zeal of Congress for the newly enfranchised slaves carry it in 1866, when all the public lands in the five Southern land States—Alabama, Mississippi, Louisiana, Florida, and Arkansas—were reserved for homestead entry.*

But this growing liberality to the settler has been accompanied by a still more rapidly growing liberality to speculators and corporations, and since the pre-emption and homestead laws were passed, land monopolisation has gone on at a faster rate than ever. Without dwelling on the special means, such as the exercise of the treaty-making power, by which large tracts of land in some of the Western States have been given to railroad corporations and individuals for a few cents per acre, let us look at the general methods by which the monopolisation of Government land has been and is being accomplished.

## PUBLIC SALE AND PRIVATE ENTRY

The first method adopted for the disposal of public lands was their sale to the highest bidder. This theory has never been abandoned. After lands have been surveyed, they may, at any time, be ordered to be offered at public sale. This public sale is only a matter of form, purchasers at more than the minimum price seldom or never appearing. But the offering makes an important difference in the disposition of the lands. Before being offered at public sale they are open only to pre-emption and

---

* This reservation has been broken through by the passage of the Southern Pacific Railroad bill, which gives 5,000,000 acres to a branch road in Louisiana, which would be sure to be constructed without any aid.

homestead entry–that is, to actual settlers, in tracts not exceeding 160 acres. After being offered, they are open to private entry–that is, they may be purchased by any one in any amount, at the minimum price, $1.25 per acre.

Whether by the misrepresentations of speculators or the inadvertence of the authorities, public sales, as a general thing, have been ordered before the line of settlement had fairly reached the land, and thus the speculator has been able to keep in advance, picking out the choice lands in quantities to retail at a largely advanced price, or to hold back from improvement for years.

By means of cabins built on wheels or at the intersection of quarter section lines, and false affidavits, a good deal of land grabbing has also been done under the pre-emption and homestead laws. More, however, in the Mississippi Valley States than elsewhere.

## DONATIONS OF PUBLIC LANDS

Thus land monopolisation has gone on in the ordinary course of our land dealings. But the extraordinary means which have done most to hasten it, have been the donations of land in immense bodies.

It is a trite saying that men are always disposed to be liberal with that which is not their own–a saying which has had exemplifications enough in the history of all our legislative bodies. But there is a check to the appropriation of money, in the taxation involved, which, if not felt by those who vote the money away, is felt by their constituents. Not so with appropriations of land. No extra taxation is caused, and the people at whose expense the appropriations are made–the settlers upon the land–have not yet appeared. And so Congress has always been extremely liberal in giving away the public lands on all pretexts, and its liberality has generally been sanctioned, or at least never seriously questioned by public opinion.

The donations of land by Congress have been to individuals, to States, and to corporations.

## THE BOUNTY LAND GRANTS

The grants to individuals consist chiefly of bounties to soldiers and sailors of the War of 1812 and the Mexican War, and amount to about 73,000,000 acres, for which transferable warrants were issued. Nearly all of this scrip passed into the hands of speculators, not one warrant in five hundred having been located by or for the original holder. It has been estimated that, on an average, the warrants did not yield the donees twenty-five cents per acre. But taking fifty cents as a basis, we are able to form an idea of the disproportion between the cost of the gift to the nation and the benefit to the soldiers. Leaving out of the calculation the few that have taken the land given them, we find that the Government gave up a revenue of $91,067,500, which it would have received from the sale of the land at $1.25 per acre, in order to give the soldiers $36,427,000, or, in other words, every dollar the soldiers got cost the nation $2.50! Nor does this tell the whole story. Though some of this scrip was located by settlers who purchased it from brokers at an advance on the price paid soldiers, most of it has been located by speculators who, with the same capital, have been enabled to monopolise much more land than they could otherwise have monopolised, and to monopolise land even before it was offered at public sale. If we estimate the advance which settlers have had to pay in consequence of this speculation at $2 per acre for the amount of transferred scrip, we have a tax upon settlers of $145,708,000, which, added to the loss of the Government, gives a total of $236,775,500, given by the Government and exacted from settlers in order to give the soldiers $36,427,000! And yet the story is not told. To get at the true cost of this comparatively insignificant gift, we should also have to estimate the loss caused by dispersion—by the widening of the distance between producer and consumer—which the land speculation, resulting from the issue of bounty warrants, has caused. But here figures fail us.

## GRANTS TO STATES

The donations of land by the general Government to individual States have been large. Besides special donations to particular States, the general donations are 500,000 acres for internal improvements, ten sections for public buildings, seventy-two sections for seminaries, two sections in each township (or 1-18th) for common schools, and all the swamp and overflowed lands, for purposes of reclamation. These grants have been made to the States which contain public land, of land within their borders. In addition, all the States have been given 30,000 acres for each of their Senators and Representatives, for the establishment of agricultural colleges.

If land is to be sold, it is certainly more just that the proceeds should go to the States in which it is located than to the general Government, and the purposes for which these grants have been made are of the best. Yet judging from the standpoint of a right land policy, which would give the settler his land at the mere cost of surveying and book-keeping, even in theory, they are bad. For why should the cost of public buildings, or even of public education, be saddled upon the men who are just making themselves farms, who, as a class, have the least capital, and to whom their capital is of the most importance?

But whether right or wrong in theory, in practice, like the military bounties, these grants have proved of but little benefit to the States in comparison with their cost to the nation and to settlers. As a general rule they have been squandered by the States, and their principal effect has been to aid in the monopolisation of land. How true this is will be seen more clearly when we come to look at the land policy of the State of California.

## THE AGRICULTURAL COLLEGE GRANT

The Agricultural College grant was made in 1862, and has since been extended as the Representatives of other States have been admitted.[9] It aggregates 9,510,000 acres, and if extended to the Territories as they come in, will take at least 11,000,000 acres. This grant differs from the other State grants in this: that it is given to all States, whether they contain public land or not; those in which there is no public land being permitted to take their land in other States which do contain it. This feature makes this grant, in theory at least, the very worst of the grants, for it throws upon the settlers in new and poor States the burden of supporting colleges not merely for their own State but for other and far richer States.

For instance, the State of New York, the most populous and wealthy member of the Union, receives 990,000 acres, which must all be located in the poor far-Western States. Thus to this old and rich State is given the power of taxing the settlers upon nearly a million acres in far-off and poor States for the maintenance of a college which she is far more able to support than they are. If New York has located this land well, and retains it (as I believe is the intention), in a very few years she will be able to rent it for one fourth or even one third of the crop. That is, for the support of one of her own institutions, New York will be privileged to tax 50,000 people, fifteen hundred or two thousand miles away, to the amount of one fourth or one third of their gross earnings. And as time passes, and population becomes denser, and land more valuable, the number of people thus taxed will increase and the tax become larger. The Cornell University, to which the New York grant has been made over, is a noble and beneficent institution; but will any one say that it is just to throw the burden of its support upon the labouring classes of far-off States?

The same thing is true of all the old and rich States which are thus given the right to tax the producers of new and poorer States. That most of these States have sold this right to speculators at rates ranging from 37 $^1/_2$ to 80 cents per acre, only makes the matter worse.

But perhaps this injustice is even more evident in the case of those Southern States which do contain public land. The public land of Texas (of which there are some 80,000,000 acres left) belongs to the State; that in the other Southern land States was reserved for homestead entry by the Act of 1866.[10] These States get the same amount of land under this grant as the others; but none of it is taken from their own lands, and their college scrip is now being plastered over the public lands in California and the Northwest, much of it being located here.

California gets 150,000 acres under the Act. Yet, besides this, there have been located here up to June of last year more than 750,000 acres of the land scrip of other States, and large amounts have since been located or are here ready for location as soon as immigration sets in. This scrip brought to the States to which it was issued an average of, probably, 50 cents per acre. What the giving of this paltry donation has cost us we know too well. A great deal of the land thus located at a cost to the speculator of 50 cents per acre has been sold to settlers at prices ranging from $5 to $10 per acre, much of it is held for higher prices than can now be obtained; and a great deal of it is being rented for one fourth of the gross produce, the renter supplying all the labour and furnishing all the seed; while the land monopolisation, of which this agricultural scrip has been one of the causes, has turned back immigration from California, has made business of all kinds dull, and kept idle thousands of mechanics and producers who would gladly have been adding to the general wealth.

Badly as California has suffered, other States have suffered worse. Wisconsin is entitled to 210,000 acres; yet, up to June, 1870, 1,111,385 acres had been located in that State with agricultural scrip. Nebraska gets only 90,000 acres, yet the agricultural scrip locations in Nebraska up to the same time were nearly a million acres.

## RAILROAD GRANTS

Some four millions of acres have been donated for the construction of various wagon roads, and some four millions and a half for the construction of canals; but by far the largest grants have been to railroads– the amount given to these companies within the last ten years aggregating nearly one half as much as all the public lands disposed of in other ways since the formation of the Government.[11] This policy was not commenced until 1850, when six sections per mile, or in all 2,595,053 acres, were granted for the construction of the Illinois Central road. This donation was made to the State, and by it assigned to the company on condition of the payment to the State of seven per cent. of its gross receipts in lieu of taxation. This grant, which now seems so insignificant, was then regarded as princely, and so it was, as it has more than paid for the building and equipment of the road. The example being set, other grants of course followed. In 1862, a long leap ahead in the rapidity of the disposal of the public lands was taken in the passage of the first Pacific Railroad bill, giving directly, without the intervention of States, to the Union, Central and Kansas companies ten sections of land per mile (at that time the largest amount ever granted), and $16,000 per mile in bonds. In 1864 this grant was doubled, making it twenty sections or 12,800 acres per mile, and at the same time the bonded subsidy was trebled for the mountain districts and doubled for the interior basin while the Government first mortgage for the payment of the bonds was changed into a second mortgage.

But the disposition to give away lands kept on increasing, and the Northern and Southern Pacific getting no bonds, the land grant to them was again doubled–making it forty sections or 25,600 acres per mile, or, to speak exactly, twenty sections in the States and forty sections in the Territories. To these three Pacific roads alone have been given 150,000,000 acres in round numbers–more than is contained in all Germany, Holland and Belgium, with their population of over fifty millions–more land than that of any single European state except Russia. The largest single grant–and it is a grant unparalleled in the history of the world–is that to the Northern Pacific, which aggregates 58,000,000 acres. And besides this these roads get 400 feet right of way (which in the case of the Northern Pacific amounts to 100,000 acres), what land they want for depots, stations, etc., and the privilege of taking material from Government land, which means that they may cut all the timber they wish off Government sections, reserving that on their own. With these later grants has also been inaugurated the plan of setting aside a tract on each side of the grant in which the companies may make up any deficiency within the original limits by reason of settlement. Thus the grant to the Southern Pacific withdraws from settlement a belt of land sixty miles wide in California and one hundred miles wide in the Territories, and that to the Northern Pacific withdraws a belt one hundred and twenty miles wide from the western boundary of Minnesota to Puget Sound and the Columbia River.

Since the day when Esau sold his birthright for a mess of pottage we may search history in vain for any parallel to such concessions.[12] Munificence, we call it! Why, our common use of words leaves no term in the English tongue strong enough to express such reckless prodigality. Just think of it! 25,600 acres of land for the building of one mile of railroad—land enough to make 256 good-sized American farms; land enough to make 4,400 such farms as in Belgium support a family each in independence and comfort. And this given to a corporation, not for building a railroad for the Government or for the people, but for building a railroad for themselves; a railroad which they will own as absolutely as they will own the land—a railroad for the use of which both Government and people must pay as much as though they had given nothing for its construction.

### THE VALUE OF THESE GRANTS

If we look but a few years ahead, to the time when we shall begin to feel the pressure of a population of one hundred millions, the value of these enormous grants is simply incalculable. But their immediate value is greatly underestimated. Land was given to the first Pacific roads as though it had not and never would have any value. Money enough to build the roads and leave princely fortunes besides was placed in the hands of the companies, and the land was thrown in as a liberal grocer might throw an extra lump of sugar into the already falling scale. Yet it is already apparent that by far the most valuable part of these franchises are these land grants. The timber which the Central Pacific gets in the Sierras will of itself yield more than the cost of the whole road. In addition, it has large amounts of good agricultural lands in California and along the Nevada river bottoms, and millions of acres of the best grazing lands in the sage-brush plains of Nevada and Utah, while there are thousands of acres of its lands which will have enormous value from the coal, salt, iron, lead, copper and other minerals they contain. The Union Pacific lands in the Platte Valley have, so far as sold, yielded it an average of $5 per acre; and though it gets no timber to speak of, it has millions of acres which will soon be valuable for grazing, and for a long distance its route passes through the greatest coal and iron deposits of the continent, where much of its 12,600 acres per mile will in time be valued at thousands of dollars per acre.

Twenty years ago, when the Illinois Central received its grant, its lands were worth no more than those now given the Northern Pacific. Yet the lands sold by the Illinois Central have averaged over $12 per acre, and those yet remaining on hand are held at a still higher price. Counting at the company's price what is held, the grant has yielded over $30,000,000–much more than the cost of the road. If *six* sections per mile will do this in twenty years, what should *forty* sections per mile do?

The Directors of the Northern Pacific have themselves estimated their grant to be worth $10 per acre on the completion of the road. I think they rather under- than over-estimated it, and for an obvious reason. A true statement of the real value of the grant would tend to discredit the whole affair in the eyes of the cautious foreign capitalists, from whom the company seeks to borrow money, for they would not believe that any Government could be extravagant enough to make such a donation. But it must be remembered that the line of the Northern Pacific passes for nearly its whole length through as fine an agricultural country as that of Illinois; that its grant consists, in large part, of immensely valuable timber and mineral land, and that it will build up town after town, one of them at least a great commercial city, on its own soil.

Furthermore, for reasons before stated, the increase in the value of land during the next twenty years must be much greater than it has been in the last twenty years. Taking these things into consideration, is it too much to say that in twenty years from now the lands of the company will have sold for or will be worth an average of at least $20 per acre? At this rate the grant amounts to over *half a million dollars per mile,* or in the aggregate to the enormous sum of $1,160,000,000–a sum more than half the national debt. This donated absolutely to one corporation. And for what? For building a road which cannot cost more than eighty millions, and for building it for themselves!

No keener satire upon our land-grant policy could be written than that which is to be found in the published advertisement of this Northern Pacific Company. The Directors show that if they get an average of but $2 per acre for their land, they can pay the whole cost of building and equipping the road and have a surplus of some $20,000,000 left. That is to say, the Government might have built the road by merely raising the average price of the lands $1 per acre, and have made a profit by the operation, while it would then own the road, and could give or lease it to the company which would agree to charge the lowest rates. As it is, the Government has raised the price to settlers on one half the land $1.25 per acre; the other half it has given to the company to charge settlers just what it pleases; and then on this railroad which it has made the settlers pay for over and over again both Government and settlers must pay for transportation just as though the road had been built by private means.

## THE ARGUMENT FOR RAILROAD GRANTS

So plausible and so ably urged are the arguments for these grants, such general acceptance have they gained, and so seldom are they challenged (for the opposition which has been made has been rather against the extravagance than the theory of the grants) that it is worth while to consider them with some care.

The plea for railroad land grants is about this: By giving land to secure the building of railroads, we develop the country without expense, or at least at the expense of those who largely profit by the operation. The land which we give is useless as it is; the railroad makes it useful and valuable. The Government giving really nothing of present value, does not even deprive itself of that which it might receive in the future, for it is reimbursed for the selling price of the land it gives by doubling the price of the land it retains. The Government in fact acts like a sagacious individual, who having an unsaleable estate, gives half of it away to secure improvements which will enable him to sell the other half for as much as he at first asked for the whole. The settler is also the gainer, for land at $2.50 per acre with a railroad is worth more to him than land at $1.25 per acre without a railroad, and vast stretches of territory are opened to him to which he could not otherwise go for lack of means to transport his produce to market; while the country at large is greatly the gainer by the enormous wealth which railroads always create.

"Here are thousands of square miles of fertile land," cries an eloquent Senator, "the haunt of the bear, the buffalo and the wandering savage, but of no use whatever to civilised man, for there is no railroad to furnish cheap and quick communication with the rest of the world. Give away a few millions of these acres for the building of a railroad and all this land may be used. People will go there to settle, farms will be tilled and towns will arise, and these square miles, now worth nothing, will have a market and a taxable value, while their productions will stream across the continent, making your existing cities still greater and their people still richer; giving freight to your ships and work to your mills."

All this sounds very eloquent to the land-grant man who stands in the lobby waiting for the little bill to go through which is to make him a millionaire, and really convinces him that he is a benefactor of humanity, the Joshua of the hardy settler and the Moses of the downtrodden immigrant.[13] And backed up, as it is, by columns of figures showing the saving in railroad over wagon transportation, the rapidity of settlement where land grants have been already made, and the increase in the value of real estate, it sounds very plausible to those who have not anything like the reason to be as easily convinced as has the land-grant man. But will it bear the test of examination? Let us see:

In the first place it must be observed that the consideration for which we make these grants is purely one of time—to get railroads built before they would otherwise be built. No one will seriously pretend that without land grants railroads would never be built; all that can be claimed is that without grants they would not be built so soon—that is, until the prospective business would warrant the outlay. This is what we get, or rather expect to get, for we do not always get it. What do we give? We give land. That is, we give the company, in addition to the power of charging (practically what it pleases) for the carrying it does, the unlimited power of charging the people who are to settle upon one half the land for the privilege of settling there. If the Government loses nothing, it is because the settlers on one half of the land must pay double price to reimburse it, while the settlers on the other half must pay just what the company chooses to ask them.

Now, in the course of the settlement of this land there comes a time when there are enough settlers, together with the prospective increase of settlers, to warrant the building of a railroad without a land grant.

Admitting that the settlers who come upon the land before that time are gainers by the land grant in getting a railroad before they otherwise would,* it is evident that the settlers after that time are losers by the amount of the additional price which they must pay for their land, for *they* would have had a railroad anyhow.

And this point where the gain of settlers ceases, and the loss of settlers commences, is very much nearer the beginning of settlement–that is to say, there are fewer gainers and more losers, than might at first glance be supposed. For if there were no land grants at all, the land would be open to settlers as homesteads, or at $1.25 per acre, and therefore the number of actual settlers which would justify the construction of a non-land-grant railroad would be very much smaller than that which would suffice to furnish a land-grant railroad with a paying business, as the prospective increase during and upon the completion of the road would be very much greater.

* But as to this it must be remembered that the gain to the settler is not to be measured by the increased advantage which the railroad gives to the new land through which it is built, but by the difference in advantage which that land offers over the land on which he would otherwise have settled. Thus we cannot estimate the gain from the building of the Northern Pacific road to the people now settling along its route in Minnesota and Dakota by the saving in the cost of transportation the produce of that land; for had the road not been projected, they would not have settled there, but would have settled in Iowa or Nebraska, where railroads are already built; and thus the gain they derive from the building of the Northern Pacific is not to be measured by the increased advantage which the railroad gives for the cultivation of the land on which they are settling, but by the advantage which the railroad gives that land over land in Iowa or Nebraska, on which they would otherwise have settled.

At first look, it would appear that all the people who go where a new railroad is built must gain something that they could not gain elsewhere, as otherwise they would not go there. This is doubtless true as regards such gain as inures to the individual without regard to other individuals, but not always true as regards such individual gain as is also a gain to the community. For some part of the population which accompanies the building of a railroad through an unsettled country comes to minister to the needs and desires of those who build it, and is merely to be regarded as an appendage of the building force, and with many of the others the expectation of advantage is prospective and speculative. They settle in the new country which the road is opening up, not because their labour will yield them a larger return than in other places to which they might go, but because they can get choice locations or a larger amount of land, which population afterwards to come will make valuable. That is, the gain which they expect is not from the increased productiveness of their own labour, but from the appropriation of some portion of other people's labour—and is not a gain to the community, though it may be a loss.

So therefore, when, by giving a land grant, we get a railroad to pre-
cede settlement, if the first settlers gain at all, the others lose. The gain
of the first is lessened by their having to pay double price for their lands;
the loss of the others is mitigated by no gain. So that, as far as settlers
are concerned, we are sacrificing the future for the present; we are taxing the many for the very questionable benefit of the few. And even in
the case of the gainers, their first advantage, in having a railroad before
its natural time, is offset by the subsequent retardation of settlement in
their neighbourhood which the land grant causes.

For if the first effect of the land grant is to hasten settlement by getting
a railroad built, its second effect is to retard it by enhancing the price of
lands. Illinois, where the first railroad land grant was made, may in a
year or two after have had more people, but for years back her population has certainly been less because of it. For nearly half a million acres–
one fifth of this grant–remained unoccupied in 1870, the company
holding it at an average price of $13 per acre. If this land could have been
had for $1.25 per acre, it would have been occupied years ago. This is the
case wherever land grants have been made, and long before the
Territories, in which we are now giving away 25,000 acres per mile for
the building of railroads, are one tenth settled, we will be asked to give
away like amounts of other unappropriated territory (if there is any by
that time left) in order to furnish "cheap homes to the settlers!"

Considering *all* the people who are to come upon our now unoccupied lands, weighing the near future with the present, is it not evident
that the policy of land grants is a most ruinous one even in theory–even
when we get by it that which we bargain to get? Let us see how it affects
the community at large in the present.

Where a land grant is necessary to induce the building of a road, it is
because the enterprise itself will not pay–that is to say, at least, that it
will not yield as large a return for the investment as the same amount
of capital would yield if invested somewhere else. The land grant is a
subsidy which we give to the investors to make up this loss.

Is it not too plain for argument, that where capital is invested in a less
remunerative enterprise than it otherwise would be, there is a loss to the
whole community? Whether that loss is made up to the individuals by a
subsidy or not, only affects the distribution of the loss among individuals–
the loss to the community, which includes all its individuals, is the same.

But it will be said: Though this may be true so far as the direct
returns of the railroad are concerned, there are other advantages from

railroad building besides the receipts from fares and freights. The owners of the land through which the road passes, the producer and the consumer of the freight which it carries, and the passenger who rides upon it, are all benefited to an amount far exceeding the sums paid as fares and freight. When we give a land grant, we merely give the railroad company a share in these *diffused* profits, which will make up to it the loss which would accrue were it confined to its legitimate share. Thus: Here is a railroad, the business of which would not pay for building it for five years yet. The loss to the unsubsidised company which would build it now and run it for five years would be $10,000,000. But the gain to landowners and others would be $100,000,000. Now, if by a land grant or otherwise, we secure to the railroad company a share of this collateral gain, amounting to $20,000,000, the railroad company will make a profit of $10,000,000, instead of a loss of $10,000,000, by building the road, and others would make a profit of $80,000,000.

But it must be remembered that every productive enterprise, besides its return to those who undertake it, yields collateral advantages to others. It is the law of the universe—each for all, and all for each. If a man only plant a fruit tree, *his* gain is that he gathers its fruit in its time and its season. But in addition to his gain, there is a gain to the whole community in the increased supply of fruit, and in the beneficial effect of the tree upon the climate. If he build a factory, besides his own profit he furnishes others with employment and with profit; he adds to the value of the surrounding property. And if he build a railroad, whether it be here or there, there are diffused benefits, besides the direct benefit to himself from its receipts.

Now, as a general rule, is it not safe to assume that the direct profits of any enterprise are the test of its *diffused* profits? For instance: It will pay to put up an ice-making machine rather in New Orleans than in Bangor. Why? *Because* more people in New Orleans need ice, and they need it more than those in Bangor. The individual profit will be greater, *because* the general profit will be greater. It will pay capitalists better to build a railroad between San Francisco and Santa Cruz than it will to build a like railroad in Washington Territory.[14] Why? Because there are more people who will ride, and more freight to be carried, on the one than on the other. And as the diffused benefit of a railroad can only inure from the carrying of passengers and freight, is it not evident that the diffused benefit is greater in the one case than in the other, just in proportion as the direct benefit is greater?

In the second place, in any particular case in which we have to offer a subsidy to get a railroad built, the question is not, shall we have this railroad or nothing?—but, shall we have this road in preference to something else?—for the investment of capital in one enterprise prevents its investment in another. No legislative act, no issue of bonds, no grant of lands, can create capital. Capital, so to speak, is stored-up labour, and only labour can create it. The available capital of the United States at any given time is but a given quantity. It may be invested here or it may be invested there, but it is only here *or* there that it can be invested. Nor is there any illimitable supply abroad to borrow from. The amount of foreign capital seeking investment in the United States is about so much each year; and if by increasing our offers we get any more, we must pay more, not merely for the increased amount which we get, but for all which we get.

To recur, now, to our former example: Here is a railroad through an unsettled country, which to build now would, relying upon its direct receipts, entail a loss of $10,000,000, the diffused benefits of which may be estimated at $100,000,000. Here is another railroad which it would take the same capital to build, which, in the same time, would yield a direct profit of $5,000,000, and the diffused benefits of which it is fair to presume might be expressed by $300,000,000. Now if we offer to the builders of the first road a land grant which will enable them to obtain one fifth of the diffused benefits of the road, we could induce them to build that road rather than the other, for they would make twice as much by doing so. But what would be the net result to the community? Clearly a loss of $215,000,000. That is to say: By offering a land grant we could induce capitalists to build a road in Washington Territory, rather than between San Francisco and Santa Cruz. But if we did do so, the people between San Francisco and Santa Cruz would lose far more than the capitalists and the Washington Territory settlers would gain; the people of the Pacific Coast, as a whole, and the United States, as a whole, would be poorer than if we had left capital free to seek the investments which would of themselves return to it the largest profits.

The comparison between an individual and the nation is fallacious. The one is a part, the other is the whole. The individual lives but a few years, the lifetime of the nation is counted by centuries. It may profit an individual to induce people to settle or capital to be invested in certain places; the nation can only profit by having its population and its capital so located and invested that the largest returns will be realised. It may profit an individual to sacrifice the near future to the present, but it cannot profit a nation.

As concerns the statistics by which the benefits of land-grant railroads are attempted to be shown, it must be remembered, first, that the population of the United States is growing at the rate of a million per year, and next, that an increase in the value of land is not increase in wealth. That whatever population railroads have brought to new States and Territories is dispersion, not increase, is proven by the fact that the population of the United States is not increasing faster than it did before railroad building commenced, while the slightest consideration of economic laws shows that whatever gain has resulted from their building is at the expense of a greater gain which would have resulted from the investment of the same capital where it was more needed—in fact, that there is no gain, but a loss. We have been supposing that land grants secure the consideration for which they are given—the building of roads before they would otherwise be built; but this is far from being always the case. With the exception, perhaps, of the little Stockton and Copperopolis road, the California grants have not hastened the building of railroads, but have actually retarded it, by retarding settlement. The fact is, that in nearly all the cases these land grants are made to men who do not propose, and who have not the means, to build the road. They keep them (procuring extensions of time, when necessary*) until they can sell out to others who wish to build, and who, on their part, generally delay until they can see a profit in the regular business.

To sum up: When we give a land grant for the building of a railroad, we either get a railroad built before it would be built by private enterprise, or we do not.

If we do not, our land is given for nothing; if we do, capital is diverted from more to less productive investments, and we are the poorer for the operation.

In either case the land grant tends to disperse population; in either case it causes the monopolisation of land; in either case it makes the many poorer, and a few the richer.

I have devoted this much space to answering directly the argument for railroad land grants, because they are constantly urged, and are seldom squarely met, and because so long as we admit that we may profit

---

* Congress, in 1870, actually passed a bill extending the time for the completion of the first twenty miles of Western road to which a land grant was made in 1853.

by thus granting away land in "reasonable amounts," we shall certainly find our lands going in "unreasonable amounts." But surely it requires no argument to show that this thing of giving away from twelve to twenty-five thousand acres per mile of road in order to get people to build a railroad for themselves, is a wicked extravagance for which no satisfactory excuse can be made. This land, now so worthless that we give it away by the million acres without a thought, is only worthless because the people who are to cultivate it have not yet arrived. They are coming fast–we have seen how fast. While there is plenty of uncultivated land in the older States, we are giving away the land in the Territories under the plea of hastening settlement, and when the time comes that these lands are really needed for cultivation, they will all be monopolised, and the settler, go where he will, must pay largely for the privilege of cultivating soil which since the dawn of creation has been waiting his coming. We need not trouble ourselves about railroads; settlement will go on without them–as it went on in Ohio and Indiana, as it has gone on since our Aryan forefathers left the Asiatic cradle of the race on their long westward journey. Without any giving away of the land, railroads, with every other appliance of civilisation, will come in their own good time. Of all people, the American people need no paternal Government to direct their enterprise. All they ask is fair play, as between man and man; all the best Government can do for them is to preserve order and administer justice.

There may be cases in which political or other non-economic reasons may make the giving of a subsidy for the building of a road advisable. In such cases, a money subsidy is the best, a land subsidy the worst. But if the policy of selling our lands is continued, and it is desirable to make the payment of the subsidy contingent upon the sale of the land, then the proceeds of the land, not the land itself, should be granted.

There is one argument for railroad land grants which I have neglected to notice. Senator Stewart pleads that these grants have kept the land from passing into the hands of speculators, who would have taken more than the railroad companies, and have treated the settlers less liberally than the companies. Perhaps he is right; there is certainly some truth in his plea. But if he is right, what does that prove? Not the goodness of railroad grants; but the badness of the laws which allow speculation in the public lands.

# II. THE LANDS OF CALIFORNIA

## HOW FAR LAND MONOPOLISATION HAS ALREADY GONE

In all the new States of the Union land monopolisation has gone on at an alarming rate, but in none of them so fast as in California, and in none of them, perhaps, are its evil effects so manifest.

California is the greatest land State in the Union, both in extent (for Texas owns her own land) and in the amount of land still credited to the Government in Department reports.[15] With an area of 188,981 square miles, or, in round numbers, 121,000,000 acres, she has a population of less than 600,000—that is to say, with an area twenty-four times as large as Massachusetts, she has a population not half as great. Of this population not one third is engaged in agriculture, and the amount of land under cultivation does not exceed 2,500,000 acres. Surely land should here be cheap, and the immigrant should come with the certainty of getting a homestead at Government price! But this is not so. Of the 100,000,000 acres of public land which, according to the last report of the Department, yet remain in California (which of course includes all the mountains and sterile plains), some 20,000,000 acres are withheld from settlement by railroad reservations, and millions of acres more are held under unsettled Mexican grants, or by individuals under the possessory laws of the State, without color of title.[16] Though here or there, if he knew where to find it, there may be a little piece of Government land left, the notorious fact is that the immigrant coming to the State to-day must, as a general thing, pay their price to the middlemen before he can begin to cultivate the soil. Although the population of California, all told—miners, city residents, Chinamen and Diggers—does not amount to three to the square mile; although the arable land of the State has hardly been scratched (and with all her mountains and dry plains California has an arable surface greater than the entire area of Ohio), it is already

24

so far monopolised that a large part of the farming is done by renters, or by men who cultivate their thousands of acres in a single field. For the land of California is already to a great extent monopolised by a few individuals, who hold thousands and hundreds of thousands of acres apiece. Across many of these vast estates a strong horse cannot gallop in a day, and one may travel for miles and miles over fertile ground where no plough has ever struck, but which is all owned, and on which no settler can come to make himself a home, unless he pay such tribute as the lord of the domain chooses to exact.

Nor is there any State in the Union in which settlers in good faith have been so persecuted, so robbed, as in California. Men have grown rich, and men still make a regular business of blackmailing settlers upon public land, or of appropriating their homes, and this by the power of the law and in the name of justice. Land grabbers have had it pretty much their own way in California–they have moulded the policy of the general Government; have dictated the legislation of the State; have run the land offices and used the courts.

Let us look briefly at the modes by which this land monopolisation has been carried on.

### THE MEXICAN GRANTS

California has had one curse which the other States have not had*–the Mexican grants. The Mexican land policy was a good one for a sparsely settled pastoral country, such as California before the American occupation. To every citizen who would settle on it, a town lot was given; to every citizen who wanted it, a cattle range was granted. By the terms of the cession of California to the United States it was provided that these rights should be recognised.

It would have been better, far better, if the American Government had agreed to permit these grant-holders to retain a certain definite amount of land around their improvements, and compounded for the rest of the grants called for by the payment of a certain sum per acre, turning it into the public domain. This would have been best, not only for the future population of California, but for the grant-holders themselves as the event has proved.

---

* The Territory of New Mexico is afflicted in the same way.

Or, if means had been taken for a summary and definite settlement of these claims, the evils entailed by them would have been infinitesimal compared with what have resulted. For it is not the extent of the grants (and all told the *bona fide* ones call for probably nine or ten million acres of the best land of California) which has wrought the mischief, so much as their unsettled condition–not the treaty with Mexico, but our own subsequent policy.

It is difficult in a brief space to give anything like an adequate idea of the villainies for which these grants have been made the cover. If the history of the Mexican grants of California is ever written, it will be a history of greed, of perjury, of corruption, of spoliation and high-handed robbery, for which it will be difficult to find a parallel.

The Mexican grants were vague, running merely for so many leagues within certain natural boundaries, or between other grants, though they were generally marked out in rough fashion.[17] It is this indefiniteness which has given such an opportunity for rascality, and has made them such a curse to California, and which, at the same time, has prevented in nearly all cases their original owners from reaping from them any commensurate benefit. Between the Commission which first passed upon the validity of the grants and final patent, a thousand places were found where the grant could be tied up, and where, indeed, after twenty-three years of litigation the majority of them still rest.[18] Ignorant of the language, of the customs, of the laws of the new rulers of their country, without the slightest idea of technical subtleties and legal delays, mere children as to business–the native grant-holders–were completely at the mercy of shrewd lawyers and sharp speculators, and at a very early day nearly all the grants passed into other hands.

## HOW THE GRANTS FLOAT

As soon as settlers began to cultivate farms and make improvements, the grants began to float. The grant-holders watched the farmers coming into their neighbourhood, much as a robber chief of the Middle Ages might have watched a rich Jew taking up his abode within striking distance of his castle. The settler may have been absolutely certain that he was on Government land, and may even have been so assured by the grant-holder himself; but so soon as he had built his house and fenced his land and planted his orchard, he would wake up some morning to find that the grant had been floated upon him, and that his land and improvements were claimed by some land shark who had gouged a native Californian out of his claim to a cattle-run, or wanting an opportunity to do this, had set up a fraudulent grant, supported by forged papers and suborned witnesses. Then he must either pay the blackmailer's price, abandon the results of his hard labour, or fight the claim before surveyor-general, courts, commissioner, secretary, and Congress itself, while his own property, parcelled out into contingent fees, furnished the means for carrying the case from one tribunal to another, for buying witnesses and bribing corrupt officials. And then, frequently, after one set of settlers had been thus robbed, new testimony would be discovered, a new survey would be ordered, and the grant would stretch out in another direction over another body of settlers, who would then suffer in the same way, while in many cases, as soon as one grant had been bought off or beaten away, another grant would come, and there are pieces of land in California for which four or five different titles have been purchased.

The ruling of the courts has been, that so long as the grants had not been finally located, their owners might hold possession within their exterior boundaries and eject settlers. Thus, if a grant is for one league, within certain natural boundaries which include fifty, the claimant can put settlers off any part of the fifty leagues.

Whenever any valuable mine or spring is discovered in the neighbourhood of any of these grants, then the grant jumps. If they prove worthless, then it floats back again. Thus the celebrated Mariposa claim, after two or three locations in the valley, was finally carried up into the mountains, where it had as much business as it would have had in Massachusetts or Ohio, and stretched out into the shape of a boot to cover a rich mining district.[19] Among the property given to John Charles Frémont and his partners, by this location, was the Ophir mine and mill, upon which an English company had spent over $100,000, after assurances from the Mariposa people that the mine was outside their claim.[20] In the southern half of California, where these grants run, there has been hardly a valuable spring or mine discovered that was not pounced upon by a grant. One of the latest instances was the attempt to float the Cuyamaca grant over the new San Diego mining district, and to include some sixty-five mines—one of them, the Pioneer, on which $200,000 has been expended. Another was the attempt to float a grant over the noted Geyser Springs, in Sonoma [C]ounty. In both these cases the attempt was defeated, General Hardenburgh refusing to approve the surveys. In the latter case, however, it was dog eat dog, the great scrip locator, W. S. Chapman, having plastered a Sioux warrant over the wonderful springs.[21] He has since obtained a patent, though I understand that somebody else laid a school-land warrant on the springs before Chapman.

## HOW THE GRANTS ARE STRETCHED OUT

Hardly any attention seems to have been paid to the amount of land granted by the Mexican authorities. Though, under the colonisation laws, eleven leagues (a Mexican league contains 4,438 acres) constituted the largest amount that could be granted, many of these grants have been confirmed and patented for much more (in the teeth of a decision of the United States Supreme Court), and under others yet unsettled, much larger amounts are still held. Grants for one league have been confirmed for eleven. Claims rejected by the Commission have been confirmed by the District Courts, and claims rejected by other decisions of the Supreme Court have been got through by the connivance of law officers of the Government who would suffer the time for appeal to lapse or take it so that it would be thrown out on a technicality.

As for the surveys they might almost as well have been made by the grant-holders themselves, and seem, as a general thing, to have run about as the grant-holders wished. The grants have been extended here, contracted there, made to assume all sorts of fantastic shapes, for the purpose of covering the improvements of settlers and taking in the best land. There is one of them that on the map looks for all the world like a tarantula—a fit emblem of the whole class. In numbers of cases, the names of which might be recited, grants of four leagues have been stretched in the survey to eight; grants of two leagues to six; grants of five to ten; and in one case it has been attempted to stretch one league to forty. In one case, the Saucal Redondo, where a two-league grant had been confirmed to five, and a survey of 22,190 acres made, a new survey was ordered by a clerk of the surveyor-general, and a survey taking in 25,000 acres more of United States land covered by settlers *was made and fixed up in the office;* and it was not until after some years of litigation before the Department that this fact was discovered. In some cases speculators who were "on the inside" would buy from a Spanish grantee the use of the name of his claim, and get a new survey which would take in for them thousands of acres more. The original claimant of Rancho la Laguna asked for three leagues, or 13,314 acres; the survey was made and confirmed for 18,000. Afterwards it was set aside, on the pretence that the Santa Barbara paper, in which the advertisement of survey had been published, was printed for part of the time in San Francisco, and a survey taking in 48,703 acres made, which, after being rejected by Commissioner Edwards, was patented by Commissioner Wilson. The Rancho Guadaloupe, a grant of 21,520 acres, was surveyed for 32,408 acres in 1860, the survey approved, a patent issued, and the ranch sold. Now the new owner, supported by an affidavit from the surveyor that objection was made to the 32,000 acre survey in 1860 by the two Mexican owners (one of whom died in 1858), is trying to get a new survey confirmed which takes in 11,000 acres more. The survey of Los Nogales was made in 1861, under a decree for one league and no more, and now an application for a new survey which will include 11,000 acres more is being pushed. The land is covered by settlers.

## THE BIG GRAPE-VINE RANCHO

Perhaps the most daring attempt to grab lands and rob settlers under pretence of a Mexican grant–so daring that it has almost a touch of the comic–is the case of Los Prietos y Najalayegua, which was shown up first in a little pamphlet by James F. Stuart, of San Francisco, and afterwards in Congress by Mr. Julian, to whom the settlers of California are indebted for many signal services.[22] In Santa Barbara [C]ounty there is living an old Mexican, named José Dominguez, on whose little ranch grows an immense grape-vine. In the old times Dominguez had petitioned for another tract of land of about a league and a half, but he neglected to comply with the conditions, and sold it for the sum of one dollar. In fact he seems to have sold it twice. Finally the claim passed into the hands of Thomas A. Scott, the Pennsylvania railroad king, and Edward J. Pringle, of San Francisco.[23] It had never been presented to the United States Commission, and was consequently barred. But in 1866 a bill confirming the grant, and accompanied by a memorial purporting to be from Dominguez, but which Dominguez swears he never saw, was introduced by Mr. Conness, and slipped quietly through, under pretence of giving the old man, with his sixty children and grandchildren, the big grape-vine which his mother had planted.

The bill was assisted in the House by the reading of a letter from Mr. Levi Parsons, in which a visit to the Mexican Patriarch and his great grape-vine, the only support of a greater family, was most touchingly described, and the intervention of Congress asked as a matter of justice and humanity. Then came the survey; and the speculators, emboldened by their success with Congress, went in for a big grab, taking in the modest amount of 208,742 acres*–a pretty good dollar's worth of land, considering that it included many valuable farms and vineyards. They asked too much, for an outcry was made and a resurvey was ordered, which is now pending.

## BOGUS GRANTS

The real grants have been bad enough, the bogus grants have been worse. Their manufacture commenced early–the signatures of living ex-Mexican officials being sometimes procured. Of this class was the famous Limantour claim to a great portion of San Francisco. It was finally defeated, but not until a large amount had been paid to its holders, and enormous expenses incurred in fighting it. Many of these claims have been pressed to final patent, and settlers driven from their homes by sheriff's posses or the bayonets of the United States troops. Others have only been used for purposes of blackmail, the owners of threatened property being compelled to remove the shadow from their title when obliged to borrow or to sell, and finding it cheaper to pay the sums asked than to incur the expense of long and tedious litigation, many steps in which had to be taken in Washington.

Thanks to the possessory law of the State, as interpreted by State courts, where the holders of a bogus claim secure possession they have been all right as long as they could delay final action. After the action of the District Court five years are allowed for appeal to the Supreme Court, and then a smart attorney can easily keep the case hanging from year to year. In one case where a modest demand for some forty leagues was rejected, because in forging the Mexican seal on the grant, the head of the cactus-mounted eagle had been carelessly put where his tail ought to be, the appeal has been kept at the foot of the docket for years, while the claimants are enjoying the land just as fully as if they had paid the Government for it, and are actually selling it to settlers, who know

---

* The survey was not strictly official, though made by a United States Deputy, he having reported that the calls were uncertain, and the grantees asking a survey according to their views.

the claim to be fraudulent, at from $2 to $10 per acre. If the Supreme Court ever does reach the case, the appeal will be dismissed. A new motion will then be made, and finally, when all the law's delays are exhausted, the settlers will have to pay the Government $1.25 per acre for the land. Meantime they can get it only by paying his price to the holder of this notoriously fraudulent claim.

It has at all times been within the power of Congress to end this uncertainty as to land titles, and settle these Mexican claims. There has been a great deal of legislation on the subject, but somehow or other it has always turned out for the benefit of the land grabbers. Modes of procedure have been changed; cases have been thrown from the courts into the land offices; from the land offices back to the courts, and then from the courts back to the land offices again. Always some excuse for delay; always some loophole in the law, through which the land grabber could easily pass, but in which the settler would be crushed. The majority of these Mexican grants are yet unsettled. Their owners do not want them settled so long as they can hold thousands of acres more than they have a shadow of claim to, and delay as much as possible. These are cases where the last step to secure patent can be taken at any time, by the making of a motion or the payment of a fee; but which are suffered to remain in that condition, while in the meantime the claim holders are selling quitclaim deeds to settlers, for land which their patents would show they do not own.[24]

## THE PUEBLO OF SAN FRANCISCO

For the injuries which these Mexican grants have done to California, the Mexican land policy is not responsible. That merely furnished the pretext under cover of which *our* policy has fostered land monopolisation. What of the Mexican policy was bad under our different conditions, we have made infinitely worse; what would still have been good, we have discarded. The same colonisation laws under which these great grants were made gave four square leagues to each town in which to provide homes for its inhabitants, the only conditions being good character and occupancy. The American city of San Francisco, as the successor of the Mexican pueblo, came into a heritage such as no great city of modern times has enjoyed—land enough for a city as large as London, dedicated to the purpose of providing every family with a free homestead.[25] Here was an opportunity to build up a great city, in which tenement houses and blind alleys would be unknown; in which there would be less poverty, suffering, crime and social and political corruption than in any city of our time, of equal numbers. This magnificent opportunity has been thrown away, and with the exception of a great sand bank, the worst that could be found, reserved for a part, and a few squares reserved for public buildings, the heritage of *all* the people of San Francisco has been divided among a few hundred. Of the successive steps, culminating in the United States law of 1866, by which this was accomplished, of the battles of land grabbers to take and to keep, and of the municipal corruption engendered, it is not worth while here to speak. The deed is done. We have made a few millionaires, and now the citizen of San Francisco who needs a home must pay a large sum for permission to build it on land dedicated to its use ere the American flag had been raised in California.

## THE RAILROAD GRANTS OF CALIFORNIA

The grants made to railroads of public lands in the State of California are: The grant to the Western Pacific and Central Pacific, of ten alternate sections on each side per mile (12,800 acres), made to half that amount in 1862, and doubled in 1864; the grants to the Southern Pacific and to the California and Oregon, of ten alternate sections on each side, with ten miles on each side in which to make up deficiencies, made in 1866; the grant to the Stockton and Copperopolis, of five alternate sections on each side, with twenty miles on each side in which to make up deficiencies, made in 1867; the grants to the Texas Pacific* and to the connecting branch of the Southern Pacific, of ten alternate sections on each side, with ten miles for deficiencies, made in 1871. A grant was also made in 1866 to the Sacramento and Placerville road, but the idea of building the road was abandoned, and the grant has lapsed.

Upon the map of California (see frontispiece) the reservations for these grants are marked in red. This marking does not show the *exact* limits of the reservations, as they follow the rectilinear section lines, which it is, of course, impossible to show on so small a scale—nor are the routes of the roads *precisely* drawn. But it gives a perfectly correct idea of the extent and general course of these reservations. The exhibit is absolutely startling—a commentary on the railroad land-grant policy of Congress to the

---

* Between the line of the road and the Mexican boundary this company gets all the public land.

force of which no words can add. Observe the proportion which these reservations bear to the total area of the State, and observe at the same time the topography of California—how the railroad reservations cover nearly all the great central valleys, and leave but the mountains, and you may get an idea of how these reservations are cursing the State.

It is true that the companies do not get all of the land included in these reservations, nor even half of it; but for the present, at least, so far as the greater part of it is concerned, they might as well get it all. Preemption or homestead settlers may still go upon the even sections, but the trouble is to find them. The greater part of this land is unsurveyed, or having been once surveyed, the *vaqueros,* who share in the prejudices of their employers against settlers, have pulled up the stakes, and the settler cannot tell whether he gets on Government or on railroad land.[26] If on Government land, he is all right, and can get 80 acres for $22, as a homestead; or 160 acres for $400 by pre-emption. But it is an even chance that he is on railroad land, and if so, he is at the mercy of a corporation which will make with him no terms, in advance. Settlers will not take such chances.

These railroad grants have worked nothing but evil to California.[27] Though given under pretext of aiding settlement, they have really retarded it. Of all the roads ever subsidised in the United States, the Central Pacific is the one to which the giving of a subsidy is the most defensible. But so large was the subsidy, in money and bonds, that the road could have been built, and would have been built, just as soon without the land grant. The Western Pacific land grant became the property of a single individual, who did nothing towards building the road—the company that did build the road (the Central) buying the franchise minus the land grant. The Southern Pacific land grant has actually postponed the building of a road southward through California, and had the grant never been made, it is certain that an unsubsidised road would already have been running farther into Southern California than the land-grant road yet does. Of the California and Oregon land grant, the same thing may be said. The Stockton and Copperopolis grant was made in 1867, but the building of the road has only been commenced this year. And it is exceedingly probable that had this land been open to settlers, the business, actual and prospective, would by this time have offered sufficient inducements for the building of the road.

All these land grants, with the exception perhaps of that from the Eastern boundary to San Diego, and with the exception of the Western

Pacific grant, are owned by a single firm, who also own all the railroads in California, having bought what they did not build.

It is generally argued when land grants are made, that it is to the interest of the companies to sell their lands cheaply, because settlement will bring them business. But the land-grant companies of California seem in no hurry to sell their lands, preferring to wait for the greater promise of the future. Neither the Southern Pacific nor the California and Oregon will make any terms with settlers until their lands are sur- veyed and listed over to them. It is, of course, to their interest to have the Government sections settled first, and to reserve their own land for higher prices after the Government land is gone. The Central Pacific advertises to sell good farming land for $2.50 per acre; but when one goes to buy good farming land for that price, he finds that it has been sold to the Sacramento Land Company, a convenient corporation, which stands to the company in its land business just as the Contract and Finance Company did in the building of the road.

## PRIVATE ENTRY AND SCRIP LOCATIONS

Large bodies of the public lands of California were offered at public sale long before there was any demand for them. When the failure of placer mining directed industry towards agriculture, and the beginnings of the railroad system led to hopes of a large immigration, these lands were gobbled up by a few large speculators, by the hundred thousand acres.[28] The larger part of the available portion of the great San Joaquin Valley went in this way, and the process has gone on from Siskiyou on the north to San Diego on the south.

According to common report, the speculators have received every facility in the [L]and [O]ffices. While the poor settler who wanted a farm would have to trudge off to look at the land himself, the speculator or his agent had all the information which could be furnished. Land, which had never been sold or applied for, would be marked on the maps as taken, in order to keep it from settlers and reserve it for speculators; and in some cases, it is even said that settlers selecting land and going to the Land Office to apply for it, would be put off for a few minutes while the land they wanted would be taken up in behalf of the speculator, and then they would be referred to him, if they desired to purchase.

A great deal of this land has been located with the Agricultural College scrip of Eastern States, bought by the speculators at an average of about fifty cents per acre, in greenbacks, when greenbacks were low, and sold or held at prices varying from $4 to $20 per acre, in gold.[29] Whole townships have been taken up at once in this way; but the law was amended in 1867, so that only three sections in the same township can now be located with this scrip. The Agricultural scrip of California has been sold at about $5 per acre, having special privileges.

The Act of last year, making this California scrip locatable on unsurveyed land, within railroad reservations, etc., is a good sample of the recklessness of Congressional legislation on land matters. It is so loosely drawn that by the purchase of forty acres a speculator can tie up a whole township. The Land Agent of the University has only to give notice to the United States Register that he has an application for land (without specifying amount or locality) in a certain township, and the Register must hold the plats of survey for sixty days after their return. Should a pre-emptor go on before this time, there is nothing to prevent the speculator from swooping down upon him and asserting that *his* farm is the particular piece of ground he wanted. Happily, nearly all this scrip will be used for locating timber land, for which the scrip of other States is not available, as it can only be located on surveyed land, and the surveyed timber land has long since been taken up.

Besides the Agricultural scrip, a large amount of Half Breed scrip has been located by speculators. This scrip was issued to Indians in lieu of their lands, and was made by law locatable only by the Indians themselves, and though the speculators pretended to locate as the attorneys of the Indians, the location was illegal. However, it was made, and patents have been issued.

In this way millions of acres in California have been monopolised by a handful of men. The chief of these speculators now holds some 350,000 acres, while thousands and thousands of acres which he located with scrip or paid $1.25 per acre for, have been sold to settlers at rates varying from $5 to $20 per acre, the settlers paying cash enough to clear him and leave a balance, and then giving a mortgage for and paying interest on the remainder; and a large quantity of his land is rented—cultivators furnishing everything and paying the landlord one fourth of their crop.

And as has been the case in all the methods of land monopolisation in California, these scrip locations have been used not only to grab unoccupied lands, but to rob actual settlers of their improved farms. In one instance, a large scrip speculator got a tool of his appointed to make the survey of a tract of land in one of the southern counties which had been long occupied by actual settlers. This deputy surveyor persuaded the settlers that it would be cheaper for them to get a State title to their lands than to file pre-emption claims, and they accordingly proceeded to do this. But as the clock struck nine, and the doors of the Land Office in San Francisco were thrown open on the morning the plats were filed, another agent of the speculator entered with an armful of scrip which he proceeded to plaster over the settlers' farms.

## Management of the California State Lands

We have seen what Federal legislation has done to inflict the curse of land monopoly upon California. Let us now see what has been done by the State herself. We shall find that reckless as have been the dealings of the general Government with our lands, the dealings of the State have been even worse.

And here let it be remarked that for most of these wrong acts of the Federal Government, the people of California are themselves largely responsible. For the public manifestation of a strong sentiment here could not have failed to exert great influence upon Congress. But, for instance, instead of objecting to railroad grants, we have, for the most part, hailed them as an evidence of Congressional liberality; and when the Southern Pacific had once forfeited its grant, the California Legislature asked Congress to give it back without suggesting a single restriction on the sale or management of the lands. In 1870, a bill actually passed the House reserving the public lands of California for homestead entry, as the lands of the Southern States had been reserved, but it went over in the Senate on the objection of Senator Nye, of Nevada.[30] There is little doubt that the manifestation of a strong desire on our part would, at any time, secure the passage of such a bill.

The specific grants made to California, in common with other land States, which have been before enumerated, amount to an aggregate of 7,421,804 acres—an area almost as large as that of Massachusetts and Connecticut combined. Besides these grants, all the swamp lands are given to the State for purposes of reclamation, of which 3,581,691 acres have already been sold—about all there is.

These large donations have proved an evil rather than a benefit to the people of California; for in disposing of them, the State has given even greater facilities for monopoly than has the Federal Government, and the practical effect of the creation of two sources of title to public land has been to harass settlers and to give opportunity for a great deal of robbery and rascality.

The land policy of the State of California must be traced through some thirty-five or forty Acts, in whose changes and technicalities the non-expert will soon become bewildered. It is only necessary here to give its salient features.

It must be understood in the first place that the only grant of specific pieces of land is that of the 16th and 36th sections of each township. When these are occupied or otherwise disposed of, other sections are given in lieu of them. These lieu lands, as well as the lands granted in specific amounts, the State has had the privilege of taking from any unappropriated Government land, the ownership of the swamp lands being decided by the nature of the land itself. With this large floating grant, as it may be termed, the general policy of the State has been, not to select the lands and then to sell them, but in effect to sell to individuals its right of selection.

Now, under the general laws of the United States, until land is offered at public sale, there is no way of getting title to it save by actual settlement, and then in tracts of not over 160 acres to each individual. And though since 1862 the pre-emption right has applied to unsurveyed lands, yet until land is surveyed and the plats filed, the settler can make no record of his pre-emption.

To this land thus reserved by the general laws for the small farms of actual settlers, the State grants gave an opportunity of obtaining title without regard to settlement or amount—an opportunity which speculators have well improved. In defiance of the laws of the United States, and even of the Act admitting California into the Union, the State at first sold even unsurveyed land, a policy which continued until the courts declared it illegal in 1863.[31] In 1852, to dispose of the 500,000 acre grant (which the Constitution of the State gave to the School Fund), warrants were issued purchasable at $2 per acre in depreciated scrip, and locatable on any unoccupied Government land, surveyed or unsurveyed. These warrants, however, were not saleable to any one person in amounts of more than 640 acres, and the buyer had to make affidavit that he intended to make permanent settlement on the land. But as the warrants were assignable, and affidavits cheap, these restrictions were of but little avail. Passing for the most part into the hands of speculators, the warrants enabled them to forestall the settler and even in many cases to take his farm from him; for though by the terms of the law the warrants could only be laid on unoccupied land, yet when once laid, they were *prima facie* evidence of title, and the difficulty could be got over only by collusion with county officers and false affidavits. These school-land warrants have been a terror to the California settler, and many a man who has made himself a home, relying upon the general laws of the Federal Government, has seen the results of his years of toil and privation pass into the hands of some soulless cormorant, who, without his knowledge, had plastered over his farm with school-land warrants. The law under which the warrants were issued was repealed in 1858, and the policy adopted of settling the State title to applicants for land, in amounts not to exceed 320 acres to each individual, at the rate of $1.25 per acre, payable either in cash, or twenty per cent. in cash, and the balance on credit with interest at ten per cent. The 16th and 36th sections, or the lands in lieu of them, were at first given to the respective townships, to be sold for the benefit of the Township School Fund; but were afterwards made saleable as other lands for the benefit of the General Fund.

The swamp lands were from the first made saleable in tracts not exceeding 320 acres to each person, for $1 per acre, cash or credit, the proceeds to be applied to the reclamation of the land, under regulations varied by different laws, from time to time. This was virtually giving them away–the true policy; but the trouble is that for the most part they have been given to a few men.

Up to 1868, the State had always, in words at least, recognised the principle that one man should not be permitted to take more than a certain amount of land; but by the Act of March 28th, of that year, which repealed all previous laws, and is still, with some trifling amendments, the land law of the State, all restrictions of amount, except as to the 16th and 36th sections proper, were swept away; and with reference to those lands, the form of affidavit was so changed that the applicant was not required to swear that he wanted the land for settlement, or wanted it for himself. This Act has some good features; but from enacting clause to repealing section, its central idea seems to be the making easy of land monopolisation, and the favouring of speculators at the expense of settlers. In addition to sweeping away the restrictions as to amount and to use, it provided that the settlers upon the 16th and 36th sections should only be protected in their occupancy for six months after the passage of the Act, after which the protection should only be for sixty days; and changed the affidavit previously required, from a denial of other settlement to a denial of valid adverse claim. Under this provision a regular business has been driven in robbing settlers of their homes. Unless a new law is very generally discussed in the newspapers (and land laws seldom are) it takes a long time for the people to become acquainted with it; and there were many settlers on State land who knew nothing of the limitation until they received notification that somebody else had possession of a clear title to their farms. Did space permit, numbers of cases of this kind of robbery might be cited—some of them of widows and orphans, whose all was ruthlessly taken from them; but I will confine myself to one case of recent occurrence, where the looked-for plunder is unusually large.

The town of Amador, and the very valuable Keystone Mine, are situated on the east half of a 36th section. The survey which developed this fact was only made in the early part of the present year. The Deputy Surveyor, who was evidently in the plot, returned to the United States Land Office the plat of the township, with the mine and the town marked in the west half. Application was at the same time made to the State Surveyor-General, in the name of Henry Casey, for the east half. In regular course, the Surveyor-General sent the application to the United States Land Office, whence it was returned, with a certificate that the land was free; whereupon, the Surveyor-General approved the application, and twenty-five cents per acre was paid the State. And thus for $80 cash, and $32 per annum interest, a little knot of speculators have secured title to the Keystone Mine, worth at least a million dollars, and the whole town of Amador, besides.

And as further evidence of the recklessness of California land legislation, and of the lengths to which the land grabbers are prepared to go, two facts may be cited: The last Legislature, instead of repealing or removing the objectionable features from this Green [L]aw, actually passed a special bill legalising all applications for State lands, even where the affidavits by which they were supported did not conform to the requirements of the law, *either in form or in substance*.[32] After this had been passed, on the last day of the session a bill was got through and was signed by the Governor,[33] designed to restrict applicants for lieu lands to 320 acres. But after the Legislature had adjourned, when the Act came to be copied in the Secretary of State's office, lo, and behold! it was discovered that the engrossed and signed copy did not contain this provision.

Yet, to understand fully what a premium the State has offered for the monopolisation of her school lands, there is another thing to be explained. To purchase land of the State, an application must be filed in the State Land Office, describing the land by range, township and section, and stating under what grant the title is asked. This application must be accompanied by a fee of five dollars. The Surveyor-General then issues a certificate to the applicant, and sends the application to the United States Land Office, for certification that the land is free, before he approves the application and demands payment for the land. If there be no record in his office of pre-emption, homestead or other occupation, the United States Register thereupon marks the land off on his map, but he does not certify to the State Surveyor-General until he gets his fee. The State Surveyor-General has no appropriation to pay the fee, although the present incumbent asked for one in his first report; and so the payment of the fee and the return of the United States certificate depend upon the applicant, whose interest it is, of course, not to get it until he wishes to pay for his land. And thus, by the payment of five dollars, a whole section of United States land can be shut up from the settler. There are 1,244,696 acres monopolised in California to-day in this way. For thousands and thousands of the acres which are offered for sale on California and Montgomery streets there is no other title than the payment of this five dollars. When the immigrant buys of the speculator for two, five, ten or twenty dollars an acre, as the case may be, then the speculator goes to the United States Land Office, pays the Register's fee, gets his certificate and the State Surveyor-General's approval, and pays the State $1.25 per acre; or, if with the immigrant he has made a bargain of that kind, he pays twenty-five cents per acre, and leaves his purchaser to pay the dollar at some future time, with interest at ten per cent.

## SWAMP LAND GRABBING

And as the speculator has had a far better opportunity in dealing with the State than with the United States, there has been every inducement to get as much land as possible under the jurisdiction of the State, by declaring it swamp land. The certificate of United States officers as to the character of the land has not been waited for; but the State has sold to every purchaser who would get the County Surveyor to segregate the land he wanted, and procure a couple of affidavits as to its swampy character. Probably one half of the land sold (or rather given, as the money is returned) by the State as swamp, is not swamp at all, but good dry land, that has been sworn to as swamp, in order to take it out of the control of the pre-emption laws of the United States. The State has been made the catspaw of speculators, and her name used as the cover under which the richest lands in California might be monopolised and settlers robbed. The seizure of these lands of the State (or rather by speculators in the name of the State) is for the most part entirely illegal; but by the Act of 1866, previous seizures were confirmed, and the land grabbers of California, though Mr. Julian occasionally makes them some trouble, have powerful friends in Washington, and unless energetic remonstrance is made, generally get what they ask. This swamp land grant has not yielded a cent to the State, but it has enabled speculators to monopolise hundreds of thousands of acres of the most valuable lands in California, and, of course, to rob settlers. For the settler, though he has a right under United States laws, can get no record nor evidence of title until his land is surveyed and the plats filed. In the meantime, if the speculator comes along and can get a couple of affidavits as to the swampy character of the settler's farm, he has been able to buy the title of the State. Lands thousands of feet above the level of the sea have been purchased as swamp; lands over which a heavily loaded wagon can be driven in the month of May; and even lands which cannot be cultivated without irrigation.

Sierra Valley is in Plumas [C]ounty, in the very heart of the mountains. Standing on its edge, you may at your option toss a biscuit into a stream which finally sinks in the great Nevada Basin, or into the waters which join the Pacific. When the snow melts in the early spring, the mountain streams which run through the valley overflow and spread over a portion of the land; but after a freshet has passed, water has to be turned in through irrigating ditches to enable the lands to produce their most valuable crop, hay. The valley is filled with pre-emption and homestead settlers, who, besides their own homes and improvements, have built two churches and seven schoolhouses. Many of their farms are worth $20 per acre. The swamp land robbers cast their eyes on this pretty little valley and its thrifty settlement, and the first thing the settlers knew their farms had been bought of the State as swamp lands, and the United States was asked to list them over. Energetic remonstrance was made, and the matter was referred by the Department to the United States Surveyor-General to take testimony. His investigation has just been concluded, and the attempted grab has probably failed. But in hundreds of cases, similar ones on a smaller scale have succeeded.

Another recent attempt has been made to get hold of 46,000 acres adjoining Sacramento. This land was formerly overshadowed by the rejected Sutter grant, and for some time has been all pre-empted.[34] Something like a year ago it was surveyed and the plats returned to the United States Land Office, with this land marked as swamp; applications being at the same time made to the State for the land. The ex-Surveyor-General, Sherman Day, signed the plats, and the land had actually been listed over by the Department, when a protest was made and forwarded to Washington, accompanied by his own personal testimony, by the new Surveyor-General, Hardenburgh, who, having been long a resident of Sacramento, knew the character of the land. This forced the suspension of the lists, very much, it seems, to the indignation of the Acting Commissioner of the General Land Office, W. W. Curtis, who wrote a letter to the Surveyor-General, which has been published in the newspapers (which is a curiosity of official impudence), and which betrays a very suspicious anger with what the Acting Commissioner seems to consider the interference of the Surveyor-General.

Mr. Julian, in his speech entitled "Swamp Land Swindles," has detailed how a party of speculators, one of whom was ex-State Surveyor-General Houghton, and another the son of the then United States Surveyor-General Upson, got hold of sixteen thousand acres in Colusa (as to the dry character of which he gives affidavits), under the swamp-land laws, by having the survey of two townships made and approved in a few days, just before the map of the California and Oregon Railroad Company was filed. These swamp-land speculators are in many cases attempting to shelter themselves behind the growing feeling against railroad grants; but bad as the railroad grants are, the operations of these speculators are worse. The railroad companies can only take half the lands; the speculators take it all. The railroad companies cannot easily disturb previous settlers; but the speculators take the settler's home from under his feet.

## WHO HAVE OUR LANDS

The State Surveyor-General ought to give in his next report (and if he does not the Legislature ought to call for it) a list of the amounts of State lands taken in large quantities by single individuals (with their names) under the Act of 1868. Such a list would go far to open the eyes of the people of California to the extent their State Government has been used to foster the land monopoly of which they are beginning to complain. Yet such a list would not fully show what has been done, as a great deal of land has been taken by means of dummies. Of the 16th and 36th sections proper, to which even now one individual cannot apply for more than 320 acres, one speculator has secured 8000 acres in Colusa [C]ounty alone. Among those who have secured the largest amount from the State, either in their own names or as attorneys for others, are[:] W. S. Chapman, George W. Roberts, ex-Surveyor-General Houghton, John Mullan, Will S. Green, H. C. Logan, George H. Thompson, B. F. Maulden, I. N. Chapman, Leander Ransom, N. N. Clay, E. H. Miller and James W. Shanklin. The larger amounts secured by single individuals range from 20,000 acres to over 100,000.

## WHAT SHOULD HAVE BEEN DONE

The true course in regard to State lands is that urged upon the Legislature by the present Surveyor-General in his first annual report–to issue title only to the actual settler who has resided on the land three years, and who has shown his intention to make it his home by placing upon it at least $500 worth of improvements.* Had this course been adopted from the start, California would to-day have had thousands more of people and millions more of property. Had it even been adopted when urged by General Bost, over half a million acres of land would have been saved to settlers–that is to say, *four thousand* families might have found homesteads in California at nominal rates–at rates so much lower than that which they must now pay that the difference would more than have sufficed for all the expenses of their transportation from the East.

To amend our policy in regard to sales of State land now, is a good deal like locking the stable door after the horse is stolen. Still it should

---

* In his biennial message to the same Legislature (the last) Governor Haight speaks in the same strain. He says: "Our land system seems to be mainly framed to facilitate the acquisition of large bodies of land by capitalists and corporations, either as donations or at nominal prices. It is to be regretted that the land granted by Congress to railroad corporations had not been subject to continued pre-emption by settlers, giving to the corporation the proceeds at some fixed price, and it would have been much better for the State and country if the public lands had never been disposed of except to actual settlers under the pre-emption law."

be done. Our swamp lands are all gone, and the most available of the school lands have gone also. Yet there may be a million acres of good land left. These we cannot guard with too jealous care.

## THE POSSESSORY LAW

But the catalogue of what the State of California has done towards the monopolisation of her land does not end with a recital of her acts as trustee of the land donated her by the general Government. Besides giving these lands for the most part to monopolists, she has, by her legislation, made possible the monopolisation of other vast bodies of the public lands. Under her possessory laws before alluded to, millions of acres are shut out from settlement, without their holders having the least shadow of title. It is Government land, but unsurveyed. The only way of getting title to it is to go upon it and live; but the laws of California say that no one can go upon it until he has a better title than the holder—that of possession. Tracts of from two to ten thousand acres thus held are common, and in one case at least (in Lake [C]ounty) a single firm has 28,000 acres of Government land, open by the laws of the United States to pre-emption settlers, enclosed by a board fence, and held under the State laws. It is these laws that enable the Mexican grant owners to hold all the land they can possibly shadow with their claims, and that offer them a premium to delay the adjustment of their titles, in order that they may continue to hold, and in many cases, to sell, far more than their grants call for.

## HOW A LARGE QUANTITY OF PUBLIC LAND MAY BE FREED

A large appropriation for the survey of the public lands in California, managed by a Surveyor-General who really wished to do his duty,* would open to settlers millions of acres from which they are now excluded by railroad reservations or the monopolisation of individuals. If our Representatives in Congress desire to really benefit their State, they will neglect the works at Mare Island, the erection of public buildings in San Francisco, and the appropriations for useless fortifications, until they can get this. And one of the first acts of the next Legislature should be to limit the possessory law to 160 acres, which would be a

---

* And we seem to have secured one in the present Surveyor-General.

quick method of breaking up possessory monopolisations. In the meantime there is a remedy, though a slower and more cumbrous one. At the
last session of Congress an Act was passed (introduced by Mr. Sargent)
authorising the credit to settlers, on payments for their lands, of money
advanced for surveying them.[35] Here is a means by which, with combined effort, a large amount of public land may be freed. Let a number
of settlers, sufficient to bear the expense, go upon one of these large possessory claims. If ejected, let them deposit the money for a survey with
the United States Surveyor-General, and the moment the lines are run
and the plats are filed they have a sure title to the land.

## MORE MONOPOLISATION THREATENED—FOOD AND WATER

There is little doubt that one of the greatest attempts at monopolisation
yet made in California would have followed the passage of Sargent's bill
for the sale of the Pacific Coast timber lands, which was rushed through
the House at the last session, but was passed over by the Senate, and
which has been re-introduced. These timber lands are of incalculable
value, for from them must come the timber supply, not of the Pacific
States alone, but of the whole Interior Basin, and nearly all the Southern
Coast. The present value of these lands when they can be got at, may be
judged by the fact that there are single trees upon the railroad lands
which yield at present prices over $500 worth of lumber. Under this bill,
these lands would have been saleable at $2.50 per acre. The limitation
of each purchaser to 640 acres would of course amount to nothing, and
within a short time after the passage of the bill, the available timber
lands would have passed into the hands of a small ring of large capitalists, who would then have put the price of lumber at what figure they
pleased. The amount of capital required to do this would be by no
means large when compared with the returns, which would be enormous, for though some estimates of the timber lands of California go as
high as 30,000,000 acres, the means of transportation as yet make but a
small portion of this available. And it would be only necessary to buy
the land as it is opened, to virtually control the whole of it. There is,
however, a good deal to be said in favour of the sale of these lands, and
some legislation is needed, as there is a great deal of land of no use but
for its timber, but upon which individuals cannot cut, except as tres-
passers, while the railroad company in the Sierras, having been given
the privilege of taking timber off Government land for construction, has

a monopoly there, and is clearing Government land in preference to its own. If waste could be prevented, it would perhaps be best to leave the timber free to all who chose to cut, on the principle that all the gifts of nature, whenever possible, should be free. This is problematical, perhaps impossible. If so, the plan proposed by Honourable Will S. Green, of Colusa, seems to be the best of those yet brought forward; that is, to sell the lands only to the builders of saw-mills, in amounts proportioned to the capacity of the mill. At all events, almost anything would be better than the creation of such a monstrous monopoly as would at once have sprung up under the Sargent bill–a monopoly which would have taxed the people of California millions annually, and would have raised the price of timber on the whole coast.

It is not only the land and the timber, but even the water of California that is threatened with monopoly, as by virtue of laws designed to encourage the construction of mining and irrigation ditches, the mountain streams and natural reservoirs are being made private property, and already we are told that all the water of a large section of the State is the property of a corporation of San Francisco capitalists.

### THE EFFECT OF LAND MONOPOLISATION IN CALIFORNIA

It is not we, of this generation, but our children of the next, who will fully realise the evils of the land monopolisation which we have permitted and encouraged; for those evils do not begin to fully show themselves until population becomes dense.

But already, while our great State, with an area larger than that of France or Spain or Turkey–with an area equal to that of all of Great Britain, Holland, Belgium, Denmark and Greece combined–does not contain the population of a third-class modern city; already, ere we have commenced to manure our lands or to more than prospect the treasures of our hills, the evils of land monopolisation are showing themselves in such unmistakable signs that he who runs may read. This is the blight that has fallen upon California, stunting her growth and mocking her golden promise, offsetting to the immigrant the richness of her soil and the beneficence of her climate.

It has already impressed its mark upon the character of our agriculture–more shiftless, perhaps, than that of any State in the Union where slavery has not reigned. For California is not a country of farms, but a country of plantations and estates. Agriculture is a speculation. The farm-houses, as a class, are unpainted frame shanties, without garden or flower or tree. The farmer raises wheat; he buys his meat, his flour, his butter, his vegetables, and, frequently, even his eggs. He has too much land to spare time for such little things, or for beautifying his home, or he is merely a renter, or an occupant of land menaced by some adverse title, and his interest is but to get for this season the greatest crop that can be made to grow with the least labour. He hires labour for his planting and his reaping, and his hands shift for themselves at other seasons of the year. His plough he leaves standing in the furrow, when the year's ploughing is done; his mustangs he turns upon the hills, to be lassoed when again needed. He buys on credit at the nearest store, and when his crop is gathered must sell it to the Grain King's agent, at the Grain King's prices.[36]

And there is another type of California farmer. He boards at the San Francisco hotels, and drives a spanking team over the Cliff House road; or, perhaps, he spends his time in the gayer capitals of the East or Europe. His land is rented for one third or one fourth of the crop, or is covered by scraggy cattle, which need to look after them only a few half-civilised *vaqueros;* or his great wheat fields, of from ten to twenty thousand acres, are ploughed and sown and reaped by contract. And over our ill-kept, shadeless, dusty roads, where a house is an unwonted landmark, and which run frequently for miles through the same man's land, plod the tramps, with blankets on back–the labourers of the California farmer–looking for work, in its seasons, or toiling back to the city when the ploughing is ended or the wheat crop is gathered. I do not say that this picture is a universal one, but it is a characteristic one.*

It is not only in agriculture, but in all other avocations, and in all the manifestations of social life, that the effect of land monopoly may be seen–in the knotting up of business into the control of little rings, in the concentration of capital into a few hands, in the reduction of wages in

---

* An old Californian, a gentleman of high intelligence, who has recently travelled extensively through the State upon official business, which compelled him to pay particular attention to the material condition of the people, writes: "The whole country is poverty-stricken; the farmers shiftless, and crazy on wheat. I have seen farms cropped for eighteen years with wheat, and not a vine, tree, shrub or flower on the place. The roads are too wide, and are unworked, and a nest for noxious weeds. The effect of going through California is to make you wish to leave it, if you are poor and want to farm."

the mechanical trades, in the gradual decadence of that independent personal habit both of thought and action which gave to California life its greatest charm, in the palpable differentiation of our people into the classes of rich and poor. Of the "general stagnation" of which we of California have been so long complaining, this is the most efficient cause. Had the unused land of California been free, at Government terms, to those who would cultivate it, instead of this "general stagnation" of the past two years, we should have seen a growth unexampled in the history of even the American States. For with all our hyperbole, it is almost impossible to overestimate the advantages with which nature has so lavishly endowed this Empire State of ours. "God's Country," the returning prospectors used to call it, and the strong expression loses half of its irreverence as, coming over sage-brush plains, from the still frost-bound East, the traveller winds, in the early spring, down the slope of the Sierras, through interminable ranks of evergreen giants, past laughing rills and banks of wild flowers, and sees under their cloudless sky the vast fertile valleys stretching out to the dark blue Coast Range in the distance. But while nature has done her best to invite newcomers, our land policy has done its best to repel them. We have said to the immigrant: "It is a fair country which God has made between the Sierras and the sea, but before you settle in it and begin to reap His bounty, you must pay a forestaller roundly for *his* permission." And the immigrant having far to come and but scanty capital, has as a general thing stayed away.

## THE LANDED ARISTOCRACY OF CALIFORNIA

Though California is a young State; though she is a poor State, and though a few years ago she was a State in which there was less class distinction than in any State in the Union, she can already boast of an aristocracy based on the surest foundation—that of landownership.

I have been at some trouble to secure a list of the large landowners of California, but find exact and reliable information on that point difficult to obtain. The property of most of the largest landowners is scattered through various counties of the State, and a comparison of the books of the various assessors would be the only means of forming even an approximate list. These returns, however, are far from reliable. It has not been the custom to list land held by mere possessory title, and the practice of most of the assessors has been to favour large landholders.

The Board of Equalisation have ferreted out many interesting facts in this regard, which will probably be set forth in their coming report. Some remarkable discrepancies, of which the proportion is frequently as one to ten, are shown between the assessors' lists and the inventories of deceased landowners. In San Luis Obispo, one of the largest landowners and land speculators in the State returns to the assessor a total of 4366 acres. Reference to the United States Land Offices shows that he holds in that county, of United States land, 43,266 acres.

The largest landowners in California are probably the members of the great Central-Southern Pacific Railroad Corporation. Were the company land divided, it would give them something like two million acres apiece; and in addition to their company land, most of the individual members own considerable tracts in their own name.

McLaughlin, who got the Western Pacific land grant, has some three or four hundred thousand acres. Outside of these railroad grants, the largest single holder is, probably, Wm. S. Chapman, of San Francisco, the "pioneer" scrip speculator, who has some 350,000 acres; though ex-State Surveyor-General Houghton is said by some to own still more. Ex-United States Surveyor-General Beals has some 300,000 acres. Across his estate one may ride for seventy-five miles. Miller & Lux, San Francisco wholesale butchers, have 450,000. Around one of their patches of ground there are 160 miles of fence. Another San Francisco firm, Bixby, Flint & Co., have between 150,000 and 200,000 acres. George W. Roberts & Co. own some 120,000 acres of swamp land. Isaac Friedlander, San Francisco grain merchant, has about 100,000 acres. Throckmorton, of Mendocino, some 146,000; the Murphy family of Santa Clara, about 150,000; John Foster of Los Angeles, 120,000; Thomas Fowler, of Fresno, Tulare and Kern, about 200,000. Abel Stearns, of Los Angeles, had some 200,000 acres, but has sold a good deal. A firm in Santa Barbara advertises for sale 200,000 acres, owned by Philadelphia capitalists.

As for the poorer members of our California peerage—the Marquises, Counts, Viscounts, Lords and Barons—who hold but from 80,000 to 20,000 acres, they are so numerous, that, though I have a long list, I am afraid to name them for fear of making invidious distinctions, while the simple country squires, who hold but from five to twenty thousand acres, are more numerous still.

These men are the lords of California—lords as truly as ever were ribboned Dukes or belted Barons in any country under the sun. We have discarded the titles of an earlier age; but we have preserved the substance, and, though instead of "your grace," or "my lord," we may style them simply "Mr.," the difference is only in a name. They are our Land Lords just as truly. If they do not exert the same influence and wield the same power, and enjoy the same wealth, it is merely because our population is but six hundred thousand, and their tenantry have not yet arrived. Of the millions of acres of our virgin soil which their vast domains enclose, they are absolute masters, and upon it no human creature can come, save by their permission and upon their terms.* From the zenith above, to the centre of the earth below (so our laws run), the universe is theirs.

It must not be imagined that these large landholders are merely speculators—that they have got hold of land for the purpose of quickly selling it again. On the contrary, as a class, they have a far better appreciation of the future value of land and the power which its ownership gives, than have the people at large who have thoughtlessly permitted this monopolisation to go on. Many of the largest landholders do not desire to sell, and will not sell for anything like current prices; but on the contrary are continually adding to their domains. Among these, is one Irish family, who have seen at home what the ownership of the soil of a country means. They *rent* their land; they will not sell it; and this is true of many others. Sometimes this indisposition to sell is merely the result of considerations of present interest. As for instance: An agent of a society of settlers recently went to a large landholder in a southern county, and offered him a good price for enough land to provide about two hundred people with small farms. The landholder refused the offer, and the agent proceeded to call his attention to the increase in the value of his remaining land which this settlement would cause. "It may be," said the landholder, "but I should lose money. If you bring two hundred settlers here, they will begin agitating for a repeal of the fence law, and will soon compel it by their votes. Then I will be obliged to spend two or three hundred thousand dollars to fence in the rest of my ranch, and as fences do not fatten cattle, it will be worth no more to me than now."

Let me not be understood as reproaching the men who have *honestly* acquired large tracts of land. As the world goes, they are not to be blamed. If the people put saddles on their backs, they must expect

---

* They are coming. According to Government statisticians, California will, in 1890, contain a population of 3,500,000. [In 1890 the population of California was 1,213,000.]

somebody to jump astride to ride. If we must have an aristocracy, I would prefer that my children should be members of it, rather than of the common herd. While as for the men who have resorted to dishonest means, the probabilities are that most of them enjoy more of the respect of their fellows, and its fruits, than if they had been honest and got less land.

The division of our land into these vast estates derives additional significance from the threatening wave of Asiatic immigration whose first ripples are already breaking upon our shores. What the barbarians enslaved by foreign wars were to the great landlords of ancient Italy, what the blacks of the African coast were to the great landlords of the Southern States, the Chinese coolies may be, in fact are already beginning to be, to the great landlords of our Pacific slope.[37]

# III. Land and Labour

## What Land Is

L and, for our purpose, may be defined as that part of the globe's surface habitable by man–not merely his habitation, but the storehouse upon which he must draw for all his needs, and the material to which his labour must be applied for the supply of all his desires, for even the products of the sea cannot be taken, or any of the forces of nature utilised without the aid of land or its products. On the land we are born, from it we live, to it we return again–children of the soil as truly as is the blade of grass or the flower of the field.

## Of the Value of Land

Though land is the basis of all that we have, yet neither land nor its natural products constitute wealth. Wealth is the product–or to speak more precisely, the equivalent of labour. That which may be had without labour has no value, for the value of any object is measured by the labour for which it will exchange.* And when in speaking of "natural wealth," we mean anything else than the general possibilities which nature offers to labour, we mean such peculiar natural advantages as will yield to labour a larger return than the ordinary, and which are thus equivalent to the amount of labour dispensed with–that is, such natural objects or advantages as are scarce as well as desirable. If I find a diamond, I may not have expended much labour, but I am rich because I have something which it usually takes an immense amount of labour to obtain. If I own a coal mine which is valuable, it is because

---

\* I use the word ["]value["] throughout in the sense in which it is used by the writers on political economy—that of exchangeable power, not of utility.

52

other people have not coal mines, and cannot obtain fuel with as little expenditure of labour as I can, and will therefore give me the equivalent of more labour for my coal than I have to bestow to get it. If diamonds were as plenty as pebbles, they would be worth by the cart-load just the cost of loading and hauling. If coal could everywhere be had by digging a hole in the ground, the possession of a coal mine would make nobody rich.

And so it is with land. It is only valuable as it is scarce. Land (of the average quality) is not naturally scarce, but abundant, and it may be doubted whether there is any country, even the most populous, where the soil could not easily support in comfort all the people, though the law of diminishing return, as laid down by the English economists, is doubtless true.[38] But the density of population permits other economies which go far to make up for, and which, probably, in a right social state would fully make up for, any increase in the amount of labour necessarily devoted to agricultural production.

But land is a fixed quantity, which man can neither increase nor diminish, and is therefore very easily made artificially scarce by monopolisation. And artificial scarcity arising from unequal division produces the same effect as real scarcity in giving land a value. There is no scarcity of building lots in San Francisco, for there is room yet within the settled limits for ten thousand more houses. But if I want to put up a house I must pay for the privilege, just as if there were more people wanting to put up houses than there is room to put them up on.

And the value of land is the power which its ownership gives of appropriating the labour of those who have it not; and in proportion as those who own are few, and those who do not own are many, so does this power which is expressed by the selling price of land increase. We speak of railroads raising the value of land by reducing the time and cost of transportation. But if we analyse the operation by imagining the construction of a railroad through a country in which there are few settlers and land can be had for the taking, we will see that the direct effect of the railroad or other improvement which increases the value of the product of land is to increase the value of labour–or to speak more precisely, of the value of labour and capital, in the relative proportions determined by the circumstances which fix the shares of each–and that it is only when the land is so far monopolised as to enable the landowners to appropriate to themselves this benefit that the value of land is increased. No matter how few people there might be, if the land were all in private hands the owners might appropriate to themselves the whole benefit. This is the result in a country like England, but in a new country, those owners having more land than they can work or desire to work, will, in selling or renting their lands, yield some of the new advantage in order to induce people to take their surplus land. It will be said: If the value of land is the power which its ownership gives of appropriating the labour of others, so is the value of everything else, from a twenty-dollar piece to a keg of nails. But in this is the distinction: The twenty-dollar piece or the keg of nails are themselves the result of labour, and when given for labour the transaction is an exchange. Land is not the result of labour, but is the creation of God, and when labour must be given for it the transaction is an appropriation. In the one case labour is given for labour; in the other, labour is given for something that existed before labour was.

### OF THE VALUE OF LAND AND THE COMMON WEALTH

And thus we see that the value of land, being intrinsically merely the power which its ownership gives to appropriate the fruits of labour, is not an element of the wealth of a community. This principle is as self-evident as that two and two make four, yet we seem to have lost sight of it altogether. All over the country the increase in the value of land is cited as an increase of wealth. Year after year we add up the increased price which land will bring, and exclaim, Behold how rapidly the United States is growing rich! Yet we might with equal propriety count the debts which men owe each other, in estimating the assets of a community. The increased price of his land may be increased wealth to the owner, because it enables him to obtain a larger share in the distribution of its products, but it is not increased wealth to the community, because the shares of other people are at the same time cut down. The wealth of a community depends upon the product of the community. But the productive powers of land are precisely the same whether its price is low or high. In other words, the price of land indicates the distribution of wealth, not the production. The manner of distribution certainly reacts on production, and so the price of land indirectly and gradually affects the wealth of the community; but this effect is the reverse of what seems generally imagined. High prices for land tend to decrease instead of adding to the wealth of a community. For high priced land means luxury on the one side, and low wages on the other.

Luxury means waste, and low wages mean unintelligent and inefficient labour.

## OF THE VALUE OF LAND AND THE VALUE OF LABOUR

The value of land and of labour must bear to each other an inverse ratio. These two are the "terms" of production, and while production remains the same, to give more to the one is to give less to the other. The value of land is the power which its ownership gives to appropriate the product of labour, and, as a sequence, where rents (the share of the landowner) are high, wages (the share of the labourer) are low. And thus we see it all over the world, in the countries where land is high, wages are low, and where land is low, wages are high. In a new country the value of labour is at first at its maximum, the value of land at its minimum. As population grows and land becomes monopolised and increases in value, the value of labour steadily decreases. And the higher land and the lower wages, the stronger the tendency towards still lower wages, until this tendency is met by the very necessities of existence. For the higher land and the lower wages, the more difficult is it for the man who starts with nothing but his labour to become his own employer, and the more he is at the mercy of the landowner and the capitalist.

## OF SPECULATION IN LAND

The old prejudice against speculators in food and other articles of necessity is passing away, for more exact habits of thought have shown that where speculators do not control all the sources and means of production (which is impossible as to most things in this age of the world),* and speculation does not become monopoly, instead of causing scarcity, it tends to alleviate it; and this, on the one side, by giving notice of the impending scarcity, and thus inducing economy, and on the other by stimulating production.

But land not being a thing of human production, speculation in land cannot have this result. A country may export people, but it cannot

---

* Possible as to some things. The Rothschilds and the Bank of California control the quicksilver production of the world, and sell quicksilver in China cheaper than in California, where it is produced. [The Rothschilds were a prominent international family of bankers. Their name has become synonymous with wealth.]

import land. Whatever be the price put upon it, the number of acres in any given place is just so many, with just such capabilities. And though high prices for land may lessen the demand by driving people farther away, this is not economy, but waste, as the labour of a diffused population cannot be so productive as that of a more concentrated population, combined action cannot be so effective and economical, and exchanges must be much more difficult and at a greater cost. It is sometimes said (and the English landlords piously believe that in raising their rents to the highest figure they are doing their best for their fellowmen) that the increase in the price of land leads to increased thoroughness of cultivation, yet how can that be when the increase in the price of land must take from the means of the cultivator, either by reducing his capital when he buys, or by reducing his earnings when he rents?* That the two things go together is undoubtedly true; but it seems to me that the increased thoroughness of cultivation is due to the increased pressure of population–to higher prices for produce and lower prices for labour rather than directly to the increased price of land.

There is another attribute in which land differs from things of human production. It is imperishable. The speculator in grain must sell quickly, not merely because he knows another crop will soon come in, but because his grain will spoil by keeping; the speculator in a manufactured article must also sell quickly, not merely because the mills are at work, but because the articles in which he is speculating will spoil or go out of fashion. Not so with land. The speculator in land can wait; his land will still be there as good as ever. If he dies before he reaps the benefit, the land will be there for his children.

Thus land, being a thing of limited quantity, of imperishable nature and of unchanging demand, is a thing in which there are more inducements for speculation than in anything else. And being, not the result of human labour, but the field for human labour, the increased price caused by speculation is a tax for which there can be no beneficial return.

---

* It may be said (and it is probably to some extent true in new countries), that where land is low a man will buy as much as he can; where land is higher, and he must take less for the same money, he will cultivate it better. But if a man takes more than he can well use, this in itself is speculation, and another remedy should be looked for than the increase of speculation. Whereas, if by high prices a man is driven to bestow the same labour on a smaller piece of ground than he would with greater profit expend on a larger piece—the increased thoroughness of cultivation reduces production instead of increasing it—is an evil, not a benefit.

Speculation in land is, in fact, but a shutting out from the land of those who want to use it, until they agree to pay the price demanded—the land speculator is a true "dog in the manger." He does not want to use the land himself, but he finds his profit in preventing other people from using it. The speculator knows that more people are coming, and that they must have land, and he gets hold of the land which they will want to use, in order that he may force them to pay him a price for which he gives them no return—that is, that he may appropriate a portion of their labour. Our emigrating race may be likened to a caravan crossing the desert, and the land speculator to one of their number who rides a little in advance, taking possession of the springs as they are reached and exacting a price from his comrades for the water which nature furnishes without price.

#### OF PROSPECTIVE VALUE AS AFFECTING THE PRESENT VALUE OF LAND

According to the doctrine of rent advanced by Ricardo and Malthus,* and generally accepted by the best authorities on political economy, the value of land should be determined by the advantages which it possesses over the least advantageous land in use. This would be true, though subject to the modifications arising from custom and the inertia of population, were it not for the influence which prospective value exercises upon present value. Where speculation in land is permitted— more so, where it is encouraged, as it is with us—the prospective value of land (the incentive to speculation) must exercise a very great influence upon the present value of land, and the value of land be determined, not by its actual advantages over the poorest land in use, but by its advantages, prospective as well as actual, over land which offers just sufficient prospective advantage to make its possession desirable. The prices of land in the United States to-day are not warranted by our present population, but are sustained by speculation founded upon the certainty of the greater population which is coming. Every promise, every hope, is discounted by land speculation. And land being indestructible and costing less to keep than anything else (for the taxes on unimproved land are generally lighter than on anything else), and being limited in amount (so that no increase in price brings about an increase in

---

* Henry George made no real study of the authorities on political economy until the "Progress and Poverty" period.—H. G., Jr. [George wrote *Progress and Poverty* between 1877 and 1879.]

supply), these anticipations form a firm basis for price. Land has no intrinsic value. It is not like a keg of nails, which costs about so much to produce, and the price of which cannot, therefore, go much above or fall much below that point. It is worth just what can be had for it. If a man must have land where speculative prices rule, he must pay the price asked, and the price he pays is the gauge by which all the surrounding holders measure the value and assess the price of their lands. One rise encourages another rise, and the course of prices is up and up, so long as there is expectation of future demand. And whenever a temporary panic comes, the land prices recover as quickly as it is natural for hope to reassert itself in the human breast. A great singer buys a lot in a little Illinois town and real estate advances fifty per cent.; a train of cars comes to Oakland, and for miles around land cannot be bought for less than a thousand dollars an acre; a few men in San Francisco say to each other that the city is sure to be the second on the continent, and straightway the hill-tops for long distances are being bought and sold at rates which would be exorbitant if San Francisco really contained a million people, and he who wants a piece of land to use must pay the speculative price. We are thus compelled to pay in the present, prices based on what people will be compelled to pay in the future.

## OF SPECULATION IN LAND, AND THE SUPPLY OF CAPITAL

We frequently hear it said: "Times are hard because land speculation has locked up so much capital." Now it is evident that no amount of buying and selling in a community can lock up capital, and the direct effect of a rise in land values, is to alter the distribution of wealth, not to affect its amount. But to some extent the same effect is produced as would be by the locking up of capital. When a rise in land values takes place, certain men find themselves much richer, without any addition to the capital of the community having been made. Some of these will employ part of their new wealth in unproductive uses–in building finer houses, buying diamonds for their wives, or travelling in the East, or in Europe. This reduces the supply of productive capital. At the same time the profits of land speculation, and the new security which the rise in values gives, will increase the number of borrowers, and competition between them will have a tendency to keep up rates of interest. But a fall in land prices does not at once increase the available supply of capital, as capitalists are made timid, and there is a tendency to hoard rather than lend.

## OF THE NECESSARY VALUE OF LAND

Where the monopolisation of land is not permitted, where a man can only take land which he wants to use, unused land can have no value–at least, none above the price fixed by the State for the privilege of occupying it. But as land becomes occupied, most of it would acquire a value–either from the possession of natural advantages superior to that still unoccupied, or from its more central position as respects to population. This we may call the *necessary* or real value of land, in contradistinction to the *unnecessary* or fictitious value of land which results from monopolisation. To illustrate: If, on the outskirts of San Francisco, any one who wished to build a house might take a lot from the unused ground, outside land would be worth nothing, but Montgomery or Kearney street property would still be very valuable, as, being in the heart of the city, it is more convenient for residences or more useful for business purposes. The difference, however, between this *necessary* value of the land of the United States and the aggregate value at which it is held must be most enormous, and the difference represents the unnecessary tax which land monopolisation levies upon labour.

## OF PROPERTY IN LAND

The right of every human being to himself is the foundation of the right of property. That which a man produces is rightfully his own, to keep, to sell, to give, or to bequeath, and upon this sure title alone can ownership of anything rightfully rest. But man has also another right, declared by the fact of his existence–the right to the use of so much of the free gifts of nature as may be necessary to supply all the wants of that existence, and as he may use without interfering with the equal rights of any one else, and to this he has a title as against all the world.

This right is natural; it cannot be alienated. It is the free gift of his Creator to every man that comes into the world–a right as sacred, as indefeasible as his right to life itself.

Land being the creation of God and the natural habitation of man, the reservoir from which man must draw the means of maintaining his life and satisfying his wants; the material to which it was pre-ordained that his labour should be applied, it follows that every man born into this world has a natural right to as much land as is necessary for his own uses, and that no man has a right to any more. To deny this is to deny the right of man to himself, to assert the atrocious doctrine that the Almighty has created some men to be the slaves of others.

For, to permit one man to monopolise the land from which the support of others is to be drawn, is to permit him to appropriate their labour, and, in so far as he is permitted to do this, to appropriate them. It is to institute slavery.

For whether a man owns the bodies of his fellow beings, or owns only the land from which they must obtain a subsistence, makes but little difference to him or to them. In the one case it is slavery just as much as the other. And of the two forms of slavery, that which pretends to the ownership of flesh and blood seems to me, on the whole, far the more preferable. For in England, where the monopolisation of land has reached a point which gives to the mere labourer a share of the product of his labour just sufficient to maintain his existence, the land-owner gets from the labourer all that any master can get from his slave, while he is not affected by the selfish interest which prompts the master to look out for the well-being of his slave, and is not influenced by those warmer feelings which any ordinarily well-disposed man feels towards any living thing of which he claims the ownership, be it even a dog. For in free, rich England of the Nineteenth Century–England, whose boast it is that no slave can breathe her air–England, that has spent millions of pounds for the abolition of slavery in far-off lands, and that sends abroad annually hundreds of thousands of pounds for the conversion of the heathen–the condition of the agricultural labourer is to-day harder, more hopeless and more brutalising than that of the average slave under any system of slavery which has prevailed in modern times.[39] And, going even further, I do not believe that the cold-blooded horrors brought to light by the various Parliamentary Commissions which have investigated the condition of the labouring poor of England, can be matched even by the records of ancient slavery, under which system slaves were sometimes fed to fishes, or tortured for sport, or even by the annals of Spanish conquests in the New World.[40] Certain it is that the condition of the slaves upon our Southern plantations was not half so bad as that of the land monopoly slaves of England. Legrees there may have been in plenty, but I have yet to hear of the Legree who worked children to physical and moral death in his fields, or ground them, body and soul, in his mills.[41]

There is in nature no such thing as a fee simple in land.[42] The Almighty, who created the earth for man and man for the earth, has entailed it upon all the generations of the children of men by a decree written upon the constitution of all things–a decree which no human action can bar and no prescription determine. Let the parchments be ever so many, or possession ever so long, in the Courts of Natural Justice there can be but one title to land recognised–the using of it to satisfy reasonable wants.

Now, from this, it by no means follows that there should be no such thing as property in land, but merely that there should be no monopo-lisation–no standing between the man who is willing to work and the field which nature offers for his labour. For while it is true that the land of a country is a free gift from the Creator to all the people of that coun-try, to the enjoyment of which each has an equal natural right, it is also true that the recognition of private ownership in land is necessary to its proper use–is, in fact, a condition of civilisation. When the millennium comes, and the old savage, selfish instincts have died out in men, land may perhaps be held in common; but not till then. In our present state, at least, the "magic of property which turns even sand into gold" must be applied to our lands if we would reap the largest benefits they are capable of yielding–must be retained if we would keep from relapsing into barbarism.

And a full appreciation of the value of landownership tends to the same practical conclusion as the considerations I have been presenting. If the worker upon land is a better worker and a better man because he owns the land, it should be our effort to make this stimulus felt by all– to make, as far as possible, all land-users also landowners.

Nor is there any difficulty in combining a full recognition of private property in land with a recognition of the right of all to the benefits con-ferred by the Creator, as I will hereafter attempt to show.

We are not called upon to guarantee to all men equal conditions, and could not if we would, any more than we could guarantee to them equal intelligence, equal industry or equal prudence; but we *are* called upon to give to all men an equal chance. If we do not, our republicanism is a snare and a delusion, our clatter about the rights of man the veriest buncombe in which a people ever indulged.

# IV. The Tendency of Our Present Land Policy

## What Our Land Policy Is

Is our land policy calculated to give all men an equal chance? We have seen what it is—how we are enabling speculators to rob settlers; how we are by every means enhancing the tax which the many must pay to the few; how we are making away with the heritage of our children, and putting in immense bodies into the hands of a few individuals the soil from which the coming millions of our people must draw their support. If we continue this policy a few years, the public domain will all be gone; the homestead law and the pre-emption law will remain upon the statute books but to remind the poor man of the good time past, and we shall find ourselves embarrassed by all the difficulties which beset the statesmen of Europe—the social disease of England; the seething discontent of France.

Was there ever national blunder so great—ever national crime so tremendous as ours in dealing with our land? It is not in the heat and flush of conquest that we are thus doing what has been done in every country under the sun where a ruling class has been built up and the masses condemned to hopeless toil; it is not in ignorance of true political principles and in the conscientious belief that the God-appointed order of things is that the many should serve the few. We are monopolising our land deliberately—*our* land, not the land of a conquered nation, and we are doing it while prating of the equal rights of the citizen and of the brotherhood of men.

## The Value of Our Public Domain

This public domain that we are getting rid of as recklessly as though we esteemed its possession a curse, can never be replaced, nor are there other limitless bodies of land which we may subdue. Of the whole continent, we now occupy nearly the whole of the zone in which all the real progressive life of the world has been lived. North of us are the cold high latitudes, south of us the tropical heats. The table-lands of Mexico and the valleys of the Saskatchewan and Red rivers, which comprise almost all of the temperate portions of the continent yet unoccupied by our race, are of very small extent when compared with the vast country we have already overrun, and when our emigration is compelled to set upon them will be filled as we now populate a new State.

It is not pleasant to think of the time when the public domain will all be gone. "This will be a great country," we say, "when it is all fenced in." Great it will be–great it must be, in arts and arms, in population and in wealth. But will it be as great in all that constitutes true greatness? Will it be such a good country for the poor man? Will there be such an average of comfort and independence and virtue among the masses? And which to me is the important fact–that I am one of a nation of so many more millions, or that I can buy my children shoes when they need them? "The greatest glory of America," says Carlyle, "is that there every bootblack may have a turkey in his pot."[43] We shall be credited with no such glory when the country is all "fenced in" as we are now rapidly fencing it.

From this public domain of ours have sprung and still spring subtle influences which strengthen our national character and tinge all our thought. This vast background of unfenced land has given a consciousness of freedom even to the dweller in crowded cities, and has been a well-spring of hope even to those who never thought of taking refuge upon it. The child of the people as he grows to manhood in Europe finds every seat at the banquet of life marked "taken," and must struggle with his fellows for the crumbs that fall, without one chance in a thousand of forcing or sneaking his way to a seat. In America, whatever be his condition, there is always more or less clearly and vividly the consciousness that the public domain is behind him; that there is a new country where all the places are not yet taken, where opportunities are still open; and the knowledge of this fact, acting and reacting, penetrates our whole national life, giving to it generosity and independence, elasticity and ambition.

Why should we seek so diligently to get rid of this public domain as if for the mere pleasure of getting rid of it? What have the buffaloes done to us that we should sacrifice the heritage of our children to see the last of them extirpated before we die? Are the operatives of New England, the farmers of Ohio, the mechanics of San Francisco better off for the progress of this thing which we call national development–this scattering of a thousand people over the land which would suffice for a million; this fencing in for a dozen of the soil to which tens of millions must before long look for subsistence?

All that we are proud of in the American character, all that makes our condition and institutions better than those of the older countries, we may trace to the fact that land has been cheap in the United States; and yet we are doing our utmost to make it dear, and actually seem pleased to see it become dear, looking upon the lien which the few are taking upon the labour of the many as an actual increase in the wealth of all.

## No Tendency to Equalisation

Nor can we flatter ourselves that the inequality in condition which we are creating will right itself by easy and peaceful means. It is not merely present inequality which we are creating, but a tendency to further inequality. When we allow one man to take the land which should belong to a hundred, and give to a corporation the soil from which a million must shortly draw their subsistence, we are not only giving in the present wealth to the few by taking it from the many, but we are putting it in the power of the few to levy a constant and an increasing tax upon the many, and we are increasing the tendency to the concentration of wealth not merely upon the land which is thus monopolised, but all over the United States.

Even if the large bodies of land which we are giving away for nothing, or selling to speculators for a nominal price, are subdivided and sold for small farms, the mischief we have done is not at an end. The capital of the settlers has been taken from them, and put in large masses into the hands of the speculators or railroad kings. The many are thereafter the poorer; the few thereafter the richer. We have concentrated wealth; that is, we have concentrated the power of getting wealth. We have set in operation the law of attraction–the law that "unto him that hath shall it be given," and never in any age of the world has this law worked so powerfully as now.

It must not be thought that because we have no laws of entail and primogeniture the vast estates which we are creating will in time break up of themselves. There were no laws of entail and primogeniture in ancient Rome where the monopolisation of land and the concentration of wealth went so far that the empire, and even civilisation itself, perished of the social diseases engendered. It is not the laws of entail and primogeniture that have produced the concentration of wealth in England which makes the richest country in the world the abode of the most hopeless poverty. In spite of entail and primogeniture, wealth is constantly changing from hand to hand, but always in large masses. The richest families of a few centuries back are extinct, the blood of the noblest of a comparatively recent time flows in the veins of people who live in garrets and toil in kitchens. And the same causes which have reduced the 374,000 landholders of England in the middle of the last century to 30,000 now are working in this country as powerfully as they are working there.[44] Wealth is concentrating in a few hands as rapidly in New York as in London; the condition of the labouring classes of New England is steadily approximating to that of Old England.

Nor, if we are to have a very rich class and a very poor class, is there any particular advantage in the fact that one is constantly being recruited from the other, though there are people who seem to think that the fact that most of our millionaires were poor boys is a sufficient answer to anything that may be said of the evils of a concentration of wealth. As wealth concentrates, the chance for any particular individual to escape from one class to another becomes less and less, until practically worth nothing, while there is nothing in human nature to cause us to believe, and nothing in history to show that members of a privileged class are less grasping because they once belonged to an unprivileged class. Nor, after wealth has become concentrated, is there any tendency in this changing of the individuals who hold it to diffuse it again. The social structure is like the flame of a gas-burner, which retains its form though the particles which compose it are constantly changing.

## THE TENDENCY TO CONCENTRATION

There is no tendency yet to the breaking up of large landholdings in the United States; but the reverse is rather the case. The railroad lands are not being sold anything like as fast as they are being granted, and large private estates are increasing instead of diminishing. It is true that tracts bought for speculation are frequently cut up and sold, but it will generally be found that others are at the same time secured farther ahead, though not always by the same parties. And as wealth concentrates, population becomes denser, and the advantages of landownership greater, the tendency on the part of the rich to invest in land increases, and the same cause which has so largely reduced the number of landowners in Great Britain is put in operation. Already the custom of renting land is unmistakably gaining ground, and the concentration of landownership seems to be going on in our older States almost as fast as the monopolisation of new and goes on in the younger ones.* And at last the steam plough and the steam wagon have appeared—to develop, perhaps, in agriculture the same tendencies to concentration which the power loom and the triphammer have developed in manufacturing.[45]

We are not only putting large bodies of our new lands in the hands of the few; but we are doing our best to keep them there, and to cause the absorption of small farms into large estates. The whole pressure of our revenue system, National and State, tends to the concentration of wealth and the monopolisation of land. A hundred thousand dollars in the hands of one man pays but a slight proportion of the taxes which are paid by the same sum in the hands of fifty; a hundred thousand acres owned by a single landholder are assessed but for a fraction of the amount assessed upon the hundred thousand acres of six hundred

---

* "Our farms in older States, instead of being divided and subdivided as they ought to be, are growing larger and more unwieldy. The tendency of the times is unquestionably towards immense estates, each with a manorial mansion in the center and a dependent tenantry crouching in the shadow."—*North American Review,* 1859.

"A non-resident proprietary like that of Ireland is getting to be the characteristic of large farming districts in New England, adding yearly to the nominal value of leasehold farms, advancing yearly the rent demanded, and steadily degrading the character of the tenantry, until, in the place of the boasted intelligence of rural New England, a competent authority can to-day write: 'The general educational condition of the farm laborer is very low, even below that of the factory operative; a large percentage of them can neither read nor write.'"—*New York World, May,* 1871, *in an article on the returns for [the] New England of the Census of* 1870.

"The part of the report [Massachusetts Bureau of Labor Statistics], however, which of all is, in our opinion, the most remarkable, is that relating to agriculture in Massachusetts. It may be summed up in two words: rapid decay. Increased nominal value of land, higher rents, fewer farms occupied by owners; diminished product, general decline of prosperity, lower wages; a more ignorant population, increasing number of women employed at hard outdoor labor (surest sign of a declining civilization), and steady deterioration in the style of farming—these are the conditions described by a cumulative mass of evidence that is perfectly irresistible, and that is unfortunately only too strongly confirmed by such details of census statistics as have been so far made public."—*New York Nation, June,* 1871.

farms. Especially is this true of the State of California, where the large landholders are frequently assessed at the rate of one dollar per acre on land for which they are charging settlers twenty or thirty, and where the small farmer sometimes pays taxes at a rate one hundredfold greater than his neighbour of the eleven[-]league ranch. Our whole policy is of a piece—everything is tending with irresistible force to make us a nation of landlords and tenants—of great capitalists and their poverty-stricken employés.

The life of all the older nations shows the bitterness of the curse of land monopolisation; we cannot turn a page of their history without finding the blood stains and the tear marks it has left. But never since commerce and manufactures grew up, and men began to engage largely in other occupations than those connected directly with the soil, has it been so important to prevent land monopolisation as now. The tendency of all the improved means and forms of production and exchange—of the greater and greater subdivision of labour, of the enslavement of steam, of the utilisation of electricity, of the ten thousand great labour-saving appliances which modern invention has brought forth, is strongly and more strongly to extend the dominion of capital and to make of labour its abject slave. Once to set up in the business of making cloth required only the purchase of a hand loom and a little yarn, the means for which any journeyman could soon save from his earnings; now it requires a great factory, costly machinery, large stocks and credits, and to go into business on his own account one must be a millionaire. So it is in all branches of manufacture; so, too, it is in trade. Concentration is the law of the time. The great city is swallowing up the little towns; the great merchant is driving his poorer rivals out of business; a thousand little dealers become the clerks and shopmen of the proprietor of the marble-fronted palace; a thousand master workmen, the employés of one rich manufacturer, and the gigantic corporations, the alarming product of the new social forces which Watt and Stephenson introduced to the world, are themselves being welded into still more titanic corporations.[46] From present appearances, ten years from now we shall have but three, possibly but one railroad company in the United States, yet our young men remember the time when these giants were such feeble infants that we deemed it charity to shelter them from the cold, and feed them, as it were, with a spoon. In the new condition of things what chance will there be for a poor man if our land also is monopolised?

Of the political tendency of our land policy, it is hardly necessary to speak. To say that the land of a country shall be owned by a small class, is to say that that class shall rule it; to say—which is the same thing—that the people of a country shall consist of the very rich and the very poor, is to say that republicanism is impossible. Its forms may be preserved; but the real government which clothes itself with these forms, as if in mockery, will be many degrees worse than an avowed and intelligent despotism.

# V. What Our Land Policy Should Be

## How We Should Dispose of Our New Land

When we reflect what land is; when we consider the relations between it and labour; when we remember that to own the land on which a man *must* gain his subsistence is to all intents and purposes to own the man himself, we cannot remain in doubt as to what should be our policy in disposing of our public lands.

We have no right to dispose of them except to *actual settlers*–to the men who really want to use them; no right to sell them to speculators, to give them to railroad companies or to grant them for agricultural colleges; no more right to do so than we have to sell or to grant the labour of the people who must some day live upon them.

And to actual settlers we should *give* them. *Give*, not sell. For we have no right to step between the man who wants to use land and land which is as yet unused, and to demand of him a price for our permission to avail himself of his Creator's bounty. The cost of surveying and the cost of administering the Land Office may be proper charges; but even these it were juster and wiser to charge as general expenses, to be borne by the surplus wealth of the country, by the property which settlement will make more valuable. We can better afford to bear the necessary expenses of the Land Office than we can the expense of keeping useless men-of-war at sea or idle troops in garrison posts. When we can give a few rich bankers twenty or thirty millions a year we can afford to pay a few millions in order to make our public lands perfectly free. Let the settler keep all of his little capital; it is his seed wheat. When he has gathered his crop, then we may take our toll, with usury if need be.[47]

*And we should give but in limited quantities.* For while every man has a right to as much land as he can properly use, no man has a right to any more, and when others do or will want it, cannot take any more

69

without infringing on *their* rights. One hundred and sixty acres is too much to give one person; it is more than he can cultivate; and our great object should be to give every one an opportunity of employing his own labour, and to give no opportunity to any one to appropriate the labour of others. We cannot afford to give so much in view of the extent of the public domain and the demand for homes yet to be made upon it. While we are calling upon all the world to come in and take our land, let us save a little for our own children. Nor can we afford to give so much in view of the economic loss consequent upon the dispersion of population. Four families to the square mile are not enough to secure the greatest return to labour and the least waste in exchanges. Eighty acres is quite enough for any one, and I am inclined to think forty acres still nearer the proper amount.

There should be but this one way of disposing of the agricultural lands. None at all should be given to the States, except such as was actually needed for sites of public buildings; none at all for school funds or agricultural colleges. The earnings of a self-employing, independent people, upon which the State may at any time draw, constitute the best school fund; to diffuse wealth so that the masses may enjoy the luxury of learning is the best way to provide for colleges.

## SOME OBJECTIONS

It will be said: ["]If the public land is to be morselled out in this way, what is to be done for stock ranches and sheep farms?["] There will be the unused land, the public commons. Let the large herds and flocks keep upon that, moving farther along as it is needed for settlement. But there would be plenty of stock kept on eighty-acre or even forty-acre farms. In Belgium each six-acre farmer has his cow or two of the best breed, and kept in the best condition.

And it may be said: There is some land which requires extensive work for its reclamation. Capital cannot be induced to undertake this work if the land be given away in small pieces. But if capital cannot, labour can. The most difficult reclamation in the world—that of turning the shifting sands of the French sea-coast into gardens has been done by ten- and twelve-acre farmers. Observe that it is proposed to give the lands only to actual settlers. Is there any of our land which requires for its reclamation greater capital than that involved in the labour of sixteen men to the square mile, working to make themselves homes? The cost of reclaiming the swamp lands of California, which has been made an excuse for giving them away by the hundred thousand acres, does not in most cases equal the cost of the fencing required on the uplands. Let men be sure that they are working for themselves, give them a little stake in the general prosperity, and labour will combine intelligently and economically enough.

## How Settlement Would Go On

Under such a policy as this, settlement would go on regularly and thoroughly. Population would not in the same time spread over as much ground as under the present policy; but what it did spread over would be well settled and well cultivated. There would be no necessity for building costly railroads to connect settlers with a market. The market would accompany settlement. No one would go out into the wilderness, to brave all the hardships and discomforts of the solitary frontier life; but with the foremost line of settlement would go church and school-house and lecture-room. The ill-paid, overworked mechanic of the city could find a home on the soil, where he would not have to abandon all the comforts of civilisation, but where there would be society enough to make life attractive, and where the wants of his neighbours would give a market for his surplus labour until his land began to produce; and to tell those who complain of want of employment and low wages to make for themselves homes on the public domain would then be no idle taunt.

Consider, too, the general gain from this mode of settlement. How much of our labour is now given to transportation, and wasted in various ways, because of the scattering of our population which land grabbing has caused?

## Something Still More Radical Needed

But still the adoption of such a policy would affect only the land that is left us. It would be preventive, not remedial. It would still leave the great belts granted to railroads, the vast estates such as those with which California is cursed, and the large bodies of land which everywhere have been made the subject of speculation. It would leave, moreover, still in full force, the tendency which is concentrating the ownership of the land in a few hands in the older settled States. And further than this,

I hardly think, agitate as we may, that we can secure the adoption of such a preventive policy until we can do something to make the monopolisation of land unprofitable.

What we want, therefore, is something which shall destroy the tendency to the aggregation of land, which shall break up present monopolisation, and which shall prevent (by doing away with the temptation) future monopolisation. And as arbitrary and restrictive laws are always difficult to enforce, we want a measure which shall be equal, uniform and constant in its operation; a measure which will not restrict enterprise, which will not curtail production, and which will not offend the natural sense of justice.

When our 40,000,000 of people have to raise $800,000,000 per year for public purposes* we cannot have any difficulty in discovering such a remedy, in the adjustment of taxation.

### A LESSON FROM THE PAST

Let us turn for a moment from the glare of the Nineteenth Century to the darkness of mediæval times. The spirit of the Feudal System dealt far more wisely with the land than the system which has succeeded it, and rude outcome of a barbarous age though it was, we may, remembering the difference of times and conditions, go back to it for many valuable lessons. The Feudal System annexed duties to privileges. In theory, at least, protection was the corollary of allegiance, and honour brought with it the obligation to a good life and noble deeds, while the ownership of land involved the necessity of bearing the public expenses. One portion of the land, allotted to the Crown, defrayed the expenses of the State; out of the profits of another portion, allotted to the military tenants, the army was provided and maintained; the profits of a third portion, given to religious uses, supported the Church and relieved the sick, the indigent and the wayworn, while there was a fourth portion, the commons, of which no man was master, but which was free to all the people. The great debt, the grinding taxation, which now falls on the labouring classes of England, are but the results of a departure from this system. Before Henry VIII. suppressed the monasteries and enclosed the commons there were no poor laws in England

---

* Estimate of Commissioner Wells.

and no need for any;[48] until the Crown lands were got rid of there was no necessity for taxation for the support of the Government; until the military tenants shirked the condition on which they had been originally permitted to reap the profits of landownership, England could at any time put an army in the field without borrowing and without taxation; and a recent English writer has estimated that had the feudal tenures been continued, England would have now had at her command a completely appointed army of six hundred thousand men, without the cost of a penny to the public treasury or to the labouring classes. Had this system been continued the vast war expenses of England would have come from the surplus wealth of those who make war; the expenses of government would have borne upon the classes who direct the Government; and the deep gangrene of pauperism, which perplexes the statesman and baffles the philanthropist, would have had no existence. England would have been stronger, richer, happier. Why should *we* not go back to the old system, and charge the expenses of [G]overnment upon our lands?

If we do, we shall go far towards breaking up land monopoly and all its evils, and towards counteracting the causes now so rapidly concentrating wealth in a few hands. We shall raise our revenues by the most just and the most simple means, and with the least possible burden upon production.

## TAXATION OF LAND FALLS ONLY ON ITS OWNER

There is one peculiarity in a land tax. With a few trifling exceptions of no practical importance it is the only tax which must be paid by the holder of the thing taxed. If we impose a tax upon money loaned, the lender will charge it to the borrower, and the borrower must pay it, otherwise the money will be sent out of the country for investment, and if the borrower uses it in his business he, in his turn, must charge it to his customers or his business becomes unprofitable. If we impose a tax upon buildings, those who use them must pay it, as otherwise the erection of buildings becomes unprofitable, and will cease until rents become high enough to pay the regular profit on the cost of building as well as the tax besides. But not so with land. Land is not an article of production. Its quantity is fixed. No matter how little you tax it there will be no more of it; no matter how much you tax it there will be no less. It can neither be removed nor made scarce by cessation of production.

There is no possible way in which owners of land can shift the tax upon the user. And so while the effect of taxation upon all other things is to increase their value, and thus to make the consumer pay the tax–the effect of a tax upon land is to reduce its value–that is, its selling price, as it reduces the profit of its ownership without reducing its supply. It will not, however, reduce its renting price. The same amount of rent will be paid; but a portion of it will now go to the State instead of to the landlord. And were we to impose upon land a tax equal to the whole annual profit of its ownership, land would be worth nothing and might in many cases be abandoned by its owners. But the users would still have to pay as much as before–paying in taxes what they formerly paid as rent. And reversely, if we were to reduce or take off the taxes on land, the owner, not the user, would get the benefit. Rents would be no higher, but would leave more profit, and the value of land would be more.

## LAND TAXATION THE BEST TAXATION

The best tax is that which comes nearest to filling the three following conditions:[49]

That it bear as lightly as possible upon production.

That it can be easily and cheaply collected, and cost the people as little as possible in addition to what it yields the Government.

That it bear equally–that is, according to the ability to pay.

The tax upon land better fulfils these conditions than any tax it is possible to impose.

1.–As we have seen, it does not bear at all upon production–it adds nothing to prices, and does not affect the cost of living.

2.–As it does not add to prices, it costs the people nothing in addition to what it yields the Government; while as land cannot be hid and cannot be moved, it can be collected with more ease and certainty, and with less expense than any other tax.

3.–A tax upon the value of land is the most equal of all taxes, not that it is paid by all in equal amounts, or even in equal amounts upon equal means, but because the value of land is something which belongs to all, and in taxing land values we are merely taking for the use of the community something which belongs to the community, which by the necessities of our social organisation we are obliged to permit individuals to hold.

Of course, in speaking of the value of land, I mean the value of the land itself, not the value of any improvement which has been made upon it–I mean what I believe is sometimes called in England the *unearned* value of land.

From its very nature it must be apparent that property in land differs essentially from other property, and if the principles I have endeavoured to state in the third section of this paper are correct, it must be evident that it is not unjust to impose taxes upon land values which are not imposed on other property. But as the proposition may be somewhat startling, it may be worth while to dwell a little on this point.

## Of the Justice of Taxing Land

Here is a lot in the central part of San Francisco, which, irrespective of the building upon it, is worth $100,000. What gives that value? Not what its owner has done,* but the fact that 150,000 people have settled around it. This lot yields its owner $10,000 annually. Where does this $10,000 come from? Evidently from the earnings of the workers of the community, for it can come from nowhere else.

Here is a lot on the outskirts. It is in the same condition in which nature left it. Intrinsically it is worth no more than when there were but a hundred people at Yerba Buena Cove. Then it was worth nothing. Now that there are 150,000 people here and more coming, it is worth $3000. That is, its owner can command $3000 worth of the labour or of the wealth of the community. What does he give for this? Nothing; the land was there before he was.

Suppose a community like that of San Francisco, in which land, though in individual hands as now, has no value. Suppose, then, that all at once the land was given a value of, say, $150,000,000, which is about the present value of land in San Francisco. What would be the effect? That a tax, of which $150,000,000 is the capitalised value, would be levied upon the whole community for the benefit of a portion. There would be no more in the community than before, and no greater means of producing wealth. But of that wealth, beyond the share which they formerly had, the landowners would now command $150,000,000. That is, there would be $150,000,000 less for other people who were not land-holders.

* Though he may have done some part, as in grading, etc.

And does not this consideration of the nature and effect of land values go far to explain the puzzling fact that notwithstanding all the economies in production and distribution which a dense population admits, just as a community increases in population and wealth, so does the reward of the labourer decrease and poverty deepen?

One hundred men settle in a new place. Land has at first little or no value. The net result of their labour is divided pretty equally between them. Each one gets pretty nearly the full value of his contribution to the general stock. The community becomes 100,000. Land has become valuable, its value perhaps aggregating as much as the value of all other property. The production of the community may now be more per capita for each individual who works, but before the division is made, one half of the product must go to the landholders. How then can the labourer get so much as he could in the small community?

Now in this view of the matter—considering land values as an indication of the appropriation (though doubtless the necessary appropriation) of the wealth of all; considering land rentals a tax upon the labour of the community, is not a tax upon land values the most just and the most equal tax that can be levied? Should we not take that which rightfully belongs to the whole before we take that which rightfully belongs to the individual? Should we not tax this tax upon labour before we tax productive labour itself?

That the value of our land, even the "necessary value" which it would have when stripped of speculative value, would easily bear the whole burden of taxation, there can be no doubt. The statistics are too confused and too unreliable to enable us to judge accurately of the value of land as compared with the value of other property; but we have high authority for the belief that the value of our land is equal to the value of all other property, including the improvements upon it. The New York Commissioners for the Revision of the Revenue Laws—David A. Wells, Edwin Dodge, and George W. Cuyler, the first named of whom, as United States Special Commissioner of the Revenue, has had better opportunities for studying all matters connected with taxation than any other man in the United States—say in their report, rendered this year: "A careful consideration and study of the nature and classification of property inclines the Commissioners to indorse the correctness of an opinion which appears to have been originally proposed by a financial writer of New York [George Opdyke] as far back as 1851, viz.: '*That universally the market value of the aggregate of land and that of the aggregate of productive capital are equal."*

And it may be here remarked that these New York Commissioners in their elaborate report recommend the total abolition of the tax on personal property on the ground (which has been proved in every State in the Union, and, in fact, by every nation of ancient or modern times) that it is utterly impossible to collect it with any degree of fulness and anything like fairness, and that the attempt to do so results in injury both to the material and the moral interests of the community. They propose instead of the tax on personal property, to tax every individual on an amount three times as great as the annual rental of the house or place of business he occupies, and present a strong array of reasons to show that this would be a much more equitable and productive mode of taxation. Better still, for the reasons I have given, to abandon the attempt to tax personal property or anything in lieu of it, and to put the bulk of taxation entirely on land values.

Nevertheless, after all that can be said, it must be confessed that there would be some slight injustice in doing so. I had ten thousand dollars, let us say, which I might have put out at high interest, or invested in my business. Supposing the existing policy would be continued, I bought

---

* By "productive capital" Opdyke means all property other than land. In his ["]Treatise on Political Economy["] he says: "The statistics presented by assessments of property for the purposes of taxation invariably exhibit the estimated value of land and its meliorations under the head of 'real estate,' and the estimated value of all other productive capital under the head of 'personal estate.' Thus divided, we may readily infer that the value of real estate greatly exceeds that of personal estate, and so these statistics invariably indicate. But if we take the estimate for any given village, town or city, and from the gross value of the real estate deduct the value of the buildings, and add to it the personal estate, we shall then find them equal, provided the assessment has been correctly made, which, by the way, very rarely occurs."

After citing examples from New York and Cincinnati, he goes on to say: "It is thus of all other cities, towns and villages throughout the civilized world; and it is thus in all agricultural districts, but in these the land and its meliorations are so much more intimately blended that we cannot perceive the facts so readily. The truth is, the market value of land is merely the reflection of the value of the productive capital placed upon it and its immediate vicinity. It has no real value of its own; it costs nothing to produce; but since the laws have endowed it with the vital principle of wealth by subjecting it to individual ownership, it can no longer be obtained without giving in exchange for it an equivalent portion of the capital present and designed to concur with it in the production of wealth."

land with it, calculating that in a few years, when population became greater, people would be glad to buy it of me for a much higher price, or give me one fourth of the crop for the privilege of cultivating it. You now impose taxation, which will lower the value of my land. If you do this, you make my speculation less profitable than others that I might have gone into, and thus do me injustice, for you gave me no notice.

This is true, and it is this consideration which makes men like John Stuart Mill shrink from the practical application of deductions from their own doctrines, and propose that in resuming their ownership of the land of England, the people of England shall pay its present proprietors not only its actual value, but also the present value of its prospective increase in value.[50] But if we once do a public wrong, we can never right it without doing somebody injustice. England sought to right the wrong of slavery without injustice to the slaveholders who had invested their capital in human flesh and blood. She succeeded by making them pecuniary compensation; but in doing this she did a worse injustice to her own white slaves on whom the burden of the payment has been imposed. And by shrinking from doing this slight injustice which would affect but very few people in the community, and those most able to stand it, we continue a ten thousandfold greater injustice; and the longer we delay action, the greater will be the injustice which we must do.

### Of Some Exemptions, and Some Additions

For the purpose of making it still more sure that taxation should not bear heavily upon any one; for the purpose of still further counteracting the tendency to the concentration of wealth, and for the purpose of securing as far as possible to every citizen an interest in the soil, there should be a uniform exemption to a small amount made to each landholder—perhaps a smaller amount in the cities, where land is only used for residences and business purposes, than in the country, where labour is directly applied to the land. Those whose land did not exceed in value this minimum would have no taxes to pay; those whose land did, would pay upon the surplus. This would reverse the present effect of our revenue system, and tend to make the holding of land in large bodies less profitable than the holding of it in small bodies.

And while, perhaps, it might not be wise to attempt to limit the accumulations of any individual during his lifetime, or at any rate it is not yet necessary to try the experiment, there should be a very heavy duty, amounting to a considerable part of the whole, levied upon the estates of deceased persons, and in the case of intestates the whole should escheat to the State, where there were no heirs of the first or second degree.

There is still another source from which a large revenue might be harmlessly drawn–license taxes upon such businesses as it is public policy to restrict and discourage, such as liquor selling, the keeping of gambling houses (where this cannot be prevented), etc. All other taxes of whatever kind or nature, whether National, State, County, or Municipal, might then be swept away.

## THE EFFECTS OF SUCH A CHANGE

Consider the effects of the adoption of such a system:

The mere holder of land would be called on to pay just as much taxes as the user of land. The owner of a vacant city lot would have to pay as much for the privilege of keeping other people off it till he wanted to use it, as his neighbour who has a fine house upon his lot, and is either using or deriving rent from it. The monopoliser of agricultural land would be taxed as much as though his land were covered with improvements, with crops and with stock.

Land prices would fall; land speculation would receive its death-blow; land monopolisation would no longer pay. Millions and millions of acres from which settlers are now shut out would be abandoned by their present owners, or sold to settlers on nominal terms. It is only in rare cases that it would pay any one to get land before he wanted to use it, so that those who really wanted to use land would find it easy to get.

The whole weight of taxation would be lifted from productive industry. The million dollar manufactory, and the needle of the seamstress, the mechanic's cottage, and the grand hotel, the farmer's plough, and the ocean steamship, would be alike untaxed. All would be free to buy or sell, to make or save, unannoyed by the tax-gatherer.

Imagine this country with all taxes removed from production and exchange! How demand would spring up; how trade would increase; what a powerful stimulus would be applied to every branch of industry; what an enormous development of wealth would take place. Imagine this country free of taxation, with its unused land free to those who would use it! Would there be many industrious men walking our streets, or tramping over our roads in the vain search for employment? Would we hear much of stagnation in business, and of "over produc- tion" of the things that millions of us want? Consider the enormous gain which would result from leaving capital and labour, untrammelled by tax or restriction, to seek the most remunerative fields; the enormous saving which would result from the settling of people near each other, as they would settle, if any one could get enough unused land for his needs, and it would pay nobody to get any more.

Consider the effects of this policy on the distribution of wealth– directly, by reversing the effect of taxation–which is now to make the poor poorer, and the rich richer; indirectly, by freeing and cheapening land, and thus putting labour in a position to make better terms with capital. And consider how equalisation in the distribution of wealth would react on production–how it would lessen the great army of involuntary idlers; how it would increase the vigour and industry and skill of workers; for poorly rewarded labour is poor labour all the world over, and the greater its reward, the greater the efficiency of labour. Consider, too, the moral effects: Sharp alternations of wealth and poverty breed vice and crime, as surely as they breed misery. Personal independence is the foundation of all the virtues. Deep poverty bru- talises men. Where it exists, the preacher will preach in vain; and the philanthropist will toil in vain; they are dumping their good words and good deeds into such a Slough of Despond as Pilgrim saw.[51]

## WHO WOULD GAIN AND WHO WOULD LOSE

That the policy proposed would be to the advantage of all who do not hold land is clear enough. But it must not be imagined that all who hold land would lose. On the contrary, the large majority of landholders would be gainers. Whether a landholder would gain or lose, would depend upon whether his interest as a landholder, which would be adversely affected, was greater or less than his other interests, which would be beneficially affected. The man who owns a house and lot of equal value would have less taxes to pay if taxation were taken off of buildings and put on land, as the aggregate value of land is greater than that of buildings. His homestead would sell for less than before, but the money it sold for would buy just as good a house and lot as before; so that, if his intention is to always keep a homestead, he would not lose anything by the shrinkage in its value; or even if it was not, he would not have to keep it long before his gain on taxes would make up for the loss in value. While, if he was a mechanic, engaged in or connected with any of the building trades, he would gain in more constant work and better wages by the stimulus which the exemption of improvements from taxation, and the reduction in the value of land would give to building. Or if he kept a store, or was engaged in any business or profession, he would gain by the quickened growth and increased activity of the community.

And if taxes were removed from everything but land (with the exceptions and exemptions I have before indicated) the gain would be largely greater. Let the farmer, the mechanic, the manufacturer, or the business man, who is also a landowner, calculate how much he pays of the taxes which enter into the cost of everything he buys, or in any way uses, and how much he loses by the restrictive effect which those taxes have upon all industry and business. Then let him set against this amount, which he now pays and loses, the additional amount which he would pay as taxes on land, or which he would lose by the reduction of its value, were all taxes placed upon land. Did they make this calculation, three out of every four of those who own land would see they would be gainers. For as yet the class whose other interests are subordinate to their interest in the high value of land is really small. And it must be remembered that were our whole revenue raised by a direct land tax, the amount taken from the people in order to give the same amount to the Government would be very much smaller than now, and that there would be a positive increase in wealth, a large share of which would go to the landowners who would have additional taxes to pay.

## What Can Be Done at Once

The more the matter is considered, the more, I think, it will appear that all our taxation, or at least the largest part of it, should be placed upon land values. By doing so we would substitute the best possible revenue system for our present cumbrous, unjust, wasteful and oppressive modes of taxation; we would, without resort to special and arbitrary laws, prevent and break up land monopolisation, and we would, at the same time, and in the same simple, just way, do a great deal to counteract the alarming tendency to the concentration of wealth in a few hands, which is now so apparent.

Nevertheless, the application of this remedy is not yet practicable. We are so used to look upon land as upon other property, so accustomed to consider its enhancement in value as a public gain, that it will take some time to educate public opinion up to the proper point to permit this; and even then there will be constitutional difficulties to be removed.

But in the meantime, we can do something to check the progress of land monopolisation, and even to break it up. So far as the General Government is concerned, we can insist that no more land grants be made on any pretext or for any purpose; but that all of the public domain still left to us shall be reserved for the small farms of actual settlers. We can go further, and demand that something be done to open to settlers the great belts which have been already handed over to railroad corporations. These grants, in the first place, outraged natural justice, and Congress had no more right to make them than Catherine of Russia had to give away her subjects to her paramours and courtiers, or than the Pope had to divide the Southern Hemisphere between the Spanish and the Portuguese.[52] We should be perfectly justified in taking this land back, throwing it open to settlers upon Government terms, and paying the companies the Government price. Such an operation would largely increase our debt, but the money would be well expended. If this cannot be done, the land can at least be immediately surveyed, so that settlers can find the Government sections, and the right of the Companies to land reserved for them be declared subject to State taxation.

In this monopoly-cursed State of ours, we may at once do a great deal to free our land. By restricting possessory rights to the maximum amount allowed by the General Government to pre-emptors, and by demanding payment for the large tracts now held by speculators under five-dollar certificates, or the payment of twenty per cent. of the purchase money, the Legislature could, in the first week of its session, throw open to settlers some millions of acres now monopolised.* And millions of acres more would be forced into market if its holders were only compelled to pay upon their land the same rate of taxation levied upon other property. The Board of Equalisation created by the last Legislature is endeavouring to secure the proper assessment of these large tracts; but the law under which it works is defective, and the Constitutional requirement of the election of County Assessors is very

---

* Under the decisions of the Department, land within the exterior limits of Spanish grants, and included in railroad reservations, does not go to the Railroad Company when the grant is confined to its real limits, or is rejected, but becomes open to settlement.

much in the way of a thorough reform, perhaps makes it impossible. But as under our Constitution, as interpreted by the Supreme Court, all property must be taxed equally, we can do no more than this to break up large estates until the Constitution is amended.

## THE NECESSITY OF A RADICAL REMEDY

There are many who will think that if we do these things, or even if we merely do something to check the grosser abuses in the disposition of our new land, we shall have done all that is necessary. I wish to call the attention of those who thus think to a certain class of facts:

There is a problem which must present itself to every mind which dwells upon the industrial history of the present century; a problem into which all our great social, industrial, and even political questions run— which already perplexes us in the United States; which presses with still greater force in the older countries of Europe; which, in fact, menaces the whole civilised world, and seems like a very riddle of the Sphinx, which fate demands of modern civilisation, and which not to answer is to be destroyed—the problem of the proper distribution of wealth.[53]

How is it that the increase of productive power and the accumulation of wealth seem to bring no benefit, no relief to the working classes; that the condition of the labourer is better in the new and poor country than in the old and rich country; that in a country like Great Britain, whose productive power has been so enormously increased, whose surplus wealth is lent to all the world, and whose surplus productions are sent to every market, pauperism is increasing in England, while one third of the families of Scotland live in a single room each, and one third more in two rooms each?* How is it, though within the century steam machinery has added to the productive force of Great Britain a power greater than that of the manual labour of the whole human race, that the toil of mere infants is cruelly extorted—that cultivation in the richest districts is largely carried on by gangs of women and children, in which mere babies are worked under the lash; that little girls are to be found wielding sledge hammers, and little boys toiling night and day in the fearful heat of glass furnaces, or working to the extreme limit of human endurance in fetid garrets and damp cellars, at the most monotonous

---

* Census of 1861. See ["]Journal of Statistical Society,["] vol. 32.

employments–children who work so early and work so hard that they know nothing of God, have never heard of the Bible, call a violet a pretty bird, and when shown a cow in a picture, think it must be a lion;* children whose natural protectors have been changed by brutalising poverty and the want that knows no law, into the most cruel of taskmasters?[54]

Why is it that in the older parts of the United States we are rapidly approximating to the same state of things? Why is it that, with all our labour-saving machinery, all the new methods of increasing production which our fertile genius is constantly discovering–with all our railroads, and steamships, and power looms, and sewing machines, our mechanics cannot secure a reduction of two hours in their daily toil; that the general condition of the working classes is becoming worse instead of better; and the employment of women and children at hard labour is extending; that though wealth is accumulating, and luxury increasing, it is becoming harder and harder for the poor man to live?

A very Sodom's apple seems this "progress" of ours to the classes that have the most need to progress. We have been "developing the country" fast enough. We have been building railroads, and peopling the wilderness, and extending our cities. But what is the gain? We count up more millions of people, and more hundreds of millions of taxable property; our great cities are larger, our millionaires are more numerous, and their wealth is more enormous; but are the masses of the people any better off? Is it not so notoriously true that we accept the statement without question, that just as population increases and wealth augments– just in proportion as we near the goal for which we strive so hard, poverty extends and deepens, and it becomes harder and harder for a poor man to make a living?

That the startling change for the worse that has come over the condition of the masses of the United States in the last ten years is attributable in some part to the destruction caused by the war, and in much greater part to stupid, reckless, wicked legislation, there can be no doubt. The whole economic policy of the General Government–the management of the debt and of the currency, the imposition of a tariff which is oppressing all our industry, and actually killing many branches of it, the immense donations to corporations–has tended with irresistible force, as though devised for the purpose, to make a few the richer and the

---

* Report, Children's Employment Commission.

many the poorer; to swell the gains of a few rich capitalists, and make hundreds of thousands of willing workmen stand with idle hands.

But beneath and beyond these special causes, we may see, as could be seen before the war had given the money power an opportunity and excuse for wresting the machinery of Government to its own selfish ends, the working of some general tendency, observable all over the world, and most obvious in the countries which have made the greatest advances in productive power and in wealth.

What is the cause or the causes of this tendency? If we say, as many of the economists say, that it is overpopulation in England–that the working classes get married too early and have too many children– what is it in the United States? If we say that in the United States it is solely due to special conditions, what is it in Australia and other countries of widely differing circumstances?

Now, although there are undoubtedly other general causes, such as the tendency of modern processes to require greater capital and rarer administrative ability, to offer greater facilities for combination, and give more and more advantage to him who can work on a large scale; yet if the principles previously stated are correct, are we not led irresistibly to the conclusion that the main cause of this general tendency to the unequal division of wealth lies in the pursuance of a wrong policy in regard to land–in permitting a few to take and to keep that which belongs to all; in treating the power of appropriating labour as though it were in itself labour-produced wealth? Is not this mistake sufficient of itself to explain most of the perplexing phenomena to which I have alluded?

When land becomes fully monopolised as it is in England and Ireland–when the competition between land-users becomes greater than the competition between landowners, whatever increase of wealth there is must go to the landowner or to the capitalist; the labourer gets nothing but a subsistence. Amid lowing herds he never tastes meat; raising bounteous crops of the finest wheat, he lives on rye or potatoes; and where steam has multiplied by hundreds and by thousands manufacturing power, he is clad in rags, and sends his children to work while they are yet infants. No matter what be the increase in the fertility of the soil, no matter what the increase in product which beneficent inventions cause, no matter even if good laws succeed bad laws, as when free trade succeeds protection, as has been the case in Great Britain, all the advantage goes to the landowner; none to the landless labourer, for the ownership of the land gives the power of taking all that labour upon it will produce, except enough to keep the labourer in condition to work, and anything more that is given is charity. And so increase in productive power is greater wealth to the landowner–more splendour in his drawing rooms, more horses in his stables and hounds in his kennels, finer yachts, and pictures and books–more command of everything that makes life desirable; but to the labourer it is not an additional crust.

And where land monopolisation has not gone so far, steadily with the increase of wealth goes on the increase of land values. Every successive increase represents so much which those who do not produce may take from the results of production, measures a new tax upon the whole community for the benefit of a portion. Every successive increase indicates no addition to wealth, but a greater difference in the division of wealth, making one class the richer, the other the poorer, and tending still further to increase the inequality in the distribution of wealth–on the one side, by making the aggregations of capital larger and its power thus greater, and on the other, by increasing the number of those who cannot buy land for themselves, but must labour for or pay rent to others, and while thus swelling the number of those who must make terms with capital for permission to work, at the same time reducing their ability to make fair terms in the bargain.

Need we go any further to find the root of the difficulty? to discover the point at which we must commence the reform which will make other reforms possible? And while, on the one hand, the recognition of the main cause of the inequality in the distribution of wealth, which is becoming a disease of our civilisation, condemns the wild dreams of impracticable socialisms, and the impossible theories of governmental interference to restrict accumulation and competition and to limit the productive power of capital, by discovering a just and an easy remedy; on the other hand, the spread of such theories should admonish those who consider the remedy of a common-sense policy in regard to land as too radical, of the necessity of making some attempt at reform. This great problem of the more equal distribution of wealth must in some way be solved, if our civilisation, like those that went before it, is not to breed seeds of its own destruction. In one way or another the attempt must be made–if not in one way, then in another. The spread of education, the growth of democratic sentiment, the weakening of the influences which lead men to accept the existing condition of things as divinely appointed, insure that, and the general uneasiness of labour, the growth of trade-unionism, the spread of such societies as the International prove it![55] The terrible struggle of the Paris Commune was but such an attempt.* And in the light of burning Paris we may see how it may be that this very civilisation of ours, this second Tower of Babel, which some deem reaches so far towards heaven that we can plainly see there is no God there, may yet crumble and perish. How prophetic, in view of those recent events, seem the words of Macaulay, when, alluding to Gibbon's argument that modern civilisation could not be overturned as was the ancient, he declared that in the very heart of our great cities, in the shadow of palaces, libraries and colleges, poverty and ignorance might produce a race of Huns fiercer than any who followed Attila, and of Vandals more destructive than those led by Genseric.[56]

## THE PAST AND THE FUTURE OF THE NATION

Five years must yet pass before we can celebrate the hundredth anniversary of the Republic. A century ago, as the result of nearly two hundred years of colonisation, the scarce three million people of the thirteen colonies but fringed the Atlantic seaboard with their settlements. Pittsburgh was to them the Far West, and the Mississippi as little known as is now the great river that through a thousand miles of Arctic solitudes rolls sluggishly to its mouth in our newly acquired Northern possessions.[57]

Looking back over the history of the great nations from whom we derive our blood, our language and our institutions, and a hundred years seems but a small span. A hundred years after the foundation of

---

* And this French struggle also shows the conservative influence of the diffusion of landed property. The Radicals of Paris were beaten by the small proprietors of the provinces. Had the lands of France been in the hands of a few, as the first revolution found it, the raising of the red flag on the Hôtel de Ville would have been the signal for a Jacquerie in every part of the country. So conscious are the extreme reds of the conservative influence of property in land that they have for a long time condemned as a fatal mistake the law of the [F]irst Republic which provided for the equal distribution of land among heirs, not because it has not improved the condition of the peasantry, but because the improvement in their condition and the interest which their possession of land gives them in the maintenance of order dispose them to oppose the violent remedies which the workmen of the cities think necessary. [The Paris Commune (1871) was a revolutionary government temporarily set up at the end of the Franco-Prussian War and brutally put down by French troops. The first revolution began in 1789 and the First Republic lasted from that year until 1794.]

the city, and Rome had scarce begun her conquering mission; a hundred years after the Norman Invasion, and the England of the first Plantagenet differed but little from the England of the Bastard.[58]

How wondrous seems our growth when compared with the past! So wondrous, so unprecedented, that when the slow lapse of years shall have shortened the perspective, and when, in obedience to altered conditions, the rate of increase shall have slackened, it will seem as though in our time the very soil of America must have bred men.

We have subdued a continent in a shorter time than many a palace and cathedral of the Old World was a-building; in less than a century we have sprung to a first rank among the nations; our population is increasing in a steady ratio; and we are carrying westward the centre of power and wealth, of luxury, learning and refinement, with more rapidity than it ever moved before.

We look with wonder upon the past. When we turn to the future, imagination fails, for sober reason with her cold deductions goes far beyond the highest flights that fancy can dare, and we turn dazzled and almost awestruck from the picture that is mirrored. Judging from the past, in all human probability there will be on this continent, a century from now, four or five, perhaps five or six, hundred million English-speaking people, stretching from the isothermal line which marks the northern limit of the culture of wheat, to the southern limit of the semi-tropical clime–four or five hundred million people, with the railroad, the telegraph, and all the arts and appliances that we now have, and with all the undreamed-of inventions which another century such as the past will develop. Beside the great cities of such a people, the Paris of to-day will be a village, the London, a provincial town, and to the political power which will grow up, if these people remain under one government, the great nations of Europe will occupy such relative positions as the South American States now hold to the great Republic of the North.

Yet we should never forget that we have no exemption from the difficulties and dangers which have beset other peoples, though they may come to us in somewhat different guise. The very rapidity of our growth should admonish us that though we are still in our youth, our conditions are fast changing; the very possibilities of our future warn us that this is the appointed theatre upon which the questions that perplex the world must be worked out, or fought out. What good, or what evil, we of this generation do, will appear in the next on an enormously magnified scale. The blunders that we are carelessly making, saying "these things will right themselves in time," will indeed right themselves; but how? How was the wrong of slavery righted in the United States? The whole history of mankind, with its story of fire and sword, of suffering and destruction, is but one continued example of how national blunders and crimes work themselves out. On the smaller scale of individual life and actions, the workings of Divine justice are sometimes never seen; but sure, though not always swift, is the Nemesis that with tireless feet follows every wrong-doing of a people.

The American people have had a better chance and a fairer field than any nation that has gone before. Coming to a new world with all the experiences of the old; possessed of all the knowledge and the arts of the most advanced of the families of men, the temperate zone of an immense continent lay before them, where, unembarrassed by previous mistakes, they might work out the problem of human happiness by the light of the history of two thousand years. Yet nobly and well as our fathers reared the edifice of civil and religious liberty, true ideas as to the treatment of land, the very foundation of all other institutions, seem never to have entered their minds. In a new country where nothing was so abundant as land, and where there was nothing to suggest its monopolisation, the men who gave direction to our thought and shaped our polity shook off the idea of the divine right of kings without shaking off that of the divine right of landowners. They promulgated the grand truth that all men are born with equal rights to life, liberty, and the pursuit of happiness, without promulgating the doctrines in respect to land which alone could maintain those rights as a living reality; they instituted a form of government based on the theory of the independence and virtue of the masses of the people without imposing those restrictions upon land monopolisation which alone can keep the masses virtuous and independent. They laid the foundations for a glorious house; but they laid them in the sand.

Already we can see that the rains will come, the winds will blow. We see it in the increase of the renting system in agriculture; in the massing of men in the employ of great manufacturers; in the necessity under which thousands of our citizens lie of voting, and even of speaking on political matters, as their employers dictate;* in the marked differentiation of our people in older sections into the rich and the poor; in the evolution of "dangerous classes" in our large cities; in the growth of enormous individual fortunes; in the springing up of corporations which dwarf the

---

* See Reports, Massachusetts Bureau Labour Statistics.

States, and fairly grapple the General Government; in the increase of political corruption; in the ease with which a few great rings wrest the whole power of the nation to their aggrandisement.

Go to New York, the greatest of our American cities, the type of what many of them must soon be, the best example of the condition to which the whole country is tending–New York, where men build marble stables for their horses, and an army of women crowd the streets at night to sell their souls for the necessities which unremitting toil, such as no human being ought to endure, will not give them–where a hundred thousand men who ought to be at work are looking for employment, and a hundred thousand children who ought to be at school are at work. Notice the great blocks of warehouses, the gorgeousness of Broadway, the costly palaces which line the avenues. Notice, too, the miles of brothels which flank them, the tenement houses, where poverty festers and vice breeds, and the man from the free open West turns sick at heart; notice in the depth of winter the barefooted, ragged children in the press of the liveried equipages, and you will understand how it is that republican government has broken down in New York; how it is that republican government is impossible there; and how it is that the crucial test of our institutions is yet to come. If you say that New York is a great seaport, with different conditions from the rest of the country, go to the manufacturing towns, to the other cities, and see the same characteristics developing just in proportion to their population and wealth.

And while we may see all this, we are doing our utmost to make land dear, giving away the public domain in tracts of millions of acres, drawing great belts across it upon which the settler cannot enter; offering a premium by our taxation for the concentration of landownership, and pressing with the whole weight of our revenue system in favour of the concentration of wealth.

## HOW A GREAT PEOPLE PERISHED

In all the history of the past there is but one nation with which the great nation now growing up on this continent can be compared; but one people which has occupied the position and exerted the influence which, for good or evil, the American people must occupy and exert–a nation which has left a deeper impress upon the life of the race than any other nation that ever existed; whose sway was co-extensive with the known world; whose heroes and poets, and sages and orators, are still familiar names to us; whose literature and art still furnish us models; whose language has enriched every modern tongue, and though long dead, is still the language of science and of religion, and whose jurisprudence is the great mine from which our modern systems are wrought. That a nation so powerful in arms, so advanced in the arts, should perish as Rome perished; that a civilisation so widely diffused should be buried as was the Roman civilisation, is the greatest marvel which history presents. To the Roman citizen of the time of Augustus or the Antonines, it would have appeared as incredible, as utterly impossible that Rome could be overwhelmed by barbarians, as to the American citizen of to-day it would appear impossible that the great American Republic could be conquered by the Apaches, or the Chinooks, our arts forgotten, and our civilisation lost.[59]

How did this once incredible thing happen? What were the hidden causes that sapped the strength and ate out the heart of this world-conquering power, so that it crumbled to pieces before the shock of barbarian hordes? A Roman historian himself has told us. "Great estates ruined Italy!" In the land policy of Rome may be traced the secret of her rise, the cause of her fall.[60]

"To every citizen as much land as he himself may use; he is an enemy of the State who desires any more," was the spirit of the land policy which enabled Rome to assimilate so quickly the peoples that she conquered; that gave her a body of citizens whose arms were a bulwark against every assault, and who carried her standards in triumph in every direction. At first a single acre constituted the patrimony of a Roman; afterwards the amount was increased to three acres and a half. These were the heroic days of the Republic, when every citizen seemed animated by a public spirit and a public virtue which made the Roman name as famous as it made the Roman arms invincible; when Cincinnatus left his two-acre farm to become Dictator, and after the danger was over and the State was safe, returned to his plough; when Regulus, at the head of a conquering army in Africa, asked to be relieved, because his single slave had died, and there was no one to cultivate his little farm for his family.[61]

But, as wealth poured in from foreign conquests, and the lust for riches grew, the old policy was set aside. The Senate granted away the public domain in large tracts, just as our Senate is doing now; and the fusion of the little farms into large estates by purchase, by force and by fraud went on, until whole provinces were owned by two or three proprietors, and chained slaves had taken the place of the sturdy peasantry of Italy. The small farmers who had given her strength to Rome were driven to the cities, to swell the ranks of the proletarians, and become clients of the great families, or abroad to perish in the wars. There came to be but two classes—the enormously rich and their dependents and slaves; society thus constituted bred its destroying monsters; the old virtues vanished, population declined, art sank, the old conquering race actually died out, and Rome perished, as a modern historian puts it, from the very failure of the crop of men.

Centuries ago this happened, but the laws of the universe are to-day what they were then.

———

I have endeavoured in this paper to group together some facts which show with what rapidity, and by what methods, the monopolisation of our land is going on; to answer some arguments which are advanced in its excuse; to state some principles which prove the matter to be of the deepest interest to all of us, whether we live directly by the soil or not; and to suggest some remedies.

That land monopolisation when it reaches the point to which it has been carried in England and Ireland is productive of great evils we shall probably all agree. But popular opinion, even in so far as any attention has been paid to the subject, seems to regard the danger with us as remote. There are few who understand how rapidly our land is becoming monopolised; there are fewer still who seem to appreciate the evils which land monopolisation is already inflicting upon us, or the nearness of the greater evils which it threatens.

And so as to the remedy. There are many who will concede that the reckless grants of public land should cease, and even that the public domain should be reserved for actual settlers, but who will be startled by the proposition to put the bulk of taxation on land exclusively. But the matter will bear thinking of. It is impossible to overestimate the importance of this land question. The longer it is considered, the broader does it seem to be and the deeper does it seem to go. It imperatively demands far more attention than it has received; it is worthy of all the attention that can be given to it.

To properly treat so large a subject in so brief a space is a most difficult matter. I have merely outlined it; but if I have done something towards calling attention to the recklessness of our present land policy, and towards suggesting earnest thought as to what that policy should be, I have accomplished all I proposed.

Henry George

San Francisco, July 27, 1871

# THE STUDY OF POLITICAL ECONOMY

I take it that these lectures are intended to be more suggestive than didactic, and in what I shall have to say to you my object will be merely to induce you to think for yourselves. I shall not attempt to outline the laws of political economy, nor even, where my own views are strong and definite, to touch upon unsettled questions. But I want to show you, if I can, the simplicity and certainty of a science too generally regarded as complex and indeterminate, to point out the ease with which it may be studied, and to suggest reasons which make that study worthy of your attention.

Of the importance of the questions with which political economy deals it is hardly necessary to speak. The science which investigates the laws of the production and distribution of wealth concerns itself with matters which among us occupy more than nine tenths of human effort, and perhaps nine tenths of human thought. In its province are included all that relates to the wages of labour and the earnings of capital; all regulations of trade; all questions of currency and finance; all taxes and public disbursements—in short, everything that can in any way affect the amount of wealth which a community can secure, or the proportion in which that wealth will be distributed between individuals. Though not the science of government, it is essential to the science of government. Though it takes direct cognisance only of what are termed the selfish instincts, yet in doing so it includes the basis of all higher qualities. The laws which it aims to discover are the laws by virtue of which states wax rich and populous, or grow weak and decay; the laws upon which depend the comfort, happiness, and opportunities of our individual lives. And as the development of the nobler part of human nature is powerfully modified by material conditions, if it does not absolutely depend upon them, the laws sought for by political economy are the

*A lecture delivered before the students of the University of California, March 9, 1877, and published in "The Popular Science Monthly," March, 1880.[1]*

laws which at last control the mental and moral as well as the physical states of humanity.

Clearly, this is the science which of all sciences is of the first importance to us. Useful and sublime as are the sciences which open to us the vistas of Nature–which read for us the story of the deep past, or search out the laws of our physical or mental organisation–what is their practical importance as compared with the science which deals with the conditions that alone make the cultivation of the others possible? Compare on this ground of practical utility the science of political economy with all others, and its pre-eminence almost suggests the reply of the Greek: "No, I cannot play the fiddle; but I *can* tell you how to make of a little village a great and glorious city!"[2]

How is it, then, it will naturally be asked, that a science so important is so little regarded? Our laws persistently violate its first and plainest principles, and that the ignorance thus exemplified is not confined to what are called the uneducated classes is shown by the debates in our legislative bodies, the decisions of our courts, the speeches of our party leaders, and the editorials of our newspapers. A century has elapsed since Adam Smith published his "Wealth of Nations," and sixty years since Ricardo enunciated his theory of rent.[3] Yet not only has political economy received no substantial improvement since Ricardo, but, while thousands of new discoveries in other branches of human knowledge have been eagerly seized and generally utilised, and the most revolutionary conclusions of other sciences become part of the accepted data of thought, the truths taught by political economy seem to have made little real impression, and it is even now a matter of debate whether there is, or can be, such a science at all.

This cannot be on account of the paucity of politico-economic literature. Enough books have been written on the subject within the last hundred years to fill a large library, while all of our great institutions of learning have some sort of a chair of political economy, and matters of intense public interest in which the principles of the science are directly involved are constantly being discussed.

It seems to me that the reasons why political economy is so little regarded are referable partly to the nature of the science itself and partly to the manner in which it has been cultivated.

In the first place, the very importance of the subjects with which political economy deals raises obstacles in its way. The discoveries of other sciences may challenge pernicious ideas, but the conclusions of political economy involve pecuniary interests, and thus thrill directly the sensitive pocket-nerve.[4] For, as no social adjustment can exist without interesting a larger or smaller class in its maintenance, political economy at every point is apt to come in contact with some interest or other which regards it as the silversmiths of Ephesus did those who taught the uselessness of presenting shrines to Diana.[5] Macaulay has well said that, if any large pecuniary interest were concerned in denying the attraction of gravitation, that most obvious of physical facts would not lack disputers. This is just the difficulty that has beset and still besets the progress of political economy. The man who is, or who imagines that he is, interested in the maintenance of a protective tariff, may accept all your professors choose to tell him about the composition of the sun or the evolution of species, but, no matter how clearly you demonstrate the wasteful inutility of hampering commerce, he will not be convinced. And so, to the man who expects to make money out of a railroad-subsidy, you will in vain try to prove that such devices to change the natural direction of labour and capital must cause more loss than gain. What, then, must be the opposition which inevitably meets a science that deals with tariffs and subsidies, with banking interests and bonded debts, with trades-unions and combinations of capital, with taxes and licenses and land-tenures! It is not ignorance alone that offers opposition, but ignorance backed by interest, and made fierce by passions.

Now, while the interests thus aroused furnish the incentive, the complexity of the phenomena with which political economy deals makes it comparatively easy to palm off on the unreasoning all sorts of absurdities as political economy. And, when all kinds of diverse opinions are thus promulgated under that name, it is but natural that the great number of people who depend on others to save themselves the trouble of thinking should look upon political economy as a field wherein any one may find what he pleases. But what is far worse than any amount of pretentious quackery is that the science even as taught by the masters *is* in large measure disjointed and indeterminate. As laid down in the best text-books, political economy is like a shapely statue but half hewn from the rock–like a landscape, part of which stands out clear and distinct, but over the rest of which the mists still roll. This is a subject into which, in a lecture like this, I cannot enter; but, that it is so, you may see for yourselves in the failure of political economy to give any clear and consistent answer to most important practical questions–such as the industrial depressions which are so marked a feature of modern times,

and in confusions of thought which will be obvious to you if you carefully examine even the best treatises. Strength and subtilty have been
wasted in intellectual hair-splitting and super-refinements, in verbal
discussions and disputes, while the great highroads have remained
unexplored. And thus has been given to a simple and attractive science
an air of repellent abstruseness and uncertainty.

And springing, as it seems to me, from the same fundamental cause,
there has arisen an idea of political economy which has arrayed against
it the feelings and prejudices of those who have most to gain by its cultivation.[6] The name of political economy has been constantly invoked
against every effort of the working classes to increase their wages or
decrease their hours of labour. The impious doctrine always preached
by oppressors to oppressed–the blasphemous dogma that the Creator
has condemned one portion of his creatures to lives of toil and want,
while he has intended another portion to enjoy "all the fruits of the
earth and the fullness thereof"–has been preached to the working
classes in the name of political economy, just as the "cursed-be-Ham"
clergymen used to preach the divine sanction of slavery in the name of
Christianity.[7] In so far as the real turning questions of the day are concerned, political economy seems to be considered by most of its professors as a scientific justification of all that is, and by the convenient
formula of supply and demand they seem to mean some method which
Providence has of fixing the rate of wages so that it can never by any
action of the employed be increased. Nor is it merely ignorant pre-
tenders who thus degrade the name and terms of political economy.
This character has been so firmly stamped upon the science itself as
currently held and taught that not even men like John Stuart Mill have
been able to emancipate themselves.[8] Even the intellectually coura-
geous have shrunk from laying stress upon principles which might
threaten great vested interests; while others, less scrupulous, have exercised their ingenuity in eliminating from the science everything which
could offend those interests. Take the best and most extensively circulated text-books. While they insist upon freedom for capital, while they
justify on the ground of utility the selfish greed that seeks to pile fortune
on fortune, and the niggard spirit that steels the heart to the wail of distress, what sign of substantial promise do they hold out to the workingman save that he should refrain from rearing children?

What can we expect when hands that should offer bread thus hold
out a stone? Is it in human nature that the masses of men, vaguely but

keenly conscious of the injustice of existing social conditions, feeling that they are somehow cramped and hurt, without knowing what cramps and hurts them, should welcome truth in this partial form; that they should take to a science which, as it is presented to them, seems but to justify injustice, to canonise selfishness by throwing around it the halo of utility, and to present Herod rather than Vincent de Paul as the typical benefactor of humanity?[9] Is it to be wondered at that they should turn in their ignorance to the absurdities of protection and the crazy theories generally designated by the name of socialism?

I have lingered to inquire why political economy has in popular apprehension acquired the character of indefiniteness, abstruseness, and selfishness, merely that I may be the better able to convince you that none of these qualities properly belong to it. I want to draw you to its study by showing you how clear and simple and beneficent a science it is, or rather should be.

Although political economy deals with various and complicated phenomena, yet they are phenomena which may be resolved into simple elements, and which are but the manifestations of familiar principles. The premises from which it makes its deductions are truths of which we are all conscious and upon which in every-day life we constantly base our reasoning and our actions. Its processes, which consist chiefly in analysis, have a like certainty, although, as with all the causes of which it takes cognisance are at all times acting other causes, it can never predict exact results but only tendencies.

And, although in the study of political economy we cannot use that potent method of experiment by artificially produced conditions which is so valuable in the physical sciences, yet, not only may we find, in the diversity of human society, experiments already worked out for us, but there is at our command a method analogous to that of the chemist, in what may be called mental experiment. You may separate, combine, or eliminate conditions in your own imagination, and test in this way the working of known principles. This, it seems to me, is the great tool of political economy. It is a method with which you must be familiar and doubtless use every day, though you may never have analysed the process. Let me illustrate what I mean by something which has no reference to political economy.

When I was a boy I went down to the wharf with another boy to see the first iron steamship which had ever crossed the ocean to our port.[10] Now, hearing of an iron steamship seemed to us then a good deal like hearing of a leaden kite or a wooden cooking-stove. But, we had not been long aboard of her, before my comrade said in a tone of contemptuous disgust: "Pooh! I see how it is. She's all lined with wood; that's the reason she floats." I could not controvert him for the moment, but I was not satisfied, and, sitting down on the wharf when he left me, I set to work trying mental experiments. If it was the wood inside of her that made her float, then the more wood the higher she would float; and, mentally, I loaded her up with wood. But, as I was familiar with the process of making boats out of blocks of wood, I at once saw that, instead of floating higher, she would sink deeper. Then, I mentally took all the wood out of her, as we dug out our wooden boats, and saw that thus lightened she would float higher still. Then, in imagination, I jammed a hole in her, and saw that the water would run in and she would sink, as did our wooden boats when ballasted with leaden keels. And, thus I saw, as clearly as though I could have actually made these experiments with the steamer, that it was not the wooden lining that made her float, but her hollowness, or, as I would now phrase it, her displacement of water.

Now, just such mental operations as these you doubtless perform every day, and in doing so you employ the method of imaginative experiment, which is so useful in the investigations of political economy. You can, in this way, turn around in your mind a proposition or phenomenon and look on all sides of it, can isolate, analyse, recombine, or subject it to the action of a mental magnifying glass which will reveal incongruities as a *reductio ad absurdum*. Let me again illustrate:

Before I had ever read a line of political economy, I happened once to hear a long and well-put argument in favour of a protective tariff. Up to that time I had supposed that "protection to domestic industry" was a good thing; not that I had ever thought out the matter, but that I had accepted this conclusion because I had heard many men whom I believed wiser than I say so. But this particular speaker had, so far as one of his audience was concerned, overshot his mark. His arguments set me thinking, just as when a boy my companion's solution of the iron-ship mystery had set me thinking. I said to myself: ["]The effect of a tariff is to increase the cost of bringing goods from abroad. Now, if this benefits a country, then all difficulties, dangers, and impediments which increase the cost of bringing goods from abroad are likewise beneficial. If this theory be correct, then the city which is the hardest to get at has the most advantageous situation: pirates and shipwrecks contribute to national prosperity by raising the price of freight and the cost of insurance; and improvements in navigation, in railroads and steamships, are injurious.["] Manifestly this is absurd.

And then I looked further. The speaker had dwelt on the folly of a great country like the United States exporting raw material and importing manufactured goods which might as well be made at home, and I asked myself, What is the motive which causes a people to export raw material and import manufactured goods? I found that it could be attributed to nothing else than the fact that they could in this way get the goods cheaper, that is, with less labour. I looked to transactions between individuals for parallels to this trade between nations, and found them in plenty–the farmer selling his wheat and buying flour; the grazier sending his wool to a market and bringing back cloth and blankets; the tanner buying back leather in shoes, instead of making them himself. I saw, when I came to analyse them, that these exchanges between nations were precisely the same thing as exchanges between individuals; that they were, in fact, nothing but exchanges between individuals of different nations; that they were all prompted by the desire and led to the result of getting the greatest return for the least expenditure of labour; that the social condition in which such exchanges did not take place was the naked barbarism of the Terra del Fuegians;[11] that just in proportion to the division of labour and the increase of trade were the increase of wealth and the progress of civilisation. And so, following up, turning, analysing, and testing all the protectionist arguments, I came to conclusions which I have ever since retained.

Now, just such mental operations as this are all that is required in the study of political economy. Nothing more is needed (but this *is* needed) than the habit of careful thought–the making sure of every step without jumping to conclusions. This habit of jumping to conclusions–of considering essentially different things as the same because of some superficial resemblance–is the source of the manifold and mischievous errors which political economy has to combat.

But I can probably, by a few examples, show you what I mean more easily than in any other way. Were I to put to you the child's question, "Which is heavier, a pound of lead or a pound of feathers?" you would doubtless be offended; and were I seriously to ask you, ["]Which is the most valuable, a dollar's worth of gold or a dollar's worth of anything else?["] you might also feel that I had insulted your intelligence. Yet the belief that a dollar's worth of gold is more valuable than a dollar's worth of anything else is widespread and persistent. It has molded the policy of great nations, dictated treaties, marched armies, launched fleets, fought battles, constructed and enforced elaborate and vexatious systems of taxation, and sent men by thousands to jail and to the gallows. Certainly a large portion, probably a large majority, of the people of the United States–including many college graduates, members of what are styled the learned professions, senators, representatives, authors, and editors–seem to-day utterly unable to get it fully through their heads that a dollar's worth of anything else is as valuable as a dollar's worth of the precious metals, and are constantly reasoning, arguing, and legislating on the assumption that the community which exchanges gold for goods is suffering a loss, and that it is part of wisdom, by preventing such exchange, to "keep money in the country." On this absurd assumption the revenue system of the United States is based to-day, and, if you will notice, you will find it cropping out of current discussions in all sorts of forms. Even here, where the precious metals form one of our staples, and for a long time constituted our only staple, you may see the power of the same notion. The anti-cooly clubs complain of the "drain of money to China," but never think of complaining of the drain of flour, wheat, quicksilver, or shrimps. And the leading journals of San Francisco, who hold themselves on an immeasurably higher intellectual level than the anti-cooly clubs, never, I think, let a week pass without congratulating their readers that we have ceased to import this or that article, and are thereby keeping so much money that we used to send abroad, or lamenting that we still send money away to pay for this or that which might be made here. Yet that we send away wine or wool, fruit or honey, it is never thought of as a matter of lament, but quite the contrary. What is all this but the assumption that a dollar's worth of gold is worth more than a dollar's worth of anything else?

This fallacy is transparently absurd when we come to reduce it to a general proposition. But, nevertheless, the habit of jumping at conclusions, of which I have spoken, makes it seem very natural to people who do not stop to think. Money is our standard, or measure of values, in which we express all other values. When we speak of gaining wealth, we speak of "making money"; when we speak of losing wealth, we speak of "losing money"; when we speak of a rich man, we speak of him as possessed of much money, though as a matter of fact he may, and probably has, very little actual money. Then, again, as money is the common medium of exchange, in the process of getting things we want for things we are willing to dispose of, we generally first exchange the latter for money and then exchange the money for the things we want. And, as the number of people who want things of all sorts must manifestly be greater than the number of people who want the particular thing, whatever it may be that we have to exchange, any difficulty there may be in making our exchange will generally attend the first part of it; for, in exchanging anything for money, I must find some one who wants my particular thing, while in exchanging money for a commodity, any one who wants any commodity or service will be willing to take my money. Now, this habit of estimating wealth in money, and of speaking of gain or loss of wealth as gain or loss of money, and this habit of associating difficulties of exchange in individual cases with the difficulty of obtaining money, constantly lead people who do not think clearly to jump at the conclusion that money is more valuable than anything else. Yet the slightest consideration would show them that wealth never consists, but in a very small part, of money; that the difficulty in individual exchanges has no reference to the relative value of money, and is eliminated when the exchanges of large numbers of individuals are concentrated or considered, and, in short, a dollar in money is worth no more than a dollar's worth of wheat or cloth; and that, instead of the exchange of money for other commodities being proof of a disadvantageous bargain, it is proof of an advantageous bargain, for, if we did not want the goods more than the money, we would not make the exchange.

Or, to take another example: In connection with the discussion of Chinese immigration, you have, doubtless, over and over again heard it contended that cheap labour, which would reduce the cost of production, is precisely equivalent to labour-saving machinery, and, as machinery operates to increase wealth, so would cheap labour. This conclusion is jumped at from the fact that cheap labour and labour-saving machinery similarly reduce the cost of production to the manufacturer. But, if, instead of jumping at this conclusion, we analyse the manner in which the reduction of cost is produced in each case, we shall see the fallacy. Labour-saving machinery reduces cost by increasing the productive power of labour; a reduction of wages reduces cost by reducing the share of the product which falls to the labourer. To the employer the effect may be the same; but, to the community, which includes both employers and employed, the effect is very different. In the one case there is increase in the general wealth; in the other there is merely a change in distribution—whatever one class gains another class necessarily losing. Hence the effect of cheap labour is necessarily very different from that of improved machinery.

And precisely similar to this fallacy is that which seems so natural to men of another class–that because the introduction of cheaper labour in any community *does*, in the present organisation of society, tend to reduce the general level of wages, so does the importation of cheap goods. This, also–but I must leave you to analyse it for yourselves–springs from a confusion of thought which does not distinguish between the whole and the parts, between the distribution of wealth and the production of wealth.

Did time permit, I might go on, showing you by instance after instance how transparently fallacious are many current opinions–some, even, more widely held than any of which I have spoken–when tried by the simple tests which it is the province of political economy to apply. But my object is not to lead you to conclusions. All I wish to impress upon you is the real simplicity of what is generally deemed an abstruse science, and the exceeding ease with which it may be pursued. For the study of political economy you need no special knowledge, no extensive library, no costly laboratory. You do not even need text-books nor teachers, if you will but think for yourselves. All that you need is care in reducing complex phenomena to their elements, in distinguishing the essential from the accidental, and in applying the simple laws of human action with which you are familiar. Take nobody's opinion for granted; "try all things: hold fast that which is good." In this way, the opinions of others will help you by their suggestions, elucidations, and corrections; otherwise they will be to you but as words to a parrot.

If there were nothing more to be urged in favour of the study of political economy than the mental exercise it will give, it would still be worth your profoundest attention. The study which will teach men to think for themselves is the study of all studies most needed. Education is not the learning of facts; it is the development and training of mental powers. All this array of professors, all this paraphernalia of learning, cannot educate a man. They can but help him to educate himself. Here you may obtain the tools; but they will be useful only to him who can use them. A monkey with a microscope, a mule packing a library, are fit emblems of the men–and, unfortunately, they are plenty–who pass through the whole educational machinery, and come out but learned fools, crammed with knowledge which they cannot use–all the more pitiable, all the more contemptible, all the more in the way of real progress, because they pass, with themselves and others, as educated men.

But, while it seems to me that nothing can be more conducive to vigorous mental habits and intellectual self-reliance than the study which trains us to apply the analysis of thought to the every-day affairs of life, and to see in constantly changing phenomena the evidence of unchanging law; which leads us to distinguish the real from the apparent, and to mark, beneath the seething eddies of interest, passion, and prejudice, the great currents of our times—it is not on such incentives that I wish to dwell. There are motives as much higher than the thirst for knowledge, as that noble passion is higher than the lust for power or the greed of gold.

In its calculations the science of wealth takes little note of, nay, it often carefully excludes, the potent force of sympathy, and of those passions which lead men to toil, to struggle, even to die for the good of others. And yet it is these higher passions, these nobler impulses, that urge most strenuously to its study. The promise of political economy is not so much what it may do for you, as what it may enable you to do for others.

I trust you have felt the promptings of that highest of ambitions—the desire to be useful in your day and generation; the hope that in something, even though little, those who come after may be wiser, better, and happier that you have lived. Or, if you have never felt this, I trust the feeling is only latent, ready to spring forth when you see the need.

Gentlemen, if you but look, you will see the need! You are of the favoured few, for the fact that you are here, students in a university of this character, bespeaks for you the happy accidents that fall only to the lot of the few, and you cannot yet realise, as you may by-and-by realise, how the hard struggle which is the lot of so many may cramp and bind and distort—how it may dull the noblest faculties and chill the warmest impulses, and grind out of men the joy and poetry of life; how it may turn into the lepers of society those who should be its adornment, and transmute into vermin to prey upon it and into wild beasts to fly at its throat, the brain and muscle that should go to its enrichment! These things may never yet have forced themselves on your attention; but still, if you will think of it, you cannot fail to see enough want and wretchedness, even in our own country to-day, to move you to sadness and pity, to nerve you to high resolve; to arouse in you the sympathy that dares, and the indignation that burns to overthrow a wrong.

And seeing these things, would you fain do something to relieve distress, to eradicate ignorance, to extirpate vice? You must turn to political economy to know their causes, that you may lay the axe to the root of the evil tree. Else all your efforts will be in vain. Philanthropy, unguided by an intelligent apprehension of causes, may palliate or it may intensify, but it cannot cure. If charity could eradicate want, if preaching could make men moral, if printing books and building schools could destroy ignorance, none of these things would be known to-day.

And there is the greater need that you make yourselves acquainted with the principles of political economy from the fact that, in the immediate future, questions which come within its province must assume a greater and greater importance. To act intelligently in the struggle in which you must take part–for positively or negatively each of you must carry his weight–you must know something of this science. And this, I think, is clear to whoever considers the forces that are mustering–that the struggle to come will be fiercer and more momentous than the struggles that are past.

There is a comfortable belief prevalent among us that we have at last struck the trade-winds of time, and that by virtue of what we call progress all these evils will cure themselves. Do not accept this doctrine without examination. The history of the past does not countenance it, the signs of the present do not warrant it. Gentlemen, look at the tendencies of our time, and see if the earnest work of intelligent men be not needed.

Look even here. Can the thoughtful man view the development of our State with unmixed satisfaction? Do we not know that, under present conditions, just as that city over the bay grows in wealth and population, so will poverty deepen and vice increase; that just as the liveried carriages become more plentiful, so do the beggars; that just as the pleasant villas of wealth dot these slopes, so will rise up the noisome tenement house in the city slums. I have watched the growth of San Francisco with joy and pride, and my imagination still dwells with delight upon the image of the great city of the future, the queen of all the vast Pacific–perhaps the greatest city of the world. Yet what is the gain? San Francisco of to-day, with her three hundred thousand people, is, for the classes who depend upon their labour, not so good a place as the San Francisco of sixty thousand; and when her three hundred thousand rises to a million, San Francisco, if present tendencies are unchanged, must present the same sickening sights which in the streets of New York shock the man from the open West.

This is the dark side of our boasted progress, the Nemesis that seems to follow with untiring tread. Where wealth most abounds, there poverty is deepest; where luxury is most profuse, the gauntest want jostles it. In cities which are the storehouses of nations, starvation annually claims its victims. Where the costliest churches rear the tallest spires towards heaven, there is needed a standing army of policemen; as we build new schools, we build new prisons; where the heaviest contributions are raised to send missionaries to the ends of the earth to preach the glad tidings of peace and good-will, there may be seen squalor and vice that would affright a heathen. In mills where the giant power of steam drives machinery that multiplies by hundreds and thousands the productive forces of man, there are working little children who ought to be at play or at school; where the mechanism of exchange has been perfected to the utmost, there thousands of men are vainly trying to exchange their labour for the necessaries of life!

Whence this dark shadow that thus attends that which we are used to call "material progress," that which our current philosophy teaches us to hope for and to work for? Here is the question of all questions for us. We must answer it or be destroyed, as preceding civilisations have been destroyed. For no chain is stronger than its weakest link, and our glorious statue with its head of gold and its shoulders of brass has as yet but feet of clay!

Political economy alone can give the answer. And, if you trace out, in the way I have tried to outline, the laws of the production and exchange of wealth, you will see the causes of social weakness and disease in enactments which selfishness has imposed on ignorance, and in maladjustments entirely within our own control.

And you will see the remedies. Not in wild dreams of red destruction nor weak projects for putting men in leading-strings to a brainless abstraction called the state, but in simple measures sanctioned by justice. You will see in light the great remedy, in freedom the great solvent. You will see that the true law of social life is the law of love, the law of liberty, the law of each for all and all for each; that the golden rule of morals is also the golden rule of the science of wealth; that the highest expressions of religious truth include the widest generalisations of political economy.

There will grow on you, as no moralising could teach, a deepening realisation of the brotherhood of man; there will come to you a firmer and firmer conviction of the fatherhood of God. If you have ever thoughtlessly accepted that worse than atheistic theory that want and wretchedness and brutalising toil are ordered by the Creator, or, revolting from this idea, if you have ever felt that the only thing apparent in the ordering of the world was a blind and merciless fate careless of man's aspirations and heedless of his sufferings, these thoughts will pass from you as you see how much of all that is bad and all that is perplexing in our social conditions grows simply from our ignorance of law—as you come to realise how much better and happier men might make the life of man.

# THE AMERICAN REPUBLIC: ITS DANGERS AND POSSIBILITIES

*Mr. President, Ladies and Gentlemen:*

It is under circumstances that inspire gratitude and renew patriotism that we celebrate the completion by the American Republic of the first year of her second century. How much that year has held of the possibilities of dire calamity it may be too soon to speak.* But for the deliverance let us give thanks. Through the web woven by passion and prejudice has run the woof of a beneficent purpose. Through clash of plans and conflict of parties; through gateways hung with cloud and by paths we knew not of, have we come to this good estate!

As, when the long struggle was over, the men of the Revolution turned to pour forth their thanks to Him in whose hands are the nations, so let us turn to-day. Last year was the Centennial; but this year, if we read the times aright, marks the era, and with 1877 will the historian, in future ages, close the grand division of our history that records the long, sad strife of which slavery was the cause. Most gracious of our national anniversaries is that we keep. Never before has the great Declaration rung through the land as to-day. For the first time have its words neither fallen on the ears of a slave nor been flung back by a bayonet-guarded State House!

For year after year, while they who won our independence faded away; for year after year, while their sons grew old, and in their turn taught us to light the altar fires of the Republic, at every recurring anniversary of the nation's birth, the unexpressed thought of an inherited curse that was

*An oration delivered in the California Theatre, San Francisco, on the celebration of the 4th of July, 1877.[1]*

---

* The Hayes-Tilden Presidential contest. [Samuel J. Tilden (1814–86) was the Democratic candidate who lost to Republican Rutherford B. Hayes (1822–93) in the 1876 presidential election. Tilden won but a partisan electoral commission appointed by Congress to decide the disputed election results in a number of states gave the victory to Hayes.]

sowing the land with dragon's teeth, checked the pride and gave to the rejoicings of the thoughtful a sombre background, and between thunder of gun and voice of trumpet, the black shadow of a great wrong mocked in silence the burning words that protested to the world the inalienable rights of man. To this there came an end. In the deadly close of civil war, when all fierce and wicked passions were loosed, while the earth shook with the tread of fratricidal armies, and the heavens were red with the blaze of burning homes, amid the groans of dying men and the cry of stricken women, the great curse passed away. But still the shadow. Could we boast a Union in which State Governments were maintained by extra-State force, or glory in a republic whose forms were mocked in virtual provinces?[2]

But all this is of the past. The long strife is over. The cancer has been cut out. And may we not also say to-day that the wound of the knife has healed? To-day we celebrate the nation's birth, more truly one people than for years and years. Again in soul as in form, the many are one. Over palmetto as over pine floats the flag that typifies the glory of our common past, the promise of our common future—the flag that rose above the blood-stained snow at Valley Forge, that crossed with Washington the icy Delaware—the flag that Marion bore, that [John] Paul Jones nailed to the mast, that Lafayette saluted![3] Over our undivided heritage of a continent it floats to-day, with the free will of a united people—under its folds no slave, and in its blue no star save that of a free and sovereign State. And, as in city and town and hamlet, to-day, has been read once more the declaration of a nation's birth, again, I believe me, in the hearts of their people, has Adams signed with Jefferson and Rutledge with Livingston, pledging to the Republic one and indivisible, life and fortune and sacred honour![4]

Beside me on this platform, around me in this audience, sit men who have borne arms against each other in civil strife, again united under the folds of that flag. Men of the South and men of the North, do I not speak what is in your hearts, do I not give voice to your hope and your trust, when I say that the Union is again restored in spirit as in form—not a union of conquerors and conquered, but the union of a people—one in soul as one in blood; one in destiny as one in heritage!

Let our dead strifes bury their dead, while we cherish the feeling that makes us one. Let us spare no myrrh nor frankincense nor costly spices as we feed the sacred fire. It is not a vain thing these flags, these decorations, these miles of marching men. Stronger than armies, more potent than treasure is the sentiment of nationality they typify and inculcate!

Yet to more than the sentiment of nationality is this day sacred. It marks more than the birth of a nation—it marks a step in the progress of the race. More than national independence, more than national union, speaks out in that grand document to which we have just listened; it is the declaration of the fundamental principle of liberty—of a truth that has in it power to renovate the world.

It is meet that on this day the flags of all nations should mingle above our processions and wreathe our halls. For this is the festival of her to whom under all skies eyes have turned and hands been lifted—of her who has had in all lands her lovers and her martyrs—of her who shall yet unite the nations and bid the war drums cease! It is the festival of Liberty!

And in keeping this day to Liberty, we honour all her sacred days—those glorious days on which she has stepped forward, those sad days on which she has been stricken down by open foes, or fallen wounded in the house of her friends. Far back stretches the lineage of the Republic at whose birth Liberty was invoked—from every land have been gathered the gleams of light that unite in her beacon fire. It is kindled of the progress of mankind; it witnesses to heaven the aspirations of the ages; it shall light the nations to yet nobler heights!

Let us keep this day as the day sacred to Union and to Liberty should be kept. Let us draw closer the cords of our common brotherhood and renew our fathers' vows. Let it be honoured as John Adams predicted it would be honoured—with clangour of bells and roar of guns, with music and processions and assemblages of the people, with every mark of respect and rejoicing—that its memories of glory may entwine themselves with the earliest recollections of our children, that even the thoughtless may catch something of its inspiration!


Yet it is not enough that with all the marks of veneration we keep these holidays. It is possible to cherish the form and lose the spirit.

No matter how bright the lights behind, their usefulness is but to illumine the path before. Whatever be the causes of that enormous difference—almost a difference in kind—between the stationary and the progressive races, here is its unfailing indication—the one look[s] to the past, the other to the future. The moment we believe that all wisdom was concentrated in our ancestors, that moment the petrifaction of China is upon us. For life is growth, and growth is change, and political progress consists in getting rid of institutions we have outgrown. Aristocracy, feudality, monarchy, slavery–all the things against which human progress has been a slow and painful struggle–were, doubtless, in their times relatively if not absolutely beneficial, as have been in later times things we may have to cast away. The maxim commended to us by him who must ever remain the greatest citizen of the Republic–"Eternal vigilance is the price of liberty," embodies a truth which goes to the very core of philosophy, which must everywhere and at all times be true.[5] Ever and ever we sail an unknown sea. Old shapes of menace fade but to give place to others. Even new rocks lurk; ever in new guise the syrens sing![6]

As through the million-voiced plaudits of to-day we hear again the words that when first spoken were ominous of cord and gibbet, and amid a nation's rejoicing our pulses quicken as imagination pictures the bridge of Lexington, the slender earthworks of Bunker Hill, the charge of tattered Continentals, or the swift night-ride of Marion's men, let us not think that our own times are common-place, and make no call for the patriotism that, as it wells up in our hearts, we feel would have been strong to dare and do had we lived then.

How momentous our own times may be the future alone can tell. We are yet laying the foundations of empire, while stronger run the currents of change and mightier are the forces that marshal and meet.

Let us turn to the past, not in the belief that the great men of the past conquered for us a heritage that we have but to enjoy, but that we may catch their heroic spirit to guide and nerve us in the exigencies of the present; that we may pass it on to our children, to carry them through the dangers of the future.

Now, as a hundred years ago, the Republic has need of that spirit–of the noble sensitiveness that is jealous for Freedom; of the generous indignation that weighs our consideration of expediency against the sacrifice of one iota of popular right; of the quick sympathy that made an attack on the liberties of one colony felt in all; of the patient patriotism that worked and waited, never flagging, never tiring, seeking not recognition nor applause, looking only to the ultimate end and to the common good; of the devotion to a high ideal which led men to risk for it all things sweet and all things dear!

We shall best honour the men of the Revolution by invoking the spirit that animated them; we shall best perpetuate their memories by looking in the face whatever threatens the perpetuity of their work. Whether a century hence they shall be regarded as visionaries or as men who gave a new life to mankind, depends upon us.

For let us not disguise it–republican government is yet but an experiment. That it has worked well so far, determines nothing. That republican institutions would work well under the social conditions of the youth of the Republic–cheap land, high wages and little distinction between rich and poor–there was never any doubt, for they were working well before. Our Revolution was not a revolution in the full sense of the term, as was that great outburst of the spirit of freedom that followed it in France. The colonies but separated from Great Britain, and became an independent nation without essential change in the institutions under which they had grown up. The doubt about republican institutions is as to whether they will work when population becomes dense, wages low, and a great gulf separates rich and poor.

Can we speak of it as a doubt? Nothing in political philosophy can be clearer than that under such conditions republican government must break down.

This is not to say that these forms must be abandoned. We might and probably would go on holding our elections for years and years after our government had become essentially despotic. It was centuries after Cæsar ere the absolute master of the Roman world pretended to rule other than by authority of a Senate that trembled before him.[7] It was not till the thirteenth century that English kings dropped the formal claim of what was once the essence of their title–the choice of the people; and to this day the coronation ceremonies of European monarchs retain traces of the free election of their leader by equal warriors.[8]

But forms are nothing when substance has gone. And our forms are those from which the substance may most easily go. Extremes meet, and a republican government, based on universal suffrage and theoretical equality, is of all governments that which may most easily become a despotism of the worst kind. For there, despotism advances in the name of the people. The single source of power once secured, everything is secured. There is no unfranchised class to whom appeal may be made; no privileged orders, who in defending their own rights may defend those of all. No bulwark remains to stay the flood, no eminence to rise above it.

And where there is universal suffrage, just as the disparity of condition increases, so does it become easy to seize the source of power, for the greater is the proportion of power in the hands of those who feel no direct interest in the conduct of the government, nay, who, made bitter by hardships, may even look upon profligate government with the sort of satisfaction we may imagine the proletarians and slaves of Rome to have felt as they saw a Caligula or Nero raging among the rich patricians.[9]

Given a community with republican institutions, in which one class is too rich to be shorn of their luxuries, no matter how public affairs are administered, and another so poor that any little share of the public plunder, even though it be but a few dollars on election day, will seem more than any abstract consideration, and power must pass into the hands of jobbers who will sell it, as the prætorian legions sold the Roman purple, while the people will be forced to reimburse the purchase money with costs and profits.[10] If to the pecuniary temptation involved in the ordinary conduct of government are added those that come from the granting of subsidies, the disposition of public lands and the regulation of prices by means of a protective tariff, the process will be the swifter.

Even the accidents of hereditary succession or of selection by lot (the plan of some of the ancient republics) may sometimes place the wise and just in power, but in a corrupt republic the tendency is always to give power to the worst. Honesty and patriotism are weighted and unscrupulousness commands success. The best gravitate to the bottom, the worst float to the top; and the vile can only be ousted by the viler. And as a corrupt government always tends to make the rich richer and the poor poorer, the fundamental cause of corruption is steadily aggravated, while as national character must gradually assimilate to the qualities that command power and consequently respect, that demoralisation of opinion goes on which in the long panorama of history we may see over and over again, transmuting races of freemen into races of slaves.

As in England, in the last century, where Parliament was but a close corporation of the aristocracy, a corrupt oligarchy, where it is clearly fenced off from the masses, may exist without much effect on national character; because, in that case, power is associated in the popular mind with other things than corruption; but where there are no hereditary distinctions, and men are habitually seen to raise themselves by corrupt qualities from the lowest places to wealth and power, tolerance of these qualities finally becomes admiration. A corrupt democratic government must finally corrupt the people, and when a people become corrupt, there is no resurrection. The life has gone, only the carcass remains; and it is left but for the ploughshares of fate to bury it out of sight.


Secure in her strength and position from external dangers, with the cause gone that threatened her unity, the Republic begins to count the years of her second century with a future, to all outward seeming, secure. But may we not see already closing round her the insidious perils from which, since her birth, destruction has been predicted? Clearly, to him who will look, are we passing from the conditions under which republican government is easy, into those under which it becomes endangered, if not dangerous. While the possessor of a single million is ceasing to be noticeable in the throng of millionaires, and larger private fortunes are mounting towards hundreds of millions, we are all over the country becoming familiar with widespread poverty in its hardest aspects–not the poverty that nourishes the rugged virtues, but poverty of the kind that dispirits and embrutes.

And as we see the gulf widening between rich and poor, may we not as plainly see the symptoms of political deterioration that in a republican government must always accompany it? Social distinctions are sharpest in our great cities, and in our great cities is not republican government becoming a reproach? May we not see in these cities that the worst social influences are become the most potent political factors; that corrupt rings notoriously rule; that offices are virtually purchased– and, most ominous of all, may we not plainly see the growth of a sentiment that looks on all this as natural, if not perfectly legitimate; that either doubts the existence of an honest man in public place, or thinks of him as a fool too weak to seize his opportunity? Has not the primary system, which is simply republicanism applied to party management, already broken down in our great cities, and are not parties in their despair already calling for what in general government would be oligarchies and dictatorships?

We talk about the problem of municipal government! It is not the problem of municipal government that we have to solve, but the problem of republican government. These great cities are but the type of our development. They are growing not merely with the growth of the country, but faster than the growth of the country. There are children here today who in all human probability will see San Francisco a city as large as London, and will count through the country New Yorks by the score!

Fellow-citizens, the wind does not blow north or south because the weather-cocks turn that way. The complaints of political demoralisation that come from every quarter are not because bad men have been elected to office or corrupt men have taken to engineering parties. If bad men are elected to office, if corrupt men rule parties, is it not because the conditions are such as to give them the advantage over good and pure men? Fellow-citizens, it is not the glamour of success that makes the men whose work we celebrate to-day loom up through the mists of a century like giants. They were giants–some of them so great, that with all our eulogies we do not yet appreciate them, and their full fame must wait for yet another century. But the reason why such intellectual greatness gathered around the cradle of the Republic and guided her early steps, was not that men were greater in that day, but that the people chose their best. You will hardly find a man of that time, of high character and talent, who was not in some way in the public service. This certainly cannot be said now. And it is because power is concentrating, as it must concentrate as our institutions deteriorate. If one of those men were to come back to-day and were spoken of for high position– say for the United States Senate–instead of Jefferson's three questions, the knowing ones would ask: "Has he money to make the fight?" "Are the corporations for him?" "Can he put up the primaries?" No less a man than Benjamin Franklin–a man whose fame as a statesman and philosopher is yet growing–a man whom the French Academy, the most splendid intellectual assemblage in Europe, applauded as the modern Solon–represented the city of Philadelphia in the provincial Assembly for ten years, until, as their best man, he was sent to defend the colony in London.[11] Are there not to-day cities in the land which even a Benjamin Franklin could not represent in a State Assembly unless he put around his neck the collar of a corporation or took his orders from a local ring?

You will think of many things in this connection to which it is not necessary for me to allude. We all see them. Though we may not speak it openly, the general faith in republican institutions is narrowing and weakening–it is no longer that defiant, jubilant, boastful belief in republicanism as the source of all national blessings and the cure for all human woes that it once was. We begin to realise that corruption may cost as much as a royal family, and that the vaunted ballot, under certain conditions, may bring forth ruling classes of the worst kind, while we already see developing around us social evils that we once associated only with effete monarchies. Can we talk so proudly of welcoming the oppressed of all nations when thousands vainly seek for work at the lowest wages? Can we expect him, who must sup on charity, to rejoice that he cannot be taxed without being represented; or congratulate him who seeks shelter in a station-house that, as a citizen of the Republic, he is the peer of the monarchs of earth?


Is there any tendency to improvement?

Fellow-citizens, we have hitherto had an advantage over older nations which we can hardly overestimate. It has been our public domain, our background of unfenced land, that made our social conditions better than those of Europe; that relieved the labour market and maintained wages; that kept open a door of escape from the increasing pressure in older sections, and acting and reacting in many ways on our national character, gave it freedom and independence, elasticity and hope.

But with a folly for which coming generations may curse us, we have wasted it away. Worse than the Norman conqueror, we have repeated *the* sin of the sin-swollen Henry VIII; and already we hear in the "tramp" of the sturdy vagrant of the sixteenth century, the predecessor of the English pauper of this. We have done to the future the unutterable wrong that English rule and English law did to Ireland, and already we begin to hear of rack-rents and evictions.[12] We have repeated the crime that filled Italy with a servile population in place of the hardy farmers who had carried her eagles to victory after victory–the crime that ate out the heart of the Mistress of the World, and buried the glories of ancient civilisation in the darkness of mediæval night.[13] Instead of guarding the public domain as the most precious of our heritages; instead of preserving it for our poorer classes of to-day and for the uncounted millions who must follow us, we have made it the reward of corruption, greed, fraud and perjury. Go out in this fair land to-day and you may see great estates tilled by Chinamen, while citizens of the Republic carry their blankets through dusty roads begging for work; you may ride for miles and miles through fertile land and see no sign of human life save the ghastly chimney of an evicted settler or the miserable shanty of a poverty-stricken renter. Cross the bay, and you will see the loveliest piece of mountain scenery around this great city, though destitute of habitation, walled in with a high board fence, that none but the owner of 20,000 acres of land may look upon its beauties. Pass over these broad acres which lie as they lay ere man was born on this earth, and under penalty of fine and imprisonment you must confine yourself to the road, purchased of him with poll taxes of four dollars a head wrung from men packing their blankets in search of work at a dollar a day.

Fellow-citizens, the public domain fit for homes is almost gone, and at the rate we are parting with the rest, it is certain that by the time children now in our public schools come of age, the pre-emption law and the homestead law will remain on our statute books only to remind them of their squandered birthright. Then the influences that are at work to concentrate wealth in the hands of the few, and make dependence the lot of the many, will have free play.

How potent are these influences! Though in form everything seems tending to republican equality, a new power has entered the world that, under present social adjustments, is working with irresistible force to subject the many to the few. The tendency of all modern machinery is to give capital an overpowering advantage and make labour helpless.[14] Our boys cannot learn trades, because there are few to learn. The journeyman who, with his kit of tools, could make a living anywhere, is being replaced by the operative who performs but one part of a process, and must work with tools he can never hope to own, and who consequently must take but a bare living, while all the enormous increase of wealth which results from the economy of production must go to increase great fortunes. The undercurrents of the times seem to sweep us back again to the old conditions from which we dreamed we had escaped. The development of the artisan and commercial classes gradually broke down feudalism after it had become so complete that men thought of heaven as organised on a feudal basis, and ranked the first and second persons of the Trinity as Suzerain and Tenant-in-Chief.[15] But now the development of manufacture and exchange has reached a point which threatens to compel every worker to seek a master, as the insecurity which followed the final break up of the Roman Empire compelled every freeman to seek a lord. Nothing seems exempt from this tendency. Even errands are run by a corporation, and one company carries carpet-sacks, while another drives the hack. It is the old guilds of the middle ages over again, only that instead of all being equal, one is master and the others serve. And where one is master and the others serve, the one will control the others, even in such matters as votes.

In our constitution there is a clause prohibiting the granting of titles of nobility. In the light of the present it seems a good deal like the device of the man who, leaving a big hole for the cat, sought to keep the kitten out by blocking up the little hole. Could titles add anything to the power of the aristocracy that is here growing up? Six hundred liveried retainers followed the great Earl of Warwick to Parliament;[16] but in this young State there is already a simple citizen* who could discharge any one of thousands of men from their employment, who controls 2200 miles of railroad and telegraph, and millions of acres of land, and has the power of levying toll on traffic and travel over an area twice that of the original thirteen States. Warwick was a king-maker. Would it add to the real power of our simple citizen were we to dub him an earl?

Look at the social conditions which are growing up here in California. Land monopolised; water monopolised; a race of cheap workers crowding in, whose effect upon our own labouring classes is precisely that of slavery; all the avenues of trade and travel under one control, all wealth and power tending more and more to concentrate in a few hands. What sort of a republic will this be in a few years longer if these things go on? The idea would be ridiculous, were it not too sad.

Fellow-citizens, I am talking of things, not men. Most irrational would be any enmity towards individuals. How few are there of us who under similar circumstances would not do just what those we speak of as monopolists have done. To put a saddle on our back is to invite the booted and spurred to ride. It is not men who are to blame but the system. And who is to blame for the system, but the whole people? If the lion will suffer his teeth to be pulled and his claws to be pared, he must expect every cur to tease him.

But, fellow-citizens, while it is true that a republican government worth the name cannot exist under the social conditions in to which we are passing, it is also true that under a really republican government such conditions could not be.

I do not mean to say that we have not had enough government; I mean to say that we have had too much. It is a truth that cannot be too clearly kept in mind that the best government is that which governs least, and that the more a republican government undertakes to do, the

---

* Leland Stanford. [See endnote no. 27 on page 238.]

less republican it becomes. Unhealthy social conditions are but the result of interferences with natural rights.

There is nothing in the condition of things (it were a libel on the Creator to say so) which condemns one class to toil and want while another lives in wasteful luxury. There is enough and to spare for us all. But if one is permitted to ignore the rights of others by taking more than his share, the others must get less; a difference is created which constantly tends to become greater, and a greedy scramble ensues in which more is wasted than used.

If you will trace out the laws of the production of wealth and see how enormous are the forces now wasted, if you will follow the laws of its distribution, and see how, by human laws, one set of men are enabled to appropriate a greater or less part of the earnings of the others; if you will think how this robbery of labour degrades the labourer and makes him unable to drive a fair bargain, and how it diminishes production, you will begin to see that there is no necessity for poverty, and that the growing disparity of social conditions proceeds from laws which deny the equal rights of men.

Fellow citizens, we have just listened again to the Declaration, not merely of national independence, but of the rights of man.

Great was Magna Charta–a beacon of light through centuries of darkness, a bulwark of the oppressed through ages of wrong, and a firm rock for Liberty's feet, as she still strove onward![17]

But all charters and bills of right, all muniments and titles of Liberty, are included in that simple statement of self-evident truth that is the heart and soul of the Declaration:[18] "That all men are created equal; that they are endowed by their Creator with certain inalienable rights; that among them are life, liberty and the pursuit of happiness."

In these simple words breathes not only the spirit of the Magna Charta, but the spirit which seeks its inspiration in the eternal facts of nature–through them speak not only Stephen Langton and John Hampden, but Wat Tyler and the Mad Priest of Kent.[19]

The assertion of the equal rights of all men to life, liberty and the pursuit of happiness is the assertion of the right of each to the fullest, freest exercise of all his faculties, limited only by the equal right of every other. It includes freedom of person and security of earnings, freedom of trade and capital, freedom of conscience and speech and the press. It is the

declaration of the same equal rights of all human beings to the enjoyment of the bounty of the Creator–to light and to air, to water and to land.
It asserts these rights as inalienable–as the direct grant of the Creator to
each human being, of which he can be rightfully deprived neither by
kings nor congresses, neither by parchments nor prescriptions–neither
by the compacts of past generations nor by majority votes.

This simple yet all-embracing statement bears the stamp royal of primary truth–it includes all partial truths and co-ordinates with all other
truths. This perfect liberty, which, by giving each his rights, secures the
rights of all–is order, for violence is the infringement of right; it is justice, for injustice is the denial of right; it is equality, for one cannot have
more than his right, without another having less. It is reverence towards
God, for irreverence is the denial of His order; it is love towards man,
for it accords to others all that we ask for ourselves. It is the message
that the angels sang over Bethlehem in Judea–it is the political expression of the Golden Rule!

Like all men who build on truth, the men of the Revolution builded better than they knew. The Declaration of Independence was ahead of their
time; it is in advance of our time; it means more than perhaps even he
saw whose pen traced it–a man of the future that he was and still is! But
it has in it the generative power of truth; it has grown and still must grow.

They tore from the draft of the Declaration the page in which
Jefferson branded the execrable crime of slavery. But in vain! In those
all-embracing words that page was still there, and though it has taken
a century, they are, in this respect, vindicated at last, and human flesh
and blood can no longer be bought and sold.


It is for us to vindicate them further. Slavery is not dead, though its
grossest form be gone. What is the difference, whether my body is
legally held by another, or whether he legally holds that by which alone
I can live. Hunger is as cruel as the lash. The essence of slavery consists
in taking from a man all the fruits of his labour except a bare living, and
of how many thousands miscalled free is this the lot? Where wealth
most abounds there are classes with whom the average plantation
negro would have lost in comfort by exchanging. English villeins of the
fourteenth century were better off than English agricultural labourers
of the nineteenth.[20] There is slavery and slavery! "The widow," says
Carlyle, "is gathering nettles for her children's dinner; a perfumed

seigneur, delicately lounging in the Œil de Bœuf, has an alchemy whereby he will extract from her the third nettle, and call it rent!"

Fellow-citizens, let us not be deluded by names. What is the use of a republic if labour must stand with its hat off begging for leave to work, if "tramps" must throng the highways and children grow up in squalid tenement houses? Political institutions are but means to an end–the freedom and happiness of the individual; and just so far as they fail in that, call them what you will, they are condemned.

Our conditions are changing. The laws which impel nations to seek a larger measure of liberty, or else take from them what they have, are working silently but with irresistible force. If we would perpetuate the Republic, we must come up to the spirit of the Declaration, and fully recognise the equal rights of all men. We must free labour from its burdens and trade from its fetters; we must cease to make government an excuse for enriching the few at the expense of the many, and confine it to necessary functions. We must cease to permit the monopolisation of land and water by non-users, and apply the just rule, "No seat reserved unless occupied." We must cease the cruel wrong which, by first denying their natural rights, reduces labourers to the wages of competition, and then, under pretence of asserting the rights of another race, compels them to a competition that will not merely force them to a standard of comfort unworthy the citizen of a free republic, but ultimately deprives them of their equal right to live.

Here is the test: whatever conduces to their equal and inalienable rights to men is good–let us preserve it. Whatever denies or interferes with those equal rights is bad–let us sweep it away. If we thus make our institutions consistent with their theory, all difficulties must vanish. We will not merely have a republic, but social conditions consistent with a republic. If we will not do this, we will surrender the Republic, either to be torn by the volcanic forces that already shake the ground beneath the standing armies of Europe, or to rot by slow degrees, and in its turn undergo the fate of all its predecessors.

Liberty is not a new invention that, once secured, can never be lost. Freedom is the natural state of man. "Who is your lord?" shouted the envoys of Charles the Simple to the Northmen who had penetrated into the heart of France.[21] "We have no lord; we are all free men!" was their answer; and so in their time of vigour would have answered every people that ever made a figure in the world. But at some point in the development of every people freedom has been lost, because as fresh gains were made, or new forces developed, they were turned to the advantage of a few.

Wealth in itself is a good, not an evil; but wealth concentrated in the hands of a few, corrupts on one side, and degrades on the other. No chain is stronger than its weakest link, and the ultimate condition of any people must be the condition of its lowest class. If the low are not brought up, the high must be brought down. In the long run, no nation can be freer than its most oppressed, richer than its poorest, wiser than its most ignorant. This is the fiat of the eternal justice that rules the world. It stands forth on every page of history. It is what the Sphinx says to us as she sitteth in desert sand, while the winged bulls of Nineveh bear her witness! It is written in the undecipherable hieroglyphics of Yucatan; in the brick mounds of Babylon; in the prostrate columns of Persiopolis; in the salt-sown plain of Carthage.[22] It speaks to us from the shattered relics of Grecian art; from the mighty ruins of the Coliseum! Down through the centuries comes a warning voice from the great Republic of the ancient world to the great Republic of the new. In three Latin words Pliny sums up the genesis of the causes that ate out the heart of the mightiest power that the world ever saw, and overwhelmed a widespread civilisation: "Great estates ruined Italy!"

Let us heed the warning by laying the foundations of the Republic upon the work of the equal, inalienable rights of all. So shall dangers disappear, and forces that now threaten turn to work our bidding; so shall wealth increase, and knowledge grow, and vice, crime and misery vanish away.


They who look upon Liberty as having accomplished her mission, when she has abolished hereditary privileges and given men the ballot, who think of her as having no further relations to the every-day affairs of life, have not seen her real grandeur–to them the poets who have sung of her must seem rhapsodists, and her martyrs fools! As the sun is the lord of life, as well as of light; as his beams not merely pierce the clouds, but support all growth, supply all motion, and call forth from what would otherwise be a cold and inert mass, all the infinite diversities of being and beauty, so is liberty to mankind. It is not for an abstraction that men have toiled and died; that in every age the witnesses of liberty have stood forth, and the martyrs of liberty have suffered. It was for more than this that matrons handed the Queen Anne musket from its rest, and that maids bid their lovers go to death![23]

We speak of liberty as one thing, and of virtue, wealth, knowledge, invention, national strength and national independence as other things. But, of all these, Liberty is the source, the mother, the necessary condition. She is to virtue what light is to colour, to wealth what sunshine is to grain; to knowledge what eyes are to the sight. She is the genius of invention, the brawn of national strength, the spirit of national independence! Where Liberty rises, there virtue grows, wealth increases, knowledge expands, invention multiplies human powers, and in strength and spirit the freer nation rises among her neighbours as Saul amid his brethren–taller and fairer.[24] Where Liberty sinks, there virtue fades, wealth diminishes, knowledge is forgotten, invention ceases, and empires once mighty in arms and arts become a helpless prey to freer barbarians!

Only in broken gleams and partial light has the sun of Liberty yet beamed among men, yet all progress hath she called forth.

Liberty came to a race of slaves crouching under Egyptian whips, and led them forth from the House of Bondage. She hardened them in the desert and made of them a race of conquerors. The free spirit of the Mosaic [L]aw took their thinkers up to heights where they beheld the unity of God, and inspired their poets with strains that yet phrase the highest exaltations of thought. Liberty dawned on the Ph[o]enician coast, and ships passed the Pillars of Hercules to plough the unknown sea. She broke in partial light on Greece, and marble grew to shapes of ideal beauty, words became the instruments of subtlest thought, and against the scanty militia of free cities the countless hosts of the Great King broke like surges against a rock. She cast her beams on the four-acre farms of Italian husbandmen, and born of her strength a power came forth that conquered the world! She glinted from shields of German warriors, and Augustus wept his legions.[25] Out of the night that followed her eclipse, her slanting rays fell again on free cities, and a lost learning revived, modern civilisation began, a new world was unveiled;[26] and as Liberty grew so grew art, wealth, power, knowledge and refinement. In the history of every nation we may read the same truth. It was the strength born of Magna Charta that won Crecy and Agincourt. It was the revival of Liberty from the despotism of the Tudors that glorified the Elizabethan age. It was the spirit that brought a crowned tyrant to the block that planted here the seed of a mighty tree. It was the energy of ancient freedom that, the moment it had gained unity, made Spain the mightiest power of the world, only to fall to the lowest depth of weakness when tyranny succeeded liberty. See, in France, all intellectual vigour dying under the tyranny of the seventeenth century to revive in splendour as Liberty awoke in the eighteenth, and on the enfranchisement of the French peasants in the great revolution, basing the wonderful strength that has in our time laughed at disaster.[27]

What Liberty shall do for the nation that fully accepts and loyally cherishes her, the wondrous inventions, which are the marked features of this century, give us but a hint. Just as the condition of the working classes is improved, do we gain in productive power. Wherever labour is best paid and has most leisure, comfort, and refinement, there invention is most active and most generally utilised. Short-sighted are they who think the reduction of working hours would reduce the production of wealth. Human muscles are one of the tiniest of forces; but for the human mind the resistless powers of nature work. To enfranchise labour, to give it leisure and comfort and independence, is to substitute in production mind for muscle. When this is fully done, the power that we now exert over matter will be as nothing to that we shall have.

It has been said that, from the very increase of our numbers, the American Union must in time necessarily break up. I do not believe it. Even now, while the memories of a civil war are fresh, I do not think any part of our people regret that this continent is not bisected by an imaginary line, separating two jealous nations, two great standing armies. If we respect the equal rights of all, if we reduce the operation of our national Government to the purposes for which it is alone fitted, the preservation of the common peace, the maintenance of the common security and the promotion of the common convenience, there can be no sectional interest adverse to unity, and the blessings of the bond that makes us a nation must become more apparent as years roll on.

So far from this Union necessarily falling to pieces from its own weight, it may, if we but hold fast to justice, not merely embrace a continent, but prove in the future capable of a wider extension than we have yet dreamed.

The crazy king, the brutal ministers, the rotten Parliament, the combination of tyranny, folly, corruption and arrogance that sundered the Anglo-Saxon race, is gone, but stronger and stronger grows the influence of the deathless minds that make our common language classic.[28] The republic of Anglo-Saxon literature extends wherever the tongue of Shakespeare is spoken. The great actors who from time to time walk this stage, find their audiences over half the globe; it is to one people that our poets sing; it is one mind that responds to the thought of our thinkers. The old bitternesses are passing away. With us the hatreds, born of two wars, are beginning to soften and die out, while Englishmen, who this year honour us in honouring the citizen whom we have twice deemed worthy of our foremost place, are beginning to look upon our Revolution as the vindication of their own liberties.[29]

A hundred years have passed since the fast friend of American liberty–the great Earl Chatham–rose to make his last appeal for the preservation, on the basis of justice, of that English-speaking empire, in which he saw the grandest possibility of the future.[30] Is it too soon to hope that the future may hold the realisation of his vision in a nobler form than even he imagined, and that it may be the mission of this Republic to unite all the nations of English speech, whether they grow beneath the Northern Star or Southern Cross, in a league which, by insuring justice, promoting peace, and liberating commerce, will be the forerunner of a world-wide federation that will make war the possibility of a past age, and turn to works of usefulness the enormous forces now dedicated to destruction.

And she to whom on this day our hearts turn, our ancient ally, our generous friend–thank God we can say, our sister Republic of France! It was not alone the cold calculations of kingcraft that when our need was direst, and helped us with money and supplies, with armies and fleets. The grand idea of the equal rights of man was stirring in France, her pulses were throbbing with the new life that was soon to shake the thrones of Europe as with an earthquake, and French sympathy went out where Liberty made her stand. "They are a generous people," wrote Franklin, "they do not like to hear of advantages in return for their aid. They desire the glory of helping us." France has that glory, and more. Let her column Vendôme fall, and the memory of the butchers of mankind fade away; the great things that France has done for freedom will make her honoured of the nations, while, with increasing and increasing meaning, rings through the ages the cry with which she turned to the thunder-burst of Valmy: "Live the people!"[31]

Beset by difficulties from which we are happily exempt–on the one side those who dream of bringing back the middle ages, on the other the red spectre; compelled, or in fancy compelled, by the legacy of old hates to maintain that nightmare of prosperity and deadly foe of freedom, a large standing army–France has yet steadily made progress. Italy is one; the great Germanic race at last have unity; as out of a trance, life stirs in Spain; Russia moves as she marches. May it not be France's to again show Europe the way?[32]


Fellow-citizens: If I have sought rather to appeal to thought than to flatter vanity, it is not that I do not see the greatness and feel the love of my country. Drawing my first breath almost within the shadow of Independence Hall, the cherished traditions of the Republic entwine themselves with my earliest recollections, and her flag symbolizes to me all that I hold dear on earth. But for the very love I bear her, for the very memories I cherish, I would not dare come before you on this day and ignore the dangers I see in her path.

If I have not dwelt on her material greatness or pictured her future growth, it is because there rises before me a higher ideal of what this Republic may be than can be expressed in material symbols–an ideal so glorious that, beside it, all that we now pride ourselves on seems mean and pitiful. That ideal is not satisfied with a republic where, with all the enormous gains in productive power, labour is ground down to a bare living and must think the chance to work a favour; it is not satisfied with a republic where prisons are crowded and almshouses are built and families are housed in tiers. It is not satisfied with a republic where one tenant for a day can warn his co-tenants off more of the surface of this rolling sphere than he is using or can use, or compel them to pay him for the bounty of their common Creator; it is not satisfied with a republic where the fear of poverty on the one hand and the sight of great wealth on the other makes the lives of so many such a pitiful straining, keeps eyes to the ground that might be turned to the stars, and substitutes the worship of the Golden Calf for that of the Living God!

It hopes for a republic where all shall have plenty, where each may sit under his vine and fig tree, with none to vex him or make him afraid; where with want shall gradually disappear vice and crime; where men shall cease to spend their lives in a struggle to live, or in heaping up things they cannot take away; where talent shall be greater than wealth and character greater than talent, and where each may find free scope to develop body, mind and soul.

Is this the dream of dreamers? One brought to the world the message that it might be reality. But they crucified him between two thieves.

Not till it accepts that message can the world have peace. Look over the history of the past. What is it but a record of the woes inflicted by man on man, of wrong producing wrong, and crime fresh crime? It must be so till justice is acknowledged and liberty is law.

Some things have we done, but not all. In the words with which an eminent Frenchman closes the history of that great revolution that followed ours: "Liberty is not yet here; but she will come!"

Fellow-citizens, let us follow the star that rose above the cradle of the Republic; let us try our laws by the test of the Declaration. Let us show to the nations our faith in Liberty, nor fear she will lead us astray.

Who is Liberty that we should doubt her; that we should set bounds to her, and say, "Thus far shall thou come and no further!" Is she not peace? is she not prosperity? is she not progress? nay, is she not the goal towards which all progress strives?

Not here; but yet she cometh! Saints have seen her in their visions; seers have seen her in their trance. To heroes has she spoken, and their hearts were strong; to martyrs and the flames were cool!

She is not here, but yet she cometh. Lo! her feet are on the mountains—the call of her clarions ring on every breeze; the banners of her dawning fret the sky! Who will hear her as she calleth; who will bid her come and welcome? Who will turn to her? who will speak for her? who will stand for her while she yet hath need?

# THE CRIME OF POVERTY

*Ladies and Gentlemen:*

I propose to talk to you to-night of the Crime of Poverty. I cannot, in a short time, hope to convince you of much; but the thing of things I should like to show you is that poverty is a crime. I do not mean that it is a crime to be poor. Murder is a crime; but it is not a crime to be murdered; and a man who is in poverty, I look upon, not as a criminal in himself, so much as the victim of a crime for which others, as well perhaps as himself, are responsible. That poverty is a curse, the bitterest of curses, we all know. Carlyle was right when he said that the hell of which Englishmen are most afraid is the hell of poverty; and this is true, not of Englishmen alone, but of people all over the civilised world, no matter what their nationality. It is to escape this hell that we strive and strain and struggle; and work on oftentimes in blind habit long after the necessity for work is gone.

The curse born of poverty is not confined to the poor alone; it runs through all classes, even to the very rich. They, too, suffer; they must suffer; for there cannot be suffering in a community from which any class can totally escape. The vice, the crime, the ignorance, the meanness born of poverty, poison, so to speak, the very air which rich and poor alike must breathe.

Poverty is the mother of ignorance, the breeder of crime. I walked down one of your streets this morning, and I saw three men going along with their hands chained together. I knew for certain that those men were not rich men; and, although I do not know the offence for which they were carried in chains through your streets, this I think I can safely say, that, if you trace it up you will find it in some way to spring from

*An address delivered in the Opera House, Burlington, Iowa, April 1, 1885, under the auspices of Burlington Assembly, No. 3135, Knights of Labour, which afterwards distributed fifty thousand copies in tract form.*[1]

poverty. Nine tenths of human misery, I think you will find, if you look, to be due to poverty. If a man chooses to be poor, he commits no crime in being poor, provided his poverty hurts no one but himself. If a man has others dependent upon him; if there are a wife and children whom it is his duty to support, then, if he voluntarily chooses poverty, it is a crime–aye, and I think that, in most cases, the men who have no one to support but themselves are men that are shirking their duty. A woman comes into the world for every man; and for every man who lives a single life, caring only for himself, there is some woman who is deprived of her natural supporter. But while a man who chooses to be poor cannot be charged with crime, it is certainly a crime to force poverty on others. And it seems to me clear that the great majority of those who suffer from poverty are poor not from their own particular faults, but because of conditions imposed by society at large. Therefore I hold that poverty is a crime–not an individual crime, but a social crime, a crime for which we all, poor as well as rich, are responsible.

Two or three weeks ago I went one Sunday evening to the church of a famous Brooklyn preacher. Mr. Sankey was singing and something like a revival was going on there.[2] The clergyman told some anecdotes connected with the revival, and recounted some of the reasons why men failed to become Christians. One case he mentioned struck me. He said that he had noticed on the outskirts of the congregation, night after night, a man who listened intently and who gradually moved forward. One night, the clergyman said, he went to him, saying: "My brother, are you not ready to become a Christian?" The man said, no, he was not. He said it, not in a defiant tone, but in a sorrowful tone; the clergyman asked him why, whether he did not believe in the truths he had been hearing? Yes, he believed them all. Why, then, wouldn't he become a Christian? "Well," he said, "I can't join the church without giving up my business; and it is necessary for the support of my wife and children. If I give that up, I don't know how in the world I can get along. I had a hard time before I found my present business, and I cannot afford to give it up. Yet I can't become a Christian without giving it up." The clergyman asked, "are you a rum-seller?" No, he was not a rum-seller. Well, the clergyman said, he didn't know what in the world the man could be; it seemed to him that a rum-seller was the only man who does a business that would prevent his becoming a Christian; and he finally said: "What is your business?" The man said, "I sell soap." "Soap!" exclaimed the clergyman, "you sell soap? How in the world does that prevent your becoming a Christian?" "Well," the man said, "it is this way; the soap I sell is one of these patent soaps that are extensively advertised as enabling you to clean clothes very quickly, as containing no deleterious compound whatever. Every cake of the soap that I sell is wrapped in a paper on which is printed a statement that it contains no injurious chemicals, whereas the truth of the matter is that it does, and that though it will take the dirt out of clothes pretty quickly, it will, in a little while, rot them completely. I have to make my living in this way; and I cannot feel that I can become a Christian if I sell that soap." The minister went on, describing how he laboured unsuccessfully with that man, and finally wound up by saying: "He stuck to his soap and lost his soul."

But, if that man lost his soul, was it his fault alone? Whose fault is it that social conditions are such that men have to make that terrible choice between what conscience tells them is right, and the necessity of earning a living? I hold that it is the fault of society; that it is the fault of us all. Pestilence is a curse. The man who would bring cholera to this country, or the man who, having the power to prevent its coming here, would make no effort to do so, would be guilty of a crime. Poverty is worse than cholera; poverty kills more people than pestilence, even in the best of times. Look at the death statistics of our cities; see where the deaths come quickest; see where it is that the little children die like flies—it is in the poorer quarters. And the man who looks with careless eyes upon the ravages of this pestilence, the man who does not set himself to stay and eradicate it, he, I say, is guilty of a crime.

If poverty is appointed by the power which is above us all, then it is no crime; but if poverty is unnecessary, then it is a crime for which society is responsible and for which society must suffer.

I hold, and I think no one who looks at the facts can fail to see, that poverty is utterly unnecessary. It is not by the decree of the Almighty, but it is because of our own injustice, our own selfishness, our own ignorance, that this scourge, worse than any pestilence, ravages our civilisation, bringing want and suffering and degradation, destroying souls as well as bodies. Look over the world, in this heyday of nineteenth century civilisation. In every civilised country under the sun you will find men and women whose condition is worse than that of the savage: men and women and little children with whom the veriest savage could not afford to exchange. Even in this new city of yours with virgin soil around you, you have had this winter to institute a relief society.

Your roads have been filled with tramps, fifteen, I am told, at one time taking shelter in a round-house here. As here, so everywhere; and poverty is deepest where wealth most abounds.

What more unnatural than this? There is nothing in nature like this poverty which to-day curses us. We see rapine in nature; we see one species destroying another; but as a general thing animals do not feed on their own kind; and, wherever we see one kind enjoying plenty, all creatures of that kind share it. No man, I think, ever saw a herd of buffalo, of which a few were fat and the great majority lean. No man ever saw a flock of birds, of which two or three were swimming in grease and the others all skin and bone. Nor in savage life is there anything like the poverty that festers in our civilisation.

In a rude state of society there are seasons of want, seasons when people starve; but they are seasons when the earth has refused to yield her increase, when the rain has not fallen from the heavens, or when the land has been swept by some foe–not when there is plenty. And yet the peculiar characteristic of this modern poverty of ours is that it is deepest where wealth most abounds.

Why, to-day, while over the civilised world there is so much distress, so much want, what is the cry that goes up? What is the current explanation of the hard times? Over-production! There are so many clothes that men must go ragged, so much coal that in the bitter winters people have to shiver, such over-filled granaries that people actually die by starvation! Want due to over-production! Was a greater absurdity ever uttered? How can there be over-production till all have enough? It is not over-production; it is unjust distribution.

Poverty necessary! Why, think of the enormous powers that are latent in the human brain! Think how invention enable us to do with the power of one man what not long ago could not be done by the power of a thousand. Think that in England alone the steam machinery in operation is said to exert a productive force greater than the physical force of the population of the world, were they all adults. And yet we have only begun to invent and discover. We have not yet utilised all that has already been invented and discovered. And look at the powers of the earth. They have hardly been touched. In every direction as we look new resources seem to open. Man's ability to produce wealth seems almost infinite–we can set no bounds to it. Look at the power that is flowing by your city in the current of the Mississippi that might be set at work for you. So in every direction energy that we might utilise goes to waste; resources that we might draw upon are untouched. Yet men are delving and straining to satisfy mere animal wants; women are working, working, working their lives away, and too frequently turning in despair from that hard struggle to cast away all that makes the charm of woman.

If the animals can reason what must they think of us? Look at one of those great ocean steamers ploughing her way across the Atlantic, against wind, against wave, absolutely setting at defiance the utmost power of the elements. If the gulls that hover over her were thinking beings could they imagine that the animal that could create such a structure as that could actually want for enough to eat? Yet, so it is. How many even of those of us who find life easiest are there who really live a rational life? Think of it, you who believe that there is only one life for man—what a fool at the very best is a man to pass his life in this struggle to merely live? And you who believe, as I believe, that this is not the last of man, that this is a life that opens but another life, think how nine tenths, aye, I do not know but ninety-nine-hundredths of all our vital powers are spent in a mere effort to get a living; or to heap together that which we cannot by any possibility take away. Take the life of the average workingman. Is that the life for which the human brain was intended and the human heart was made? Look at the factories scattered through our country. They are little better than penitentiaries.

I read in the New York papers a while ago that the girls at the Yonkers factories had struck. The papers said that the girls did not seem to know why they had struck, and intimated that it must be just for the fun of striking. Then came out the girls' side of the story and it appeared that they had struck against the rules in force. They were fined if they spoke to one another, and they were fined still more heavily if they laughed. There was a heavy fine for being a minute late. I visited a lady in Philadelphia who had been a forewoman in various factories, and I asked her, "Is it possible that such rules are enforced?" She said it was so in Philadelphia. There is a fine for speaking to your next neighbour, a fine for laughing; and she told me that the girls in one place where she was employed were fined ten cents a minute for being late, though many of them had to come for miles in winter storms. She told me of one poor girl who really worked hard one week and made $3.50; but the fines against her were $5.25. That seems ridiculous; it is ridiculous, but it is pathetic and it is shameful.

But take the cases of those even who are comparatively independent and well off. Here is a man working hour after hour, day after day, week after week, in doing one thing over and over again, and for what? Just to live. He is working ten hours a day in order that he may sleep eight and may have two or three hours for himself when he is tired out and all his faculties are exhausted. That is not a reasonable life; that is not a life for a being possessed of the powers that are in man, and I think every man must have felt it for himself. I know that when I first went to my trade I thought to myself that it was incredible that a man was created to work all day long just to live. I used to read the "Scientific American," and as invention after invention was heralded in that paper I used to think to myself that when I became a man it would not be necessary to work so hard. But on the contrary, the struggle for existence has become more and more intense. People who want to prove the contrary get up masses of statistics to show that the condition of the working classes is improving. Improvement that you have to take a statistical microscope to discover does not amount to anything. But there is not improvement.

Improvement! Why, according to the last report of the Michigan Bureau of Labour Statistics, as I read yesterday in a Detroit paper, taking all the trades, including some of the very high priced ones, where the wages are from $6 to $7 a day, the average earnings amount to $1.77, and, taking out waste time, to $1.40. Now, when you consider how a man can live and bring up a family on $1.40 a day, even in Michigan, I do not think you will conclude that the condition of the working classes can have very much improved.

Here is a broad general fact that is asserted by all who have investigated the question, by such men as Hallam, the historian, and Professor Thorold Rogers, who has made a study of the history of prices as they were five centuries ago.[3] When all the productive arts were in the most primitive state, when the most prolific of our modern vegetables had not been introduced, when the breeds of cattle were small and poor, when there were hardly any roads and transportation was exceedingly difficult, when all manufacturing was done by hand–in that rude time the condition of the labourers of England was far better than it is to-day. In those rude times no man need fear want save when actual famine came, and owing to the difficulties of transportation the plenty of one district could not relieve the scarcity of another. Save in such times, no man need fear want. Pauperism, such as exists in modern times, was absolutely unknown. Everyone, save the physically disabled, could make a living, and the poorest lived in rude plenty. But perhaps the most astonishing fact brought to light by this investigation is that at that time, under those conditions in those "dark ages," as we call them, the working day was only eight hours.[4] While with all our modern inventions and improvements, our working classes have been agitating and struggling in vain to get the working day reduced to eight hours.

Do these facts show improvement? Why, in the rudest state of society in the most primitive state of the arts the labour of the natural bread-winner will suffice to provide a living for himself and for those who are dependent upon him. Amid all our inventions there are large bodies of men who cannot do this. What is the most astonishing thing in our civilisation? Why, the most astonishing thing to those Sioux chiefs who were recently brought from the Far West and taken through our manufacturing cities in the East, was not the marvelous inventions that enabled machinery to act almost as if it had intellect; it was not the growth of our cities; it was not the speed with which the railway car whirled along; it was not the telegraph or the telephone that most astonished them; but the fact that amid this marvelous development of productive power they found little children at work.[5] And astonishing that ought to be to us; a most astounding thing!

Talk about improvement in the condition of the working classes, when the facts are that a larger and larger proportion of women and children are forced to toil. Why, I am told that, even here in your own city, there are children of thirteen and fourteen working in factories. In Detroit, according to the report of the Michigan Bureau of Labour Statistics, one half of the children of school age do not go to school. In New Jersey, the report made to the legislature discloses an amount of misery and ignorance that is appalling. Children are growing up there, compelled to monotonous toil when they ought to be at play, children who do not know how to play; children who have been so long accustomed to work that they have become used to it; children growing up in such ignorance that they do not know what country New Jersey is in, that they never heard of George Washington, that some of them think Europe is in New York. Such facts are appalling; they mean that the very foundations of the Republic are being sapped. The dangerous man is not the man who tries to excite discontent; the dangerous man is the man who says that all is as it ought to be. Such a state of things cannot continue; such tendencies as we see at work here cannot go on without bringing at last an overwhelming crash.

I say that all this poverty and the ignorance that flows from it is unnecessary; I say that there is no natural reason why we should not all be rich, in the sense, not of having more than each other, but in the sense of all having enough to completely satisfy all physical wants; of all having enough to get such an easy living that we could develop the better part of humanity. There is no reason why wealth should not be so abundant, that no one should think of such a thing as little children at work, or a woman compelled to a toil that nature never intended her to perform; wealth so abundant that there would be no cause for that harassing fear that sometimes paralyses even those who are not considered "the poor," the fear that every man of us has probably felt, that if sickness should smite him, or if he should be taken away, those whom he loves better than his life would become charges upon charity. "Consider the lilies of the field, how they grow; they toil not, neither do they spin." I believe that in a really Christian community, in a society that honoured not with the lips but with the act, the doctrines of Jesus, no one would have occasion to worry about physical needs any more than do the lilies of the field. There is enough and to spare. The trouble is that, in this mad struggle, we trample in the mire what has been provided in sufficiency for us all; trample it in the mire while we tear and rend each other.

There is a cause for this poverty; and, if you trace it down, you will find its root in a primary injustice. Look over the world to-day—poverty everywhere. The cause must be a common one. You cannot attribute it to the tariff, or to the form of government, or to this thing or to that in which nations differ; because, as deep poverty is common to them all the cause that produces it must be a common cause. What is that common cause? There is one sufficient cause that is common to all nations; and that is the appropriation as the property of some of that natural element on which and from which all must live.

Take that fact I have spoken of, that appalling fact that, even now, it is harder to live than it was in the ages dark and rude five centuries ago—how do you explain it? There is no difficulty in finding the cause. Whoever reads the history of England, or the history of any other civilised nation (but I speak of the history of England because that is the history with which we are best acquainted) will see the reason. For century after century a parliament composed of aristocrats and employers passed laws endeavouring to reduce wages, but in vain. Men could not be crowded down to wages that gave a mere living because the bounty of nature was not wholly shut up from them; because some remains of the recognition of the truth that all men have equal rights on the earth still existed; because the land of that country, that which was held in private possession, was only held on a tenure derived from the nation, and for a rent payable back to the nation. The church lands supported the expenses of public worship, of the maintenance of seminaries and the care of the poor; the crown lands defrayed the expenses of the civil list; and from a third portion of the lands, those held under the military tenures, the army was provided for. There was no national debt in England at that time. They carried on wars for hundreds of years, but at the charge of the landowners. And more important still, there remained everywhere, and you can see in every old English town their traces to this day, the common lands to which any of the neighbourhood was free. It was as those lands were inclosed; it was as the commons were gradually monopolised, as the church lands were made the prey of greedy courtiers, as the crown lands were given away as absolute property to the favourites of the king, as the military tenants shirked their rents and laid the expenses they had agreed to defray, upon the nation, in taxation that bore upon industry and upon thrift–it was then that poverty began to deepen, and the tramp appeared in England; just as to-day he is appearing in our new States.[6]

Now, think of it–is not land monopolisation a sufficient reason for poverty? What is man? In the first place, he is an animal, a land animal who cannot live without land. All that man produces comes from land; all productive labour, in the final analysis, consists in working up land; or materials drawn from land, into such forms as fit them for the satisfaction of human wants and desires. Why, man's very body is drawn from the land. Children of the soil, we come from the land, and to the land we must return. Take away from man all that belongs to the land, and what have you but a disembodied spirit? Therefore he who holds the land on which and from which another man must live, is that man's master; and the man is his slave. The man who holds the land on which I must live can command me to life or to death just as absolutely as though I were his chattel. Talk about abolishing slavery–we have not abolished slavery; we have only abolished one rude form of it, chattel slavery. There is a deeper and a more insidious form, a more cursed form yet before us to abolish, in this industrial slavery that makes a man a virtual slave, while taunting him and mocking him with the name of freedom. Poverty! want! they will sting as much as the lash. Slavery! God knows there are horrors enough in slavery; but there are deeper horrors in our civilised society to-day. Bad as chattel slavery was, it did not drive slave mothers to kill their children, yet you may read in official reports that the system of child insurance which has taken root so strongly in England, and which is now spreading over our Eastern states, has perceptibly and largely increased the rate of child mortality!–What does that mean?[7]

Robinson Crusoe, as you know, when he rescued Friday from the cannibals, made him his slave.[8] Friday had to serve Crusoe. But, supposing Crusoe had said, "O man and brother, I am very glad to see you, and I welcome you to this island, and you shall be a free and independent citizen, with just as much to say as I have–except that this island is mine, and of course, as I can do as I please with my own property, you must not use it save upon my terms." Friday would have been just as much Crusoe's slave as though he had called him one. Friday was not a fish, he could not swim off through the sea; he was not a bird, and could not fly off through the air; if he lived at all, he had to live on that island. And if that island was Crusoe's, Crusoe was his master through life to death.

A friend of mine, who believes as I do upon this question, was talking a while ago with another friend of mine who is a greenbacker, but who had not paid much attention to the land question. Our greenback friend said, "Yes, yes, the land question is an important question; oh, I admit the land question is a very important question; but then there are other important questions. There is this question and that question, and the other question; and there is the money question. The money question is a very important question; it is a more important question than the land question. You give me all the money, and you can take all the land." My friend said, "Well, suppose you had all the money in the world and I had all the land in the world. What would you do if I were to give you notice to quit?"

Do you know that I do not think that the average man realises what land is? I know a little girl who has been going to school for some time, studying geography, and all that sort of thing; and one day she said to me: "Here is something about the surface of the earth. I wonder what the surface of the earth looks like?" "Well," I said, "look out into the yard there. That is the surface of the earth." She said, "That the surface of the earth? Our yard the surface of the earth? Why, I never thought of it!" That is very much the case not only with grown men, but with such wise beings as newspaper editors. They seem to think, when you talk of land, that you always refer to farms; to think that the land question is a question that relates entirely to farmers, as though land had no other use than growing crops. Now, I should like to know how a man could even edit a newspaper without having the use of some land. He might swing himself by straps and go up in a balloon, but he could not even then get along without land. What supports the balloon in the air? Land; the surface of the earth. Let the earth drop, and what would become of the balloon? The air that supports the balloon is supported in turn by land. So it is with everything else men can do. Whether a man is working away three thousand feet under the surface of the earth, or whether he is working up in the top of one of those immense buildings that they have in New York; whether he is ploughing the soil or sailing across the ocean, he is still using land.

Land! Why, in owning a piece of ground, what do you own? The lawyers will tell you that you own from the centre of the earth right up to heaven; and, so far as all human purposes go, you do. In New York they are building houses thirteen and fourteen stories high. What are men, living in those upper stories, paying for? There is a friend of mine who has an office in one of them, and he estimates that he pays by the cubic foot for air. Well, the man who owns the surface of the land has the renting of the air up there, and would have if the buildings were carried up for miles.

This land question is the bottom question. Man is a land animal. Suppose you want to build a house; can you build it without a place to put it? What is it built of? Stone, or mortar, or wood, or iron–they all come from the earth. Think of any article of wealth you choose, any of those things which men struggle for, where do they come from? From the land. It is the bottom question. The land question is simply the labour question; and when some men own that element from which all wealth must be drawn, and upon which all must live, then they have the power of living without work, and, therefore, those who do work get less of the products of work.

Did you ever think of the utter absurdity and strangeness of the fact that, all over the civilised world, the working classes are the poor classes? Go into any city in the world, and get into a cab and ask the man to drive you where the working people live. He won't take you to where the fine houses are. He will take you, on the contrary, into the squalid quarters, the poorer quarters. Did you ever think how curious that is? Think for a moment how it would strike a rational being who had never been on the earth before, if such an intelligence could come down, and you were to explain to him how we live on earth, how houses and food and clothing, and all the many things we need were all produced by work, would he not think that the working people would be the people who lived in the finest houses and had most of everything that work produces? Yet, whether you took him to London or Paris or New York, or even to Burlington, he would find that those called the working people were the people who live in the poorest houses.

All this is strange–just think of it. We naturally despise poverty; and it is reasonable that we should. I do not say–I distinctly repudiate it–that the people who are poor are poor always from their own fault, or even in most cases; but it ought to be so. If any good man or woman could create a world, it would be a sort of a world in which no one would be poor unless he was lazy or vicious. But that is just precisely the kind of a world this is; that is just precisely the kind of a world the Creator has made. Nature gives to labour, and to labour alone; there must be human work before any article of wealth can be produced; and in the natural state of things the man who toiled honestly and well would be the rich man, and he who did not work would be poor. We have so reversed the order of nature that we are accustomed to think of the workingman as a poor man.

And if you trace it out I believe you will see that the primary cause of this is that we compel those who work to pay others for permission to do so. You may buy a coat, a horse, a house; there you are paying the seller for labour exerted, for something that he has produced, or that he has got from the man who did produce it; but when you pay a man for land, what are you paying him for? You are paying for something that no man has produced; you pay him for something that was here before man was, or for a value that was created, not by him individually, but by the community of which you are a part. What is the reason that the land here, where we stand tonight, is worth more than it was twenty-five years ago? What is the reason that land in the centre of New York, that once could be bought by the mile for a jug of whiskey, is now worth so much that, though you were to cover it with gold, you would not have its value? Is it not because of the increase of population? Take away that population, and where would the value of the land be? Look at it in any way you please.

We talk about over-production. How can there be such a thing as over-production while people want? All these things that are said to be over-produced are desired by many people. Why do they not get them?

They do not get them because they have not the means to buy them; not that they do not want them. Why have not they the means to buy them? They earn too little. When the great masses of men have to work for an average of $1.40 a day, it is no wonder that great quantities of goods cannot be sold.

Now why is it that men have to work for such low wages? Because if they were to demand higher wages there are plenty of unemployed men ready to step into their places. It is this mass of unemployed men who compel that fierce competition that drives wages down to the point of bare subsistence. Why is it that there are men who cannot get employment? Did you ever think what a strange thing it is that men cannot find employment? Adam had no difficulty in finding employment; neither had Robinson Crusoe; the finding of employment was the last thing that troubled them.

If men cannot find an employer, why cannot they employ themselves? Simply because they are shut out from the element on which human labour can alone be exerted. Men are compelled to compete with each other for the wages of an employer, because they have been robbed of the natural opportunities of employing themselves; because they cannot find a piece of God's world on which to work without paying some other human creature for the privilege.

I do not mean to say that even after you had set right this fundamental injustice, there would not be many things to do; but this I do mean to say, that our treatment of land lies at the bottom of all social questions. This I do mean to say, that, do what you please, reform as you may, you never can get rid of wide-spread poverty so long as the element on which and from which all men must live is made the private property of some men. It is utterly impossible. Reform government–get taxes down to the minimum–build railroads; institute co-operative stores; divide profits, if you choose, between employers and employed–and what will be the result? The result will be that the land will increase in value–that will be the result–that and nothing else. Experience shows this. Do not all improvements simply increase the value of land–the price that some must pay others for the privilege of living?

Consider the matter, I say it with all reverence, and I merely say it because I wish to impress a truth upon your minds–it is utterly impossible, so long as His laws are what they are, that God Himself could relieve poverty–utterly impossible. Think of it and you will see. Men pray to the

Almighty to relieve poverty. But poverty comes not from God's laws–it is blasphemy of the worst kind to say that; it comes from man's injustice to his fellows. Supposing the Almighty were to hear the prayer, how could He carry out the request so long as His laws are what they are? Consider– the Almighty gives us nothing of the things that constitute wealth; He merely gives us the raw material, which must be utilised by man to produce wealth. Does He not give us enough of that now? How could He relieve poverty even if He were to give us more? Supposing in answer to these prayers He were to increase the power of the sun; or the virtue of the soil? Supposing He were to make plants more prolific, or animals to produce after their kind more abundantly? Who would get the benefit of it? Take a country where land is completely monopolised, as it is in most of the civilised countries–who would get the benefit of it? Simply the landowners. And even if God in answer to prayer were to send down out of the heavens those things that men require, who would get the benefit?

In the Old Testament we are told that when the Israelites journeyed through the desert, they were hungered, and that God sent manna down out of the heavens.[9] There was enough for all of them, and they all took it and were relieved. But supposing that desert had been held as private property, as the soil of Great Britain is held, as the soil even of our new States is being held; suppose that one of the Israelites had a square mile, and another one had twenty square miles, and another one had a hundred square miles, and the great majority of the Israelites did not have enough to set the soles of their feet upon, which they could call their own–what would become of the manna? What good would it have done to the majority? Not a whit. Though God had sent down manna enough for all, that manna would have been the property of the landholders; they would have employed some of the others perhaps, to gather it up into heaps for them, and would have sold it to their hungry brethren. Consider it; this purchase and sale of manna might have gone on until the majority of Israelites had given all they had, even to the clothes off their backs. What then? Then they would not have had anything left to buy manna with, and the consequences would have been that while they went hungry the manna would have lain in great heaps, and the landowners would have been complaining of the over-production of manna. There would have been a great harvest of manna and hungry people, just precisely the phenomenon that we see to-day.

I cannot go over all the points I would like to try, but I wish to call your attention to the utter absurdity of private property in land! Why, consider it, the idea of a man's selling the earth—the earth, our common mother. A man selling that which no man produced—a man passing title from one generation to another. Why, it is the most absurd thing in the world. Why, did you ever think of it? What right has a dead man to land? For whom was this earth created? It was created for the living, certainly, not for the dead. Well, now we treat it as though it was created for the dead. Where do our land titles come from? They come from men who for the most part are past and gone. Here in this new country you get a little nearer the original source; but go to the Eastern States and go back over the Atlantic. There you may clearly see the power that comes from landownership.

As I say, the man that owns the land is the master of those who must live on it. Here is a modern instance: you who are familiar with the history of the Scottish Church know that in the forties there was a disruption in the church. You who have read Hugh Miller's work on "The Cruise of the *Betsey*" know something about it; how a great body, led by Dr. Chalmers, came out from the Established Church and said they would set up a Free Church.[10] In the Established Church were a great many of the landowners. Some of them, like the Duke of Buccleugh, owning miles and miles of land on which no common Scotsman had a right to put his foot, save by the Duke of Buccleugh's permission. These landowners refused not only to allow these Free Churchmen to have ground upon which to erect a church, but they would not let them stand on their land and worship God. You who have read "The Cruise of the *Betsey*" know that it is the story of a clergyman who was obliged to make his home in a boat on that wild sea because he was not allowed to have land enough to live on. In many places the people had to take the sacrament with the tide coming to their knees—many a man lost his life worshipping on the roads in rain and snow. They were not permitted to go on Mr. Landlord's land and worship God, and had to take to the roads. The Duke of Buccleugh stood out for seven years compelling people to worship in the roads, until finally relenting a little, he allowed them to worship God in a gravel pit; whereupon they passed a resolution of thanks to His Grace.

But that is not what I wanted to tell you. The thing that struck me was this significant fact: As soon as the disruption occurred, the Free Church, composed of a great many able men, at once sent a delegation to the landlords to ask permission for Scotsmen to worship God in Scotland and in their own way. This delegation set out for London—they had to go to London, England, to get permission for Scotsmen to worship God in Scotland, and in their own native home!

But that is not the most absurd thing. In one place where they were refused land upon which to stand and worship God, the late landowner had died and his estate was in the hands of the trustees, and the answer of the trustees was, that so far as they were concerned they would exceedingly like to allow them to have a place to put up a church to worship God, but they could not conscientiously do it because they knew that such a course would be very displeasing to the late Mr. Monaltie! Now this dead man had gone to heaven, let us hope; at any rate he had gone away from this world, but lest it might displease him men yet living could not worship God. Is it possible for absurdity to go any further?

You may say that those Scotch people are very absurd people, but they are not a whit more so than we are. I read only a little while ago of some Long Island fishermen who had been paying as rent for the privilege of fishing there, a certain part of the catch. They paid it because they believed that James II, a dead man centuries ago, a man who never put his foot in America, a king who was kicked off the English throne, had said they had to pay it, and they got up a committee, went to the county town and searched the records. They could not find anything in the records to show that James II had ever ordered that they should give any of their fish to anybody, and so they refused to pay any longer.[11] But if they had found that James II had really said they should they would have gone on paying. Can anything be more absurd?

There is a square in New York–Stuyvesant Square–that is locked up at six o'clock every evening, even on the long summer evenings.[12] Why is it locked up? Why are the children not allowed to play there? Why because old Mr. Stuyvesant, dead and gone I don't know how many years ago, so willed it. Now can anything be more absurd?*

Yet that is not any more absurd than our land titles. From whom do they come? Dead man after dead man. Suppose you get on the cars here going to Council Bluffs or Chicago. You find a passenger with his baggage strewn over the seats. You say: "Will you give me a seat, if you please, sir?" He replies: "No; I bought this seat." "Bought this seat? From

---

* After a popular agitation, the park authorities since decided to leave the gates open later than six o'clock.

whom did you buy it?" "I bought it from the man who got out at the last station." That is the way we manage this earth of ours.

Is it not a self-evident truth, as Thomas Jefferson said, that "the land belongs in usufruct to the living," and that they who have died have left it, and have no power to say how it shall be disposed of? Title to land! Where can a man get any title which makes the earth his property? There is a sacred right to property—sacred because ordained by the laws of nature, that is to say, by the laws of God, and necessary to social order and civilisation. That is the right of property in things produced by labour; it rests on the right of a man to himself. That which a man produces, that is his against all the world, to give or to keep, to lend, to sell or to bequeath; but how can he get such a right to land when it was here before he came? Individual claims to land rest only on appropriation. I read in a recent number of the "Nineteenth Century," possibly some of you may have read it, an article by an ex-prime minister of Australia in which there was a little story that attracted my attention. It was of a man named Galahard, who in the early days got up to the top of a high hill in one of the finest parts of western Australia. He got up there, looked all around, and made this proclamation: "All the land that is in my sight from the top of this hill I claim for myself; and all the land that is out of sight I claim for my son John."

That story is of universal application. Land titles everywhere come from just such appropriations. Now, under certain circumstances, appropriation can give a right. You invite a company of gentlemen to dinner and you say to them: "Be seated, gentlemen," and I get into this chair. Well, that seat for the time being is mine by the right of appropriation. It would be very ungentlemanly, it would be very wrong for any one of the other guests to come up and say: "Get out of that chair; I want to sit there!" But that right of possession, which is good so far as the chair is concerned, for the time, does not give me a right to appropriate all there is on the table before me. Grant that a man has a right to appropriate such natural elements as he can use, has he any right to appropriate more than he can use? Has a guest in such a case as I have supposed a right to appropriate more than he needs and make other people stand up? That is what is done.

Why, look all over this country—look at this town or any other town. If men only took what they wanted to use we should all have enough; but they take what they do not want to use at all. Here are a lot of Englishmen coming over here and getting titles to our land in vast tracts; what do they want with our land? They do not want it at all; it is not the land they want; they have no use for American land. What they want is the income that they know they can in a little while get from it. Where does that income come from? It comes from labour, from the labour of American citizens. What we are selling to these people is our children, not land.

Poverty! Can there be any doubt of its cause? Go into the old countries—go into western Ireland, into the highlands of Scotland—these are purely primitive communities. There you will find people as poor as poor can be—living year after year on oatmeal or on potatoes, and often going hungry. I could tell you many a pathetic story. Speaking to a Scottish physician who was telling me how this diet was inducing among these people a disease similar to that which from the same cause is ravaging Italy (the Pellagra), I said to him: "There is plenty of fish; why don't they catch fish? There is plenty of game; I know the laws are against it, but cannot they take it on the sly?" "That," he said, "never enters their heads. Why, if a man was even suspected of having a taste for trout or grouse he would have to leave at once." There is no difficulty in discovering what makes those people poor. They have no right to anything that nature gives them. All they can make above a living they must pay to the landlord. They not only have to pay for the land that they use, but they have to pay for the seaweed that comes ashore and for the turf they dig from the bogs. They dare not improve, for any improvements they make are made an excuse for putting up the rent. These people who work hard live in hovels, and the landlords, who do not work at all—oh! they live in luxury in London or Paris. If they have hunting boxes there, why they are magnificent castles as compared with the hovels in which the men live who do the work. Is there any question as to the cause of poverty there?

Now go into the cities and what do you see! Why, you see even a lower depth of poverty; aye, if I would point out the worst of the evils of land monopoly I would not take you to Connemara; I would not take you to Skye or Kintire—I would take you to Dublin or Glasgow or London. There is something worse than physical deprivation, something worse than starvation; and that is the degradation of the mind, the death of the soul. That is what you will find in those cities.

Now, what is the cause of that? Why, it is plainly to be seen; the people driven off the land in the country are driven into the slums of the cities. For every man that is driven off the land the demand for the produce of the workmen of the cities is lessened; and the man himself with his wife and children, is forced among those workmen to compete upon any terms for a bare living and force wages down. Get work he must or starve–get work he must or do that which those people, so long as they maintain their manly feelings, dread more than death, go to the alms-houses. That is the reason, here as in Great Britain, that the cities are overcrowded. Open the land that is locked up, that is held by ["]dogs in the manger,["] who will not use it themselves and will not allow any-body else to use it, and you would see no more of tramps and hear no more of over-production.

The utter absurdity of this thing of private property in land! I defy any one to show me any good from it, look where you please. Go out in the new lands, where my attention was first called to it, or go to the heart of the capital of the world–London. Everywhere, when your eyes are once opened, you will see its inequality and you will see its absurdity. You do not have to go farther than Burlington. You have here a most beautiful site for a city, but the city itself as compared with what it might be is a miserable, straggling town. A gentleman showed me to-day a big hole alongside one of your streets. The place has been filled up all around it and this hole is left. It is neither pretty nor useful. Why does that hole stay there? Well, it stays there because somebody claims it as his private property. There is a man, this gentleman told me, who wished to grade another lot and wanted somewhere to put the dirt he took off it, and he offered to buy this hole so that he might fill it up. Now it would have been a good thing for Burlington to have it filled up, a good thing for you all–your town would look better, and you yourself would be in no dan-ger of tumbling into it some dark night. Why, my friend pointed out to me another similar hole in which water had collected and told me that two children had been drowned there. And he likewise told me that a drunken man some years ago had fallen into such a hole and had brought suit against the city which cost you taxpayers some $11,000. Clearly it is to the interest of you all to have that particular hole I am talking of filled up. The man who wanted to fill it up offered the hole owner $300. But the hole owner refused the offer and declared that he would hold out until he could get $1000; and in the meanwhile that unsightly and dangerous hole must remain. This is but an illustration of private property in land.

You may see the same thing all over this country. See how injuriously in the agricultural districts this thing of private property in land affects the roads and the distances between the people. A man does not take what land he wants, what he can use, but he takes all he can get, and the consequence is that his next neighbour has to go further along, people are separated from each other further than they ought to be, to the increased difficulty of production, to the loss of neighbourhood and companionship. They have more roads to maintain than they can decently maintain; they must do more work to get the same result, and life is in every way harder and drearier.

When you come to the cities it is just the other way. In the country the people are too much scattered; in the great cities they are too crowded. Go to a city like New York and there they are jammed together like sardines in a box, living family upon family, one above the other. It is an unnatural and unwholesome life. How can you have anything like a home in a tenement room, or two or three rooms? How can children be brought up healthily with no place to play? Two or three weeks ago I read of a New York judge who fined two little boys five dollars for playing hop-scotch on the street—where else could they play? Private property in land had robbed them of all place to play. Even a temperance man, who had investigated the subject, said that in his opinion the gin palaces of London were a positive good in this, that they enabled the people whose abodes were dark and squalid rooms to see a little brightness and thus prevent them from going wholly mad.

What is the reason for this overcrowding of cities? There is no natural reason. Take New York, one half its area is not built upon. Why, then, must people crowd together as they do there? Simply because of private ownership of land. There is plenty of room to build houses and plenty of people who want to build houses, but before anybody can build a house a blackmail price must be paid to some ["]dog in the manger.["] It costs in many cases more to get vacant ground upon which to build a house than it does to build the house. And then what happens to the man who pays this blackmail and builds a house? Down comes the tax-gatherer and fines him for building the house.

It is so all over the United States—the men who improve, the men who turn the prairie into farms and the desert into gardens, the men who beautify your cities, are taxed and fined for having done these things. Now, nothing is clearer than that the people of New York want more houses; and I think that even here in Burlington you could get along with more houses. Why, then, should you fine a man who builds one? Look all over this country—the bulk of the taxation rests upon the improver; the man who puts up a building, or establishes a factory, or cultivates a farm, he is taxed for it; and not merely taxed for it, but I think in nine cases out of ten the land which he uses, the bare land, is taxed more than the adjoining lot or the adjoining 160 acres that some speculator is holding as a mere ["]dog in the manger,["] not using it himself and not allowing anybody else to use it.

I am talking too long; but let me in a few words point out the way of getting rid of land monopoly, securing the right of all to the elements which are necessary for life. We could not divide the land. In a rude state of society, as among the ancient Hebrews, giving each family its lot and making it inalienable we might secure something like equality. But in a complex civilisation that will not suffice. It is not, however, necessary to divide up the land. All that is necessary is to divide up the income that comes from the land. In that way we can secure absolute equality; nor could the adoption of this principle involve any rude shock or violent change. It can be brought about gradually and easily by abolishing taxes that now rest upon capital, labour and improvements, and raising all our public revenues by the taxation of land values; and the longer you think of it the clearer you will see that in every possible way will it be a benefit.

Now, supposing we should abolish all other taxes direct and indirect, substituting for them a tax upon land values, what would be the effect? In the first place it would be to kill speculative values. It would be to remove from the newer parts of the country the bulk of the taxation and put it on the richer parts. It would be to exempt the pioneer from taxation and make the larger cities pay more of it. It would be to relieve energy and enterprise, capital and labour, from all those burdens that now bear upon them. What a start that would give to production! In the second place we could, from the value of the land, not merely pay all the present expenses of the government, but we could do infinitely more. In the city of San Francisco James Lick left a few blocks of ground to be used for public purposes there, and the rent amounts to so much, that out of it will be built the largest telescope in the world, large public baths and other public buildings, and various costly works.[13] If, instead of these few blocks, the whole value of the land upon which the city is built had accrued to San Francisco what could she not do?

So in this little town, where land values are very low as compared with such cities as Chicago and San Francisco, you could do many things for mutual benefit and public improvement did you appropriate to public purposes the land values that now go to individuals. You could have a great free library; you could have an art gallery; you could get yourselves a public park, a magnificent public park, too. You have here one of the finest natural sites for a beautiful town I know of, and I have travelled much. You might make on this site a city that it would be a pleasure to live in. You will not as you go now–oh, no! Why, the very fact that you have a magnificent view here will cause somebody to hold on all the more tightly to the land that commands this view and charge higher prices for it. The State of New York wants to buy a strip of land so as to enable the people to see Niagara, but what a price she must pay for it! Look at all the great cities; in Philadelphia, for instance, in order to build their great city hall they had to block up the only two wide streets they had in the city.[14] Everywhere you go you may see how private property in land prevents public as well as private improvement.

But I have not time to enter into further details. I can only ask you to think upon this thing, and the more you will see its desirability. As an English friend of mine puts it: "No taxes and a pension for everybody;" and why should it not be? To take land values for public purposes is not really to impose a tax, but to take for public purposes a value created by the community. And out of the fund which would thus accrue from the common property, we might, without degradation to anybody, provide enough to actually secure from want all who were deprived of their natural protectors or met with accident, or any man who should grow so old that he could not work. All prating that is heard from some quarters about its hurting the common people to give them what they do not work for is humbug. The truth is, that anything that injures self-respect, degrades, does harm; but if you give it as a right, as something to which every citizen is entitled to, it does not degrade. Charity schools do degrade children that are sent to them, but public schools do not.

But all such benefits as these, while great, would be incidental. The great thing would be that the reform I propose would tend to open opportunities to labour and enable men to provide employment for themselves. That is the great advantage. We should gain the enormous productive power that is going to waste all over the country, the power of idle hands that would gladly be at work. And that removed, then you would see wages begin to mount. It is not that everyone would turn farmer, or everyone would build himself a house if he had an opportunity for doing so, but so many could and would, as to relieve the pressure on the labour market and provide employment for all others. And as wages mounted to the higher levels, then you would see the productive power increased. The country where wages are high is the country of greatest productive powers. Where wages are highest, there will invention be most active; there will labour be most intelligent; there will be the greatest yield for the expenditure of exertion. The more you think of it the more clearly you will see that what I say is true. I cannot hope to convince you in an hour or two, but I shall be content if I shall put you upon inquiry. Think for yourselves; ask yourselves whether this wide-spread fact of poverty is not a crime, and a crime for which every one of us, man and woman, who does not do what he or she can do to call attention to it and do away with it, is responsible.

# LAND AND TAXATION

## A CONVERSATION BETWEEN DAVID DUDLEY FIELD AND HENRY GEORGE

MR. DAVID DUDLEY FIELD. Will you explain to me how you expect to develop, in practice, your theory of the confiscation of land to the use of the State?

MR. HENRY GEORGE. By abolishing all other taxes and concentrating taxation upon land values.

F. Then suppose A to be the proprietor of a thousand acres of land on the Hudson, chiefly farming land, but at the same time having on it houses, barns, cattle, horses, carriages, furniture; how is he to be dealt with under your theory?

G. He would be taxed upon the value of his land, and not upon the value of his improvements and stock.

F. Whether the value of his land has been increased by his cultivation or not?

G. The value of land is not really increased by cultivation. The value that cultivation adds is a value of improvement, which I would exempt. I would tax the land at its present value, excluding improvements; so that such a proprietor would have no more taxes to pay than the proprietors of one thousand acres of land, equal in capabilities, situation, etc., that remained in a state of nature.

F. But suppose the proprietor of such land to have let it lie waste for many years while the farmer that I speak of has devoted his time and money to increasing the value of his thousand acres, would you tax them exactly alike?

G. Exactly.

*Published in the "North American Review," July, 1885, and circulated in tract form in the United States, Canada, and Great Britain.*[1]

F. Let us suppose B, an adjoining proprietor, has land that has never yielded a blade of grass, or any other product than weeds; and that A, a farmer, took his in the same condition when he purchased, and by his own thrift and expenditure has improved his land, so that now, without buildings, furniture, or stock, it is worth five times as much as B's thousand acres; B is taxed at the rate of a dime an acre; would you tax A at the rate of a dime an acre?

G. I would certainly tax him no more than B, for by the additional value that A has created he has added that much to the common stock of wealth, and he ought to profit by it. The effect of our present system, which taxes a man for values created by his labour and capital, is to put a fine upon industry, and repress improvement. The more houses, the more crops, the more buildings in the country, the better for us all, and we are doing ourselves an injury by imposing taxes upon the production of such things.

F. How are you to ascertain the value of land considered as waste land?

G. By its selling price. The value of land is more easily and certainly ascertained than any other value. Land lies out of doors, everybody can see it, and in every neighbourhood a close idea of its value can be had.

F. Take the case of the owner of a thousand acres in the Adirondack wilderness that have been denuded of trees, and an adjoining thousand acres that have a fine growth of timber. How would you value them?

G. Natural timber is a part of the land; when it has value it adds to the value of the land.

F. The land denuded of timber would then be taxed less than land that has timber?

G. On general principles it would, where the value of the land was therefore lessened. But where, as in the Adirondacks, public policy forbids anything that would hasten the cutting of timber, natural timber might be considered an improvement, like planted timber, which should not add to taxable value.

F. Then suppose a man to have a thousand acres of wild timber land, and to have cut off the timber, and planted the land, and set up buildings, and generally improved it, would you tax him less than the man that has retained his land with the timber still on it?

G. I would tax the value of his land irrespective of the improvements made by him, whether they consisted in clearing, in ploughing, or in building. In other words, I would tax that value which is created by the growth of the community, not that created by individual effort. Land has no value on account of improvements made upon it, or on account of its natural capabilities. It is as population increases, and society develops, that land values appear, and they rise in proportion to the growth of population and social development. For instance, the value of the land upon which this building stands is now enormously greater than it was years ago, not because of what its owner has done, but because of the growth of New York.

F. I am not speaking of New York City in particular; I am speaking of land generally.

G. The same principle is generally true. Where a settler takes up a quarter section on a western prairie, and improves it, his land has no value so long as other land of the same quality can be had for nothing. The value he creates is merely the value of improvement. But when population comes, then arises a value that attaches to the land itself. That is the value I would tax.

F. Suppose the condition of the surrounding community in the West remained the same; two men go together and purchase two pieces of land of a thousand acres each; one leaves his with a valuable growth of timber, the other cuts off the timber, cultivates the land, and makes a well ordered farm. Would you tax the man that has left the timber upon his land more than you would tax the other man, provided that the surrounding country remained the same?

G. I would tax them both upon the value of the land at the time of taxation. At first, I take it, the clearing of the land would be a valuable improvement. On this, as on the value of his other improvements, I would not have the settler taxed. Thus taxation upon the two would be the same. In course of time the growth of population might give value to the uncut timber, which, being included in the value of land, would make the taxation upon the man that had left his land in a state of nature heavier than upon the man that had converted his land into a farm.

F. A man that goes into the western country and takes up land, paying the government price, and does nothing to the land; how is he to be taxed?

G. As heavily as the man that has taken a like amount of land and improved it. Our present system is unjust and injurious in taxing the improver and letting the mere proprietor go. Settlers take up land, clear it, build houses, and cultivate crops, and for thus adding to the general wealth are immediately punished by taxation upon their improvements. This taxation is escaped by the man that lets his land lie idle, and, in addition to that, he is generally taxed less upon the value of his land than are those who have made their land valuable. All over the country, land in use is taxed more heavily than unused land. This is wrong. The man that holds land and neglects to improve it keeps away somebody that would, and he ought to pay as much for the opportunity he wastes as the man that improves a like opportunity.

F. Then you would tax the farmer whose farm is worth $1,000 as heavily as you would tax the adjoining proprietor, who, with the same quantity of land, has added improvements worth $100,000; is that your idea?

G. It is. The improvements made by the capitalist would do no harm to the farmer, and would benefit the whole community, and I would do nothing to discourage them.

F. In whom would you have the title to land vested—in the State, or in the individuals, as now?

G. I would leave the land titles as at present.

F. Your theory does not touch the title to land, nor the mode of transferring the title, nor the enjoyment of it; but it is a theory confined altogether to the taxing of it?

G. In form. Its effect, however, if carried as far as I would like to carry it, would be to make the community the real owner of land, and the various nominal owners virtually tenants, paying ground rent in the shape of taxes.

F. Before we go to the method by which you would effect that result, let me ask you this question: A, a large landlord in New York, owns a hundred houses, each worth say $25,000 (scattered in different parts of the city); at what rate of valuation would you tax him?

G. On his houses, nothing. I would tax him on the value of the lots.

F. As vacant lots?

G. As if each particular lot were vacant, surrounding improvements remaining the same.

F. If you would have titles as now, then A, who owns a ten thousand dollar house and lot in the city, would still continue to be the owner, as he is at present?

G. He would still continue to be the owner, but as taxes were increased upon land values he would, while still continuing to enjoy the full ownership of the house, derive less and less of the pecuniary benefits of the ownership of the lot, which would go in larger and larger proportions to the State, until, if the taxation of land values were carried to the point of appropriating them entirely the State would derive all those benefits, and, though nominally still the owner, he would become in reality a tenant with assured possession, so long as he continued to pay the tax, which might then become in form, as it would be in essence, a ground rent.

F. Now, suppose A to be the owner of a city lot and building, valued at $500,000; who would give a deed to it to B?

G. A would give the deed.

F. Then supposing A to own twenty lots, with twenty buildings on them, the lots being, as vacant lots, worth each $1,000, and the buildings being worth $49,000 each; and B to own twenty lots of the same value, as vacant lots, without any buildings; would you tax A and B alike?

G. I would.

F. Suppose that B, to buy the twenty lots, had borrowed the price and mortgaged them for it; would you have the tax in that case apportioned?

G. I would hold the land for it. In cases in which it became necessary to consider the relations of mortgagee and mortgager, I would treat them as joint owners.

F. If A, the owner of a city lot with a house upon it, should sell it to B, do you suppose that the price would be graduated by the value of the improvements alone?

G. When the tax upon the land had reached the point of taking the full annual value, it would.

F. To illustrate: Suppose A has a city lot, which, as a vacant lot, is worth annually $10,000, and there is a building upon it worth $100,000, and he sells them to B; you think the price would be graduated according to the value of the building; that is to say, $100,000, after the taxation had reached the annual value of $10,000?

G. Precisely.

F. To what purpose do you contemplate that the money raised by your scheme of taxation should be applied?

G. To the ordinary expenses of government, and such purposes as the supplying of water, of light, of power, the running of railways, the maintenance of public parks, libraries, colleges, and kindred institutions, and such other beneficial objects as may from time to time suggest themselves; to the care of the sick and needy, the support of widows and orphans, and, I am inclined to think, to the payment of a fixed sum to every citizen when he came to a certain age.

F. Do you contemplate that money raised by taxation should be expended for the support of the citizen?

G. I see no reason why it should not be.

F. Would you have him fed and clothed at the public expense?

G. Not necessarily; but I think a payment might well be made to the citizen when he came to the age at which active powers decline that would enable him to feed and clothe himself for the remainder of his life.

F. Let us come to practical results. The rate of taxation now in the city of New York, we will suppose, is 2.30 upon the assessed value. The assessed value is understood to be about sixty per cent. of the real value of property. Land assessed at $60,000 is really worth $100,000, and being assessed at 2.30 when valued at $60,000, should be assessed at about 1.40 on the real value; you would increase that amount indefinitely, if I understand you, up to the annual rental value of the land?

G. I would.

F. Which we will suppose to be five per cent.; is that it?

G. Let us suppose so.

F. Then your scheme contemplates the raising of five per cent. on the true value of all real estate as vacant land, to be used for the purposes you have mentioned. Have you thought of the increase in the army of office-holders that would be required for the collection and disbursement of this enormous sum of money?

G. I have.

F. What do you say to that?

G. That as to collection, it would greatly reduce the present army of office-holders. A tax upon land values can be levied and collected with a much smaller force than is now required for our multiplicity of taxes; and I am inclined to think, that, directly and indirectly, the plan I propose would permit the dismissal of three fifths of the officials needed for the present purposes of government. This simplification of government would do very much to purify our politics; and I rely largely upon the improvement that the change I contemplate would make in social life, by lessening the intensity of the struggle for wealth, to permit the growth of such habits of thought and conduct as would enable us to get for the management of public affairs as much intelligence and as strict integrity as can now be obtained for the management of great private affairs.

F. Supposing it to be true that you would reduce the expense of collection, would you not, for the disbursement of these vast funds, require a much larger number of efficient men than are now required?

G. Not necessarily. But, whether this be so or not, the full scheme I propose can only be attained gradually. Until, at least, the total amount needed for what are now considered purely governmental purposes were obtained by taxation on land values, there would be a large reduction of office-holders, and no increase.

F. How do you propose to divide the taxation between the State and the municipalities?

G. As taxes are now divided. As to questions that might arise, there will be time enough to determine them when the principle has been accepted.

F. Your theory contemplates the raising of nearly four times as much revenue in the State of New York as is now raised; how many office-holders would it require to disburse this enormous sum of money among the various objects that you have mentioned?

G. My theory does not require that it should be disbursed among the objects I have mentioned, but simply that it should be used for public benefit.

F. Do you not think that the present rate of taxation is more than sufficient for all purposes of government?

G. Under the state of society that I believe would ensue, it would be much more than sufficient for the present purposes of government. We should need far less for expenses of revenue collection, police, penitentiaries, courts, almshouses, etc.

F. Then, to bring the matter down to a point, you propose for the present no change whatever in anything, except that the amount now raised by all methods of taxation should be imposed upon real estate considered as vacant?

G. For a beginning, yes.

F. Well, what do you contemplate as the ending of such a scheme?

G. The taking of the full annual value of land for the benefit of the whole people. I hold that land belongs equally to all, that land values arise from the presence of all, and should be shared among all.

F. And this result you propose to bring about by a tax upon land values, leaving the title, the privilege of sale, of rent, of testament, the same as at present?

G. Yes.

F. Your theory appears to be impracticable. I think that the raising of such an enormous sum of money, placing it in the coffers of the State, to be disbursed by the State in the manner you contemplate, would tend to the corruption of the government beyond all former precedent. The end you contemplate–of bettering the condition of the people–is a worthy one. I believe that we–you and I–who are well to do in the world, and others in our condition, do neglect and have neglected our duty to those in a less fortunate condition, and that it is our highest duty to endeavour to relieve, so far as we can, the burdens of those who are now suffering from poverty and want. Therefore, far from deriding or scouting your theory, I examine it with respect and attention, desirous of getting from it whatever I can that may be good, while rejecting what

I conceive to be erroneous. Taken altogether, as you have explained it, I do not see that it is a practicable scheme.

G. But your objections to it as impracticable only arise at the point, yet a long distance off, at which the revenues raised from land values would be greater than those now raised. Is there anything impracticable in substituting for the present corrupt, demoralising, and repressive methods of taxation a single tax upon land values?

F. I think it possible to concentrate all taxation upon land, if that should be thought the best method. Many economists are of opinion that taxes should be raised from land alone, conceiving that rent is really paid by every consumer, but they include in land everything placed upon it out of which rent comes.

G. Then we could go together for a long while; and when the point was reached at which we would differ, we might be able to see that a purer government than any we have yet had might be possible. Certainly here is the gist of the whole problem. If men are too selfish, too corrupt, to co-operate for mutual benefit, there must always be poverty and suffering.

F. My theory of government is that its chief function is to keep the peace between individuals and allow each to develop his own nature for his own happiness. I would never raise a dollar from the people except for necessary purposes of government. I believe that the demoralisation of our politics comes from the notion that public offices are spoils for partisans. A large class of men has grown up among us whose living is obtained from the State—that is to say, out of the people. We must get rid of those men, and instead of creating offices we must lessen their number.

G. I agree with you as to government in its repressive feature; and in no way could we so lessen the number of office-holders and take the temptation of private profit out of public affairs as by raising all public revenues by the tax upon land values, which, easily assessed and collected, does not offer opportunities for evasion or add to prices. Though in form a tax, this would be in reality a rent; not a taking from the people, but a collecting of their legitimate revenues. The first and most important function of government is to secure the full and equal liberty of individuals; but the growing complexity of civilised life and the growth of great corporations and combinations, before which the individual is powerless, convince me that government must undertake more than to keep the peace between man and man—must carry on, when it cannot regulate, businesses that involve monopoly, and in larger and larger degree assume co-operative functions. If I could see any other means of doing away with the injustice involved in growing monopolies, of which the railroad is a type, than by extension of governmental functions, I should not favour that; for all my earlier thought was in the direction you have indicated—the position occupied by the [D]emocratic [P]arty of the last generation.[2] But I see none. However, if it were to appear that further extension of the functions of government would involve demoralisation, then the surplus revenue might be divided per capita. But it seems to me that there must be in human nature the possibility of a reasonably pure government, when the ends of that government are felt by all to be the promotion of the general good.

F. I do not believe in spoliation, and I conceive that that would be spoliation which would take from one man his property and give it to another. The scheme of the communists, as I understand it, appears to me to be not only unsound, but destructive of society. I do not mean to intimate that you are one of the communists; on the contrary, I do not believe you are.

G. As to the sacredness of property, I thoroughly agree with you. As you say in your recent article on industrial co-operation in the "North American Review," "To take from one against his will that which he owns and give it to another, would be a violation of that instinct of justice which God has implanted in the heart of every human being; a violation, in short, of the supreme law of the Most High"; and my objection to the present system is that it does this. I hold that that which a man produces is rightfully his, and his alone; that it should not be taken from him for any purpose, even for public uses, so long as there is any public property that might be employed for that purpose; and therefore I would exempt from taxation everything in the nature of capital, personal property, or improvements—in short, that property which is the result of man's exertion. But I hold that land is not the rightful property of any individual. As you say again, "No one can have private property in privilege," and if the land belongs, as I hold it does belong, to all the people, the holding of any part of it is a privilege for which the individual holder should compensate the general owner according to the pecuniary value of the privilege. To exact this would not be to despoil any one of his rightful property, but to put an end to spoliation that now goes on. Your article in the "Review" shows that you see the same difficulties I see, and would seek the same end—the amelioration of the condition of labour, and the formation of society upon a basis of justice. Does it not seem to you that something more is required than any such scheme of co-operation as that which you propose, which at best could be only very limited in its application, and which is necessarily artificial in its nature?

F. Undoubtedly. The hints that I have given in the article to which you refer, would affect a certain number of persons, not by any means the whole body politic. I conceive that a great deal more is necessary. There should be more sympathy, more mutual help. I think, as I have said, that we are greatly wanting in our duty to all the people around us, and I would do everything in my power to aid them and their children. I do not think that we have arrived at the true conception of our duty—of the duty of every American citizen to all other American citizens.

G. I think you are right in that; but does it not seem as though it were out of the power of mere sympathy, mere charity, to accomplish any real good? Is it not evident that there is at the bottom of all social evils an injustice, and until that injustice is replaced by justice, charity and sympathy will do their best in vain? The fact that there are among us strong, willing men unable to find work by which to get an honest living for their families is a most portentous one. It speaks to us of an injustice that, if not remedied, must wreck society. It springs, I believe, from the fact that, while we secure to the citizen equal political rights, we do not secure to him that natural right more important still, the equal right to the land on which and from which he must live. To me it seems clear, as our Declaration of Independence asserts, that all men are endowed by their Creator with certain unalienable rights, and that the first of these rights—that which, in fact, involves all the rest, that without which none of the others can be exercised—is the equal right to land. Here are children coming into life to-day in New York; are they not endowed with the right to more than struggle along as they best can in a country where they can neither eat, sleep, work, nor lie down without buying the privilege from some of certain human creatures like themselves, who claim to own, as their private property, this part of the physical universe, from the earth's centre to the zenith?

F. I was not speaking of charity, but of sympathy leading to help—helping one to help himself—that is the help I mean, and not the charity that humbles him.

G. Then I cordially agree with you, and I look upon such sympathy as the most powerful agency for social improvement. But sympathy is little better than mockery until it is willing to do justice, and justice requires that all men shall be placed upon an equality so far as natural opportunities are concerned.

F. How would you secure that equality? Take the case of a child born to-day in a tenement house, in one of those rooms that are said to be occupied by several families, and another child born at the same time in one of the most comfortable homes in our city. The parents of the first child are wasteful, intemperate, filthy: the parents of the second are thrifty, temperate, cleanly; how would you secure equality in opportunities of the first child with that of the second?

G. Equality in all opportunities could not be secured; virtuous parents are always an advantage, vicious parents a disadvantage; but equality of natural opportunities could be secured in the way I have proposed. And in a civilisation where the equal rights of all to the bounty of their Creator were recognised, I do not believe there would be any tenement houses, and very few, if any, parents such as those of whom you speak. The vice and crime and degradation that so fester in our great cities are the effects, rather than the causes, of poverty.

F. The principle announced in the Declaration of Independence to which you have referred, is one of the cardinal principles of the American government—the unalienable right of all men to "life, liberty, and the pursuit of happiness." That, however, does not mean that all men are equal in opportunities or in positions. A child born to-day is entitled to the labours of its parents, or rather to the products of their labour, just as much as they are entitled to it until he is able to take care of himself. One of the incentives to labour is to provide for the children of the labourer. The aim of our American civilisation ought to be to furnish, so far as can be done rightfully, to every child born into the world, an equal opportunity with every other child, to work out his own good. This, however, is the theoretical proposition. It is impossible in practice to give to every child the same opportunity; what we should aim at is, to approximate to that state of things: that is the work of the philanthropist and Christian. In short, my belief is that the truest statement of political ethics and political economy is to be found in the doctrines of the Christian religion.

G. In that I thoroughly agree with you. But Christianity that does not assert the natural rights of man, that has no protest when the earth, which it declares was created by the Almighty as a dwelling-place for all his children, is made the exclusive property of some of them, while others are denied their birthright–seems to me a travesty. A Christian has something to do as a citizen and lawmaker. We must rest our social adjustments upon Christian principles if we would have a really Christian society. But to return to the Declaration of Independence; the equal right to life, liberty, and the pursuit of happiness, does it not necessarily involve the equal right to land, without which neither life, liberty, nor the freedom to pursue happiness is possible?

F. You do not propose to give to every child a piece of land; you only propose to secure its right, if I understand you, by taxing land as vacant land in the mode you propose.

G. That is all, but it is enough. In the complex civilisation we have now attained it would be impossible to secure equality by giving to each a separate piece of land, or to maintain that equality, even if once secured; but by treating all land as the property of the whole people, we would make the whole people the landlords, and the individual users the tenants of all, thus securing to each his equal right.

F. In how long a time, if you were to have such legislation as you would wish, do you think we should arrive at the condition that you have mentioned?

G. I think immediately a substantial equality would be arrived at, such an equality as would do away with the spectacle of a man unable to find work, and would secure to all a good and easy living, with a mere modicum of the hard labour and worriment now undergone by most of us. The great benefit would not be in the appropriation to public use of the unearned revenues now going to individuals, but in the opening of opportunities to labour, and the stimulus that would be given to improvement and production by the throwing open of unused land and the removal of taxation that now weighs down productive powers. And with the land made the property of the whole people, all social progress would be a progress towards equality. While other values tend to decline as civilisation progresses, the value of land steadily advances. Such a great fact bespeaks some creative intent; and what that intent may be, it seems to me we can see when we reflect that if this value–a value created not by the individual, but by the whole community–were appropriated to the common benefit, the progress of society would constantly tend to make less important the difference between the strong and the weak, and thus, instead of those monstrous extremes toward which civilisation is now hastening, bring about conditions of greater and greater equality.

F. As a conclusion of the whole matter, if I understand this explanation of your scheme, it is this, that the State should tax the soil, and the soil only; that in doing so it should consider the soil as it came from the hands of the Creator, without anything that man has put upon it; that all other property–in short, everything that man has made–is to be acquired, enjoyed, and transmitted as at present; that the rate of annual taxation should equal the rate of annual rental, and that the proceeds of the tax should be applied, not only to purposes of government, but to any other purpose that the legislature from time to time may think desirable, even to dividing them among the people at so much a head.

G. That is substantially correct.

F. I am glad to hear your explanation, though I do not agree with you, except as I have expressed myself.

# "THOU SHALL NOT STEAL"

D r. McGlynn in Chickering Hall last Sunday night said it was an his-
toric occasion.[2] He was right. That a priest of Christ, standing on
Sunday night on a public platform and addressing a great audience–an
audience embracing men and women of all creeds and beliefs–should
proclaim a crusade for the abolition of poverty, and call on men to join
together and work together to bring the kingdom of God on earth, did
mark a most important event. Great social transformations, said
Mazzini, never have been and never will be other than the application
of great religious movements.[3] The day on which democracy shall ele-
vate itself to the position of a religious party, that day will its victory
begin. And the deep significance of the meeting last Sunday night, the
meaning of this Anti-Poverty Society that we have joined together to
inaugurate, is the bringing into the struggle of democracy the religious
sentiment, the sentiment alone of all sentiments powerful enough to
regenerate the world.

The comments made on that meeting and on the institution of this
society are suggestive. We are told, in the first place by the newspapers,
that you cannot abolish poverty because there is not wealth enough to
go around. We are told that if all the wealth of the United States were
divided up there would only be some eight hundred dollars apiece.
Well, if that is the case, all the more monstrous then is the injustice
which to-day gives single men millions and tens of millions, and even
hundreds of millions. If there really is so little, then the more injustice
in these great fortunes. But we do not propose to abolish poverty by
dividing up what wealth there is, so much as by creating more wealth.
We propose to abolish poverty by setting at work that vast army of men,
estimated last year to amount in this country alone to one million, that
vast army of men only anxious to create wealth, but who are now, by a

*An address at the second public meeting of the Anti-Poverty Society, in the Academy
of Music, New York, Sunday evening, May 8, 1887.[1]*

system which permits ["]dogs in the manger["] to monopolise God's bounty, deprived of the opportunity to toil.

Then again, they tell us, you cannot abolish poverty because poverty always has existed. Well, if poverty always has existed, all the more need for our moving for its abolition. It has existed long enough. We ought to be tired of it; let us get rid of it.

But I deny that poverty–such poverty as we see on earth to-day–always has existed. Never before in the history of the world was there such an abundance of wealth, such power of producing wealth. So marked is this that the very people who tell us that we cannot abolish poverty, attribute it in almost the next breath to over-production. They virtually tell us it is because mankind produces so much wealth that so many are poor; that it is because there is so much of the things that satisfy human desires already produced, that men cannot find work, and that women must stint and strain. Poverty attributed to over-production; poverty in the midst of wealth; poverty in the midst of enlightenment; poverty when steam and electricity and a thousand labour-saving inventions have been called to the aid of man, never existed in the world before. There is manifestly no good reason for its existence, and it is time that we should do something to abolish it.

There are not charitable institutions enough to supply the demands for charity; that seems incapable of being supplied. But there are enough, at least, to show every thinking woman and every thinking man that it is utterly impossible to eradicate poverty by charity, to show everyone who will trace to its root the cause of the disease that what is needed is not charity, but justice–the conforming of human institutions to the eternal laws of right. But when we propose this, when we say that poverty exists because of the violation of God's laws, we are taunted with pretending to know more than men ought to know about the designs of Omnipotence. They have set up for themselves a God who rather likes poverty, since it affords the rich a chance to show *their* goodness and benevolence; and they point to the existence of poverty as a proof that God wills it. Our reply is that poverty exists not because of God's will, but because of man's disobedience. We say that we do know that it is God's will that there should be no poverty on earth, and that we know it as we may know any other natural fact. The laws of this universe are the laws of God, the social laws as well as the physical laws, and He, the Creator of all, has given us room for all, work for all, plenty for all. If to-day people are in places so crowded that it seems as though there were too many people in the world; if to-day thousands of men who would gladly be at work do not find the opportunity to go to work; if to-day the competition for employment crowds wages down to starvation rates; if to-day, amid abounding wealth, there are in the centres of our civilisation human beings who are worse off than savages in any normal times, it is not because the Creator has been niggardly; it is simply because of our own injustice–simply because we have not carried the idea of doing to others as we would have them do unto us into the making of our statutes.

This Anti-Poverty Society has no patent remedy for poverty. We propose no new thing. What we propose is simply to do justice. The principle that we propose to carry into our laws is neither more nor less than the principle of the golden rule. We propose to abolish poverty by the sovereign remedy of doing to others as we would have others do to us; by giving to all their just rights. And we propose to begin by assuring to every child of God who, in our country, comes into this world, his full and equal share of the common heritage.

Crowded! Is it any wonder that men are crowded together as they are in this city, when we see men taking up far more land than they can by any possibility use, and holding it for enormous prices? Why, what would have happened if, when these doors were opened, the first people who came in had claimed all the seats around them, and demanded a price of others who afterward came in by the same equal right? Yet that is precisely the way we are treating this continent. That is the reason why people are huddled together in tenement houses; that is the reason why work is difficult to get; the reason that there seems, even in good times, a surplus of labour, and that in those times that we call bad, the times of industrial depression, there are all over the country thousands and hundreds of thousands of men tramping from place to place, unable to find employment.

Not work enough! Why, what is work? Productive work is simply the application of human labour to land; it is simply the transforming into shapes adapted to gratify human desires, the raw material that the Creator has placed here. Is there not opportunity enough for work in this country? Supposing that, when thousands of men are unemployed and there are hard times everywhere, we could send a committee up to the high court of heaven to represent the misery and the poverty of the people here, consequent on their not being able to find employment. What answer would we get? "Are your lands all in use? Are your mines all worked out? Are there no natural opportunities for the employment of labour?" What could we ask the Creator to furnish us with that is not already here in abundance? He has given us the globe, amply stocked with raw material for our needs. He has given us the power of working up this raw material. If there seems scarcity, if there is want, if there are men who cannot find employment, if there are people starving in the midst of plenty, is it not simply because what the Creator intended for all has been made the property of the few?

In moving against this giant wrong, which denies to labour access to the natural opportunities for the employment of labour, we move against the cause of poverty. We propose to abolish it, to tear it up by the roots, to open free and abundant employment for every man. We propose to disturb no just right of property. As Dr. McGlynn said last Sunday night, we are defenders and upholders of the sacred right of property–that right of property which justly attaches to everything that is produced by labour; that right which gives to everyone a just right of property in what he has produced–that makes it his to give, to sell, to bequeath, to do whatever he pleases with, as long as in using it he does not injure any-one else. That right of property we insist upon, that we would uphold against all the world. To a house, a coat, a book–anything produced by labour–there is a clear individual title, which goes back to the man who made it. That is the foundation of the just, the sacred right of property. It rests on the right of the individual to the use of his own powers, on his right to profit by the exertion of his own labour; but who can carry the right of property in land that far? Who can claim a title of absolute own-ership in land coming from the man who made it? And until the man who claims the exclusive ownership of a piece of this planet can show a title originating with the Maker of this planet; until he can produce a decree from the Creator declaring that this city lot or that great tract of agricultural land, or that coal mine, or that gas-well, was made for him–until then we have a right to hold that land was intended for all of us.

Natural religion and revealed religion alike tell us that God is no respecter of persons; that He did not make this planet for a few individ-uals; that He did not give it to one generation in preference to other gen-erations, but that He made it for the use during their lives of all the people that His providence brings into the world. If this be true, the child that is born to-night in the humblest tenement in the most squalid quarter of New York, comes into life seized with as good a title to the land of this city as any Astor or Rhinelander.[4]

How do we know that the Almighty is against poverty? That it is not in accordance with His decree that poverty exists? We know it because we know this, that the Almighty has declared, "Thou shalt not steal." And we know for a truth that the poverty that exists to-day in the midst of abounding wealth is the result of a system that legalises theft.

The women who by the thousands are bending over their needles or sewing-machines, thirteen, fourteen, sixteen hours a day; these widows straining and striving to bring up the little ones deprived of their natural bread-winner; the children that are growing up in squalor and wretchedness, underclothed, underfed, undereducated even, in this city without any place to play—growing up under conditions in which only a miracle can keep them pure—under conditions which condemn them in advance to the penitentiary or the brothel—they suffer, they die, because we permit them to be robbed, robbed of their birthright, robbed by a system which disinherits the vast majority of the children that come into the world. There is enough and to spare for them. Had they the equal rights in the estate which their Creator has given them, there would be no young girls forced to unwomanly toil to eke out a mere existence, no widows finding it such a bitter, bitter struggle to put bread in the mouths of their little children; no such misery and squalor as we may see here in the greatest of American cities, misery and squalor that are deepest in the largest and richest centres of our civilisation to-day.

These things are the results of legalised theft, the fruits of a denial of that commandment that says, "Thou shalt not steal." How is this great commandment interpreted to-day, even by the men who pretend to preach the gospel? "Thou shalt not steal." Well, according to them, it means: "Thou shalt not get into the penitentiary." Not much more than that with any of them. You may steal, provided you steal enough, and you do not get caught, and you may have a front seat in the churches. Do not steal a few dollars—that may be dangerous; but if you steal millions and get away with it, you become one of our first citizens.

"Thou shalt not steal"; that is the law of God. What does it mean? Well, it does not merely mean that you shall not pick pockets! It does not merely mean that you shall not commit burglary or highway robbery! There are other forms of stealing which it prohibits as well. It certainly means (if it has any meaning) that we shall not take that to which we are not entitled, to the detriment of others.

Now, here is a desert. Here is a caravan going along over the desert. Here are a gang of robbers. They say, "Look! There is a rich caravan; let us go and rob it, kill the men if necessary, take their goods from them, their camels and horses, and walk off." But one of the robbers says, "Oh, no; that is dangerous; besides, that would be stealing! Let us, instead of doing that, go ahead to where there is a spring, the only spring at which this caravan can get water in this desert. Let us put a wall around it and call it ours, and when they come up we won't let them have any water until they have given us all the goods they have." That would be more gentlemanly, more polite and more respectable; but would it not be theft all the same?

And is it not theft of the same kind when men go ahead in advance of population and get land that they have no use whatever for, and then, as people come into the world and population increases, will not let this increasing population use the land until they pay an exorbitant price? That is the sort of theft on which our first families are founded. Do that under the false code of morality which exists here to-day and people will praise your forethought and your enterprise, and will say you have made money because you are a very superior man, and that anybody can make money if he will only work and be industrious! But is it not as clearly a violation of the command, "Thou shalt not steal," as taking the money out of a man's pocket?

"Thou shalt not steal." That means, of course, that we ourselves must not steal. But does it not also mean that we must not suffer anybody else to steal if we can help it? "Thou shalt not steal." Does it not also mean, "Thou shalt not suffer thyself or anybody else to be stolen from?" If it does, then we, all of us, rich and poor alike, are responsible for this social crime that produces poverty. Not merely the men who monopolise land—they are not to blame above any one else, but we who permit them to monopolise land are also parties to the theft. The Christianity that ignores this social responsibility has really forgotten the teachings of Christ. Where He in the [G]ospels speaks of the judgment, the question which is put to men is never, "Did you praise me?" "Did you pray to me?" "Did you believe this or did you believe that?" It is only this: "What did you do to relieve distress; to abolish poverty?" To those who are condemned, the judge is represented as saying: "I was ahungered and ye gave me not meat, I was athirst and ye gave me not drink, I was sick and in prison and ye visited me not." Then they say, "Lord, Lord, when did we fail to do these things to you?" The answer is, "Inasmuch as ye failed to do it to the least of these, so also did you fail to do it unto me; depart into the place prepared for the devil and his angels." On the other hand, what is said to the blessed is, "I was ahungered and ye gave me meat, I was thirsty and ye gave me drink, I was naked and ye clothed me, I was sick and in prison and ye visited me." And when they say, "Lord, Lord, when did we do these things to thee?" the answer is, "Inasmuch as ye have done it unto the least of these ye have done it unto me."

Here is the essential spirit of Christianity. The essence of its teaching is not, "Provide for your own body and save your own soul!" but, "Do what you can to make this a better world for all!" It was a protest against the doctrine of "each for himself and devil take the hindermost!" It was the proclamation of a common [F]atherhood of God and a common brotherhood of men. This was why the rich and the powerful, the high priests and the rulers, persecuted Christianity with fire and sword. It was not what in so many of our churches to-day is called religion that pagan Rome sought to tear out–it was what in too many of the churches of to-day is called "socialism and communism," the doctrine of the equality of human rights!

Now imagine when we men and women of to-day go before that awful bar that there we should behold the spirits of those who in our time under this accursed social system were driven into crime, of those who were starved in body and mind, of those little children that in this city of New York are being sent out of the world by thousands when they have scarcely entered it–because they did not get food enough, nor air enough, nor light enough, because they are crowded together in these tenement districts under conditions in which all diseases rage and destroy. Supposing we are confronted with those souls, what will it avail us to say that we individually were not responsible for their earthly conditions? What, in the spirit of the parable of Matthew, would be the reply from the judgment seat?[5] Would it not be, "I provided for them all. The earth that I made was broad enough to give them room. The materials that are placed in it were abundant enough for all their needs. Did you or did you not lift up your voice against the wrong that robbed them of their fair share in what I provided for all?"

"Thou shalt not steal!" It is theft, it is robbery that is producing poverty and disease and vice and crime among us. It is by virtue of laws that we uphold; and he who does not raise his voice against that crime, he is an accessory. The standard has now been raised, the cross of the new crusade at last is lifted. Some of us, aye, many of us, have sworn in our hearts that we will never rest so long as we have life and strength until we expose and abolish that wrong. We have declared war upon it. Those who are not with us, let us count them against us. For us there will be no faltering, no compromise, no turning back until the end.

There is no need for poverty in this world, and in our civilisation. There is a provision made by the laws of the Creator which would secure to the helpless all that they require, which would give enough and more than enough for all social purposes. These little children that are dying in our crowded districts for want of room and fresh air, they are the disinherited heirs of a great estate.

Did you ever consider the full meaning of the significant fact that as progress goes on, as population increases and civilisation develops, the one thing that ever increases in value is land? Speculators all over the country appreciate that. Wherever there is a chance for population coming; wherever railroads meet or a great city seems destined to grow; wherever some new evidence of the bounty of the Creator is discovered, in a rich coal or iron mine, or an oil well, or a gas deposit, there the speculator jumps in, land rises in value and a great boom takes place, and men find themselves enormously rich without ever having done a single thing to produce wealth.

Now, it is by virtue of a natural law that land steadily increases in value, that population adds to it, that invention adds to it; that the discovery of every fresh evidence of the Creator's goodness in the stores that He has implanted in the earth for our use adds to the value of land, not to the value of anything else. This natural fact is by virtue of a natural law—a law that is as much a law of the Creator as the law of gravitation. What is the intent of this law? Is there not in it a provision for social needs? That land values grow greater and greater as the community grows and common needs increase, is there not a manifest provision for social needs—a fund belonging to society as a whole, with which we may take care of the widow and the orphan and those who fall by the wayside—with which we may provide for public education, meet public expenses, and do all the things that an advancing civilisation makes more and more necessary for society to do on behalf of its members?

To-day the value of the land in New York City is over a hundred millions annually. Who has created that value? Is it because a few landowners are here that that land is worth a hundred millions a year? Is it not because the whole population of New York is here? Is it not because this great city is the centre of exchanges for a large portion of the continent? Does not every child that is born, everyone that comes to settle in New York, does he not add to the value of this land? Ought he not, therefore, to get some portion of the benefit? And is he not wronged when, instead of being used for that purpose, certain favoured individuals are allowed to appropriate it?

We might take this vast fund for common needs, we might with it make a city here such as the world has never seen before—a city spacious, clean, wholesome, beautiful—a city that should be full of parks; a city without tenement houses; a city that should own its own means of communication, railways that should carry people thirty or forty miles from the city hall in a half hour, and that could be run free, just as are the elevators in our large buildings; a city with great museums, and public libraries, and gymnasiums, and public halls, paid for out of this common fund, and not from the donations of rich citizens. We could out of this vast fund provide as a matter of right for the widow and the orphan, and assure to every citizen of this great city that if he happened to die his wife and his children should not come to want, should not be degraded with charity, but as a matter of right, as citizens of a rich community, as coheirs to a vast estate, should have enough to live on. And we could do all this, not merely without imposing any tax upon production; not merely without interfering with the just rights of property, but while at the same time securing far better than they are now the rights of property and abolishing the taxes that now weigh on production. We have but to throw off our taxes upon things of human production; to cease to fine a man that puts up a house or makes anything that adds to the wealth of the community; to cease collecting taxes from people who bring goods from abroad or make goods at home, and put all our taxes upon the value of land—to collect that enormous revenue due to the growth of the community for the benefit of the community that produced it.

Dr. Nulty, Bishop of Meath, has said in a letter addressed to the clergy and laity of his diocese that it is this provision of the Creator, the provision by which the value of land increases as the community grows, that seems to him the most beautiful of all the social adjustments;[6] and it is to me that which most clearly shows the beneficence as well as the intelligence of the creative mind; for here is a provision by virtue of which the advance of civilisation would, under the law of equal justice, be an advance towards equality, instead, as it now is, an advance towards a more and more monstrous inequality. The same good Catholic bishop in the same letter says: "Now, therefore, the land of every country is the common property of the people of that country, because its real owner, the Creator, who made it, hath given it as a voluntary gift unto them. 'The earth has He given to the children of men.' And as every human being is a creature and a child of God, and as all His creatures are equal in His sight, any settlement of the land of this or any other country that would exclude the humblest from his equal share in the common heritage is not only an injury and a wrong done to that man, but an impious violation of the benevolent intention of his Creator." And then Bishop Nulty goes on to show that the way to secure equal rights to land is not by cutting land up into equal pieces, but by taking for public use the values attaching to land. That is the method this society proposes. I wish we could get that through the heads of the editors of this city. We do not propose to divide up land. What we propose to do is to divide up the rent that comes from land; and that is a very easy thing.

We need not disturb anybody in possession, we need not interfere with anybody's building or anybody's improvement. We only need to remit taxes on all improvements, on all forms of wealth, and put the tax on the value of the land, exclusive of the improvements, so that the ["]dog in the manger["] who is holding a piece of vacant land will have to pay the same for it as though there was a building upon it. In that way we would treat the whole land of such a community as this as the common estate of the whole people of the community. And as the Sailors' Snug Harbour, for instance, out of the revenues of comparatively a little piece of land in New York can maintain that fine establishment on Staten Island, keeping in comfort a number of old seamen, so we might make a greater Snug Harbour of the whole of New York.

The people of New York could manage their estate just as well as any corporation, or any private family, for that matter. But for the people of New York to resume their estate and to treat it as their own, it is not necessary for them to go to any bother of management. It is not necessary for them to say to any landholder, this particular piece of land is ours, and no longer yours. We can leave land titles just as they are. We can leave the owners of the land to call themselves its owners; all we want is the annual value of the land. Not, mark you, that value which the owner has created, that value which has been given to it by improvements, but simply that value which is given to the bare land by the fact that we are all here—that has attached to the land because of the growth of this great community. And, when we take that, then all inducement to monopolise the land will be gone; then these very worthy gentlemen who are holding one half of the area of this city idle and vacant will find the taxes upon them so high that they either will have to go to work and build houses or sell the land, or, if they cannot sell it, give it away to somebody who will build houses.

And so all over the country. Go into Pennsylvania and there you will see great stretches of land, containing enormous deposits of the finest coal held by corporations and individuals who are working but little part of it. On these great estates the common American citizens, who mine the coal, are not allowed even to rent a piece of land, let alone buy it. They can only live in company houses; and they are permitted to stay in them only on condition (and they have to sign a paper to that effect) that they can be evicted at any time on five days' notice. The companies combine, and make coal artificially dear here and make employment artificially scarce in Pennsylvania. Now, why should not those miners, who work on it half the time, why shouldn't they dig down in the earth and get up coal for themselves? Who made that coal? There is only one answer–God made that coal. Whom did He make it for? Any child or any fool would say that God made it for the people that would be one day called into being on this earth. But the laws of Pennsylvania, like the laws of New York, say God made it for this corporation and that individual; and thus a few men are permitted to deprive miners of work and make coal artificially dear.

A few weeks ago, when I was travelling in Illinois, a young fellow got in the car at one of the mining towns, and I entered into conversation with him. He said he was going to another place to try and get work. He told me of the condition of the miners, that they could scarcely make a living, getting very small wages and only working about half the time. I said to him, "There is plenty of coal in the ground; why don't you employ yourselves in digging coal." He replied, "We did get up a co-operative company, and we went to see the owner of the land to ask what he would let us sink a shaft and get out some coal for. He wanted $7500 a year. We could not raise that much." Tax land up to its full value and how long can such ["]dogs in the manger["] afford to hold that coal land away from these men? And when any man who wants work can go and employ himself, then there will be no million or no thousand unemployed men in all the United States.

The relation of employer and employed is a relation of convenience. It is not one imposed by the natural order. Men are brought into the

world with the power to employ themselves, and they can employ themselves wherever the natural opportunities for employment are not shut
up from them. No man has a natural right to demand employment of
another, but each man has a natural right, an inalienable right, a right
given by his Creator, to demand opportunity to employ himself. And
whenever that right is acknowledged, whenever the men who want to
go to work can find natural opportunities to work upon, then there will
be as much competition among the employers who are anxious to get
men to work for them as there will be among men who are anxious to
get work. Wages will rise in every vocation to the true rate of wages, the
full, honest earnings of labour. That done, with this ever-increasing
social fund to draw upon, poverty will be abolished, and in a little while
will come to be looked upon as we are now beginning to look upon slavery—as the relic of a darker and more ignorant age.

I remember—this man here remembers (turning to Mr. James
Redpath) even better than I, for he was one of the men who brought the
atrocities of human slavery home to the heart and conscience of the
North[7]—I well remember, as he well knows, and all the older men and
women in this audience will remember, how property in human flesh
and blood was defended just as private property in land is now
defended; how the same charges were hurled upon the men who
protested against human slavery as are now made against the men who
are intending to abolish industrial slavery. We remember how the dig-
nitaries of the churches, and the opinion of the rich members of the
churches branded as a disturber, almost as a reviler of religion, any
priest or any minister who dared to get up and assert God's truth—that
there never was and there never could be rightful property in human
flesh and blood.

So it is now said that men who protest against this system, which is
simply another form of slavery, are men who propose robbery. Thus the
commandment, "Thou shalt not steal," they have made, "Thou shalt not
object to stealing." When we propose to resume our own again, when
we propose to secure its natural right to every child that comes into
being, such people talk of us advocating confiscation—charge us with
being deniers of the rights of property. The real truth is that we wish to
assert the just rights of property, that we wish to prevent theft. Chattel
slavery was incarnate theft of the worst kind. That system, which made
property of human beings, which allowed one man to sell another,
which allowed one man to take away the proceeds of another's toil,

which permitted the tearing of the child from the mother, and which permitted the so-called owner to hunt with blood-hounds the man who escaped from his tyranny—that form of slavery is abolished.

So far as that goes the command, "Thou shalt not steal," has been vindicated. But there is another form of slavery.

We are selling land now in large quantities to certain English lords and capitalists who are coming over here and buying greater estates than the greatest in Great Britain or Ireland; we are selling them land, they are buying land. Did it ever occur to you that they do not want that land? They have no use whatever for American land; they do not propose to come over here and live on it. They cannot carry it over there where they do live. It is not the land that they want. What they want is the income from it. They are buying it not that they themselves want to use it, but because by-and-by, as population increases, numbers of American citizens will want to use it, and then they can say to these American citizens, "You can use this land provided you pay us one half of all you make upon it." What we are selling those foreign lords and capitalists is not really land; we are selling them the labour of American citizens; we are selling them the privilege of taking, without giving any return for it, the proceeds of the toil of our children.

So here in New York you will read in the papers every day that the price of land is going up. John Jones or Robert Brown has made a hundred thousand dollars within a year in the increase in the value of land in New York. What does that mean? It means he has the power of getting so many more coats, so many more cigars, so much more wine, dry-goods, horses and carriages, houses or food. He has gained the power of taking for his own so much more of these products of human labour. But what has he done? He has not done anything. He may have been off in Europe or out West, or he may have been sitting at home taking it easy. If he has done nothing to get this increased income, where does it come from? The things I speak of are all products of human labour—some one has to work for them. When the man who does no work can get them, necessarily the men who do work to produce them must have less than they ought to have.

This is the system that the Anti-Poverty Society has banded together to war against, and it invites you to come and swell its ranks. It is the noblest cause in which any human being can possibly engage. What, after all, is there in life as compared with a struggle like this? One thing and only one thing is absolutely certain for every man and woman in this hall, as it is to all else of human kind—that is death. What will it profit us in a few years how much we have left? Is not the noblest and the best use we can make of life to do something to make better and happier the condition of those who come after us—by warring against injustice, by the enlightenment of public opinion, by the doing all that we possibly can do to break up the accursed system that degrades and embitters the lot of so many?

We have a long fight and hard fight before us. Possibly, probably, for many of us, we may never see it come to success. But what of that? It is a privilege to be engaged in such a struggle. This we may know, that it is but a part of that great, world-wide, long-continued struggle in which the just and the good of every age have been engaged; and that we, in taking part in it, are doing something in our humble way to bring on earth the kingdom of God, to make the conditions of life for those who come afterward, those which we trust will prevail in heaven.

# To Workingmen

I am one of those who believe that it is possible for workingmen to raise wages by an intelligent use of their votes; that this is the only way in which wages can be generally and permanently raised–the only way labour can obtain that share of wealth which is justly its due. And I am one of those who believe that this is the supreme object that workingmen should seek in politics. In seeking to raise wages, to improve the conditions of labour, we are seeking, not the good of a class, but the good of the whole. The number of those who can live on the labour of others is and can be but small as compared with the number who must labour to live. And where labour yields the largest results *to the labourer*, where the production of wealth is greatest and its distribution most equitable, where the man who has nothing but his labour is surest of making the most comfortable living and best provide for those whom nature has made dependent upon him, there, I believe, will be the best conditions of life for all–there will the general standard of intelligence and virtue be highest, and there will all that makes a nation truly great and strong and glorious most abound.

Believing this, I am glad that the presidential campaign this year is to turn, not upon sectional issues or matters of party or personal character, but upon a great question of national policy[2]–the question of protection or free trade; and that this is to be discussed, as it is most important that it should be discussed, in its relation to wages. What is thus entering our politics is more than a question of higher or lower duties, or no duties at all–it is the most important of all questions, the great labour question. And what is really involved in the decision that will be asked of you as to whether protection or free trade is best for the interests of labour, is whether the emancipation of labour is to be sought by imposing restrictions or by securing freedom. Until the men

*Article in "Belford's Magazine," New York, June, 1888, and republished in "The Standard," New York, June 16, 1888.*[1]

who would raise wages and emancipate labour settle that for themselves, they cannot unite to carry out any large measure.

In the coming campaign the most frantic appeals will be made to workingmen to vote for protection. You will be told that "protection" means "protection to American labour"; that that is what it was instituted for, and that is why it is maintained; that it is protection that makes this country so prosperous and your wages so high, and that if it is abolished, or even interfered with, mills must close, mines shut down, and poor labour stand idle and starve until American workmen are forced to work for the lowest wages that are paid in Europe.

Don't accept what any one tells you—least of all what is told you by and on behalf of those who have an enormous pecuniary interest in maintaining what is styled "protection." Hear what they say, but make up your minds for yourselves. There is nothing in the tariff question that cannot readily be mastered by any one of ordinary intelligence, and the great question whether what is called "protection" does or does not benefit the labourer can be settled for himself by any one who will ask himself what protection really is, and *how* it benefits labour.

Now what is ["]protection?["] It is a system of taxes levied on imports for the purpose of increasing the price of certain commodities in our own country so that the home producers of such commodities can get higher prices for what they sell to their own fellow-countrymen.

This is all there is to "protection." Protection can't enable any American producer to get higher prices for what he sells to people of other countries, and no duty is protective unless it so increases prices as to enable someone to get more from his fellow-citizens than he could without protection. How "protection" may thus benefit some people is perfectly clear. But how can it benefit the whole people? That it may increase the profits of the manufacturer, or the income of the owner of timber or mineral land, is plain. But *how* can it increase wages? "Protection" raises the price of commodities. That may be to the advantage of those who buy labour and sell commodities. But *how* can it be to the advantage of those who sell labour and buy commodities?

Never mind the confused and confusing claims that are put forth for protection until you can see *how* it can do what is claimed for it.

Ask yourselves what protection is and how it operates, and you will see that the only way it can benefit any one, or by "encouraging" him give him power to encourage or benefit any one else, is by enabling him to get from his fellow-citizens more than he could otherwise get. This is the essence of protection; and if it has any stimulating or beneficial effect it must be through this. The protective effect of any protective duty is precisely that of a subsidy paid by the government to some people out of taxes levied on the whole people. The only difference is, that in what is called the subsidy system the government tax-gatherers would collect the tax from the whole people and pay it over to some people, while in what is called the protective system the government tax-gatherers collect a tax on foreign goods so as to "protect" the favoured people, while they for themselves collect taxes on their fellow-citizens in increased prices.

Now if workmen get any benefit from what is thus called protection, it can only be through the protected employers and by their favour. The protective system gives nothing whatever to labour. It gives only to the employers of labour, and only to some of them. And these some are neccesarily comparatively few. It is utterly impossible that any protective tariff can "protect" the largest industries of any country, for a duty can only have a protective effect when levied upon goods some of which are produced in the country and some of which are imported or would be imported if it were not for the duty. Import duties cannot be levied upon things of which we produce enough for ourselves and consequently do not import, or of which we produce more than enough for ourselves and consequently export; and if levied upon things we do not produce and must import or go without, they can have no protective effect. In every country, therefore, the protected industries can only be those in which but a small part of the labour of that country is employed. In this country, out of over seventeen millions of labourers of one sort or another, those employed in the protected industries do not amount to more than 900,000, and these industries, it is to be observed, are those in which large capital is required and in which it is impossible for the mere labourer to employ himself.

Now, would it be possible by levying a general tax (especially a tax which, like all protective taxes, bears on the poor far more heavily than on the rich, on the labourer far more heavily than on the capitalist), and paying out the proceeds directly to the labourers engaged in certain industries, to raise wages, or even to raise wages in those industries? Everyone who thinks a moment will say no! If we were to levy such a tax and pay out the proceeds directly to glass workers or iron-ore miners or the hands in cotton or woollen factories, in addition to what they get from their employers, the consequence would simply be that labour

would be attracted from the unsubsidised to the subsidised employments, and wages would go down to a point that would give the subsidised labourers no more than they got without the subsidy!

But if such a plan of raising wages is utterly hopeless, what should
we say of a plan to raise wages by levying a tax upon all labourers and
giving the proceeds, not to all labourers, or even to some labourers, but
only to *some employers?* This is the plan of protection. If protection can
increase or maintain wages, it must be in this way. What protective
duties actually do is to increase the profits of certain employers–to
allow them to collect a tax from their fellow-citizens without any stipu-
lation as to how they shall spend it. To suppose that wages can be
increased in this way is to suppose, in the first place, that these protected employers voluntarily give up their increased profits to their
workmen, and to suppose, in the second place, that the increase of
wages which the benevolence of the protected employers thus causes in
industries which at the best employ not more than 1,500,000 people can
raise wages in occupations that employ 20,000,000 people!

Observe also that the first step in this precious scheme of plunder
which is called protection to American labour is really to reduce wages.
Wages do not really consist of money. Money is the mere flux and
counter of exchanges. What the man who works for wages really works
for are commodities and services for which he pays with the money he
receives in wages. Necessarily, therefore, to increase the price of the
commodities he buys with his money-wages is to decrease his real
wages. For instance, a good many of the highly protected American
labourers in the [S]tate of Pennsylvania (as in some other States) are
compelled by their benevolent protectionist employers to make their
purchases in what the highly protected American labourers call
"pluck-me stores." In fact, it is through these ["]pluck-me stores["] that
these highly protected American workingmen get their wages, as the
["]pluck-me bill["] is deducted before any money is turned over to them
on pay days; and many of them being kept constantly in debt, hardly
see a dollar from one year's end to another. Now, it is evident that if one
of these employers adds a dollar to the prices his men have to pay for
the goods they must buy in his "pluck-me," he just as effectually cuts
down their real earnings as though he reduced their wages by a dollar.
And so it is evident that the protective taxes which we impose for the
purpose of increasing the prices of commodities must in the same way
operate to reduce the real wages of labour. Therefore the protective

scheme for raising wages fully stated is simply this: Wages generally are in the first place reduced by taxes which increase the price of certain commodities, in order (1) that a comparatively few employers who profit by this increase in the price of what they have to sell may voluntarily increase the wages of their employees, and (2) that this benevolent raising of wages in some occupations may cause the raising of wages in all occupations!

Is it not time that American workingmen were done with such a preposterous scheme as this? There is one sense, and one sense alone, in which protection may raise wages. When real wages are low enough, it may to some extent raise nominal wages. If the protected Pennsylvania employer were to keep on raising the prices in his workmen's "protected home market," the ["]pluck-me store,["] he would come to a point where their nominal wages would not enable them to get enough food and clothing to support life, and where, consequently, he would be forced to increase their nominal wages in order to prevent their removal or starvation. In this way protection, like a depreciation of currency, may sometimes increase nominal wages. But it can never increase real wages. Whomsoever protection may benefit–and analysis will show that it cannot even benefit the employing capitalists whom it assumes to benefit, unless they are also protected from home competition by some sort of a monopoly–it cannot benefit the labourer. It is to the labourer a delusion and a fraud–a scheme of barefaced plunder that adds insult to injury; that first robs him, and then tells him to get down on his knees and thank his robber!

The impudent pretence that what is called protection is protection to labour is peculiar to the United States, and is an afterthought here. When this utterly un-American system of robbing the many for the benefit of the few was introduced into this country, it was not pretended that it was to protect labour or to compensate for high wages. It was asked for the protection of capital–to give capitalists a bonus–so that here, where interest was high, they could engage in the same sort of manufacturing businesses as in Europe, where interest was low. It was asked for the "protection of infant industries"–to give them artificial support for a few years, when, it was then claimed, they could stand alone without any more protection.

But men who once secure the enactment of laws to enable them to take the earnings of others never want an excuse for demanding the continuance of the privilege. Now that United States three per cent.

bonds are at a premium, it would be preposterous to talk of protecting American capital against the cheaper capital of Europe, and now that the great protected industries have become very industrial giants, it would be only ridiculous to talk of protecting "infant industries." So we are now told that protection is "protection for labour," and is made necessary by our higher wages. In fact, we are now told that it is *because* of protection that wages are *so* high and the country *so* prosperous.

The pretence is as hollow and insulting as the pretence of the slave-owners that slavery was for the protection of the slave. Special privilege needs protection, and monopoly needs protection, and all legalised systems of robbery that enable men who do no labour to grow rich by appropriating the earnings of those who do labour, need protection. But what is labour, that *it* should need protection? What is labour, that votes should have to be bought and coerced, and lobbyists maintained, and congressmen interested, and newspapers subsidised, and our coasts and borders lined with seizers and searchers and spies and informers and tax-gatherers, to keep *it* from falling to pauperism? Is not labour the producer of all wealth? Is it not labour that feeds all, clothes all, shelters all, and pays for all? Is not labour the one thing that can take care of itself; that requires but access to the raw materials of nature to bring forth all that man's needs require? What benevolent capitalist drew a tariff wall around Adam to enable him to get a living and bring up a family? Whatever else may need protection, labour needs no protection. What labour needs is freedom! Not the keeping up of restrictions and the perpetuation of monopolies, but the tearing of them down.

Who are these benevolent individuals, so anxious to protect the poor, helpless workingman, so fearful lest American labour may fall to the level of "the pauper labour of Europe"? The coal barons and the factory lords, the iron and steel combinations, the lumber ring, and the thousand trusts that, having secured the imposition of duties to keep out foreign productions, band themselves together to limit home production and to screw down the wages of their workmen. And are not these men who are so anxious, as they say, to protect you from the competition of "foreign pauper labour" the very men who are most ready to avail themselves of foreign labour?

Do you know of any protected employer, no matter how many millions he may have made out of the tariff, who pays any higher wages to labour than he has to? Is it not true that in all the protected industries wages are, if anything, lower than in the unprotected industries? Is it not true that in all protected industries workmen have been compelled to band themselves together to protect themselves; and that these protected industries are the industries notable above all others for their strikes and lock-outs–the bitter and oft-times disastrous industrial wars that labour is compelled to wage to prevent being crowded to starvation rates? Are these the men whose protection you need?

It is impossible for me in a brief article like this to go over all the claims and expose all the fallacies of protection. That I have already done, in anticipation of the coming before the people of this question, in a little book entitled "Protection or Free Trade?" in which I have shown the full relations of the tariff question to the labour question.[3] All I want here to do is to urge every American workingman to think over the matter for himself, and to decide whether what is called "protection" is or is not in the interests of the men who earn their daily bread by their daily labour.

For if, as protectionists tell us, our country is *so* prosperous and wages are *so* high because of the protection we already have, then we certainly ought to bend all our efforts to get more protection. However prosperous this country may be when viewed through the rose-coloured spectacles of the millionaire, and however high wages may be from the standpoint of those who think that the natural wages of labour are only enough to keep soul and body together, there will be no dispute among workingmen that this country is *not* prosperous enough and wages *not* high enough. Whoever may be satisfied with things as they are, the great mass of American citizens who work for a living are not satisfied and ought not to be satisfied. Monstrous fortunes are rolling up here faster than they ever did in the world before; but the great body of the American people get but a poor hand-to-mouth living, and find year after year passing without anything laid by for a rainy day. Our rich men astonish the rich men of Europe by their lavish expenditure, and the daughters of our millionaires are sought in marriage by European aristocrats of the bluest blood; but the tramp is known from the Atlantic to the Pacific; the proportion of our people who are maintained by charity, the proportion who are confined in prisons and lunatic asylums, the proportion of our women and children who must go to work, is steadily increasing. And the proportion of men who, starting with nothing but their ability to labour, can become their own employers, or can hope out of the earnings of their labour to maintain a family and put by a competence for old age, is steadily diminishing. "Statisticians" may pile up figures to prove to the American workingman how much better off he is than he used to be, and the editors of protection papers may picture the poverty of European workingmen in the darkest colours to show him how proud and happy and contented he ought to be. But the labour organisations, the strikes, the bitter unrest with which the whole industrial mass is seething, show that he is not contented. If protection gives prosperity, if protection raises wages, then in heaven's name let us demand more protection, even though we utterly destroy all foreign commerce, put a line of custom-houses between every State, and shut in our rich men so that they cannot go to Europe and spend their money on foreign paupers, as Mr. Blaine is doing.[4] But if it does not–then let us sweep away what protection we have. Let us raise the banner of equal rights, and try the way of freedom!

It is not protection that has made wages higher here than in Europe. If protection could make wages high, why has it not made wages high in Germany and Italy and Spain and Mexico? Why did it not make wages high in England when it was in full force there? Wages were higher in the United States than in Europe before we had any protection; and if they have on the whole remained higher, it is in spite of protection. Our higher wages are because of our cheaper land–because labour can more readily obtain access to the natural materials and opportunities of labour. The secret of our prosperity, of our rapid growth, of our better conditions of labour, is simply that we have had the temperate zone of a vast and virgin continent to overrun, and that it has taken a long while for monopoly to fence it in. As it is gradually fenced in, as the tribute that labour must pay to monopoly for the use of land becomes higher and higher, so must our social conditions, tariff or no tariff, approximate to the social conditions of Europe.

To give labour full freedom; to make wages what they ought to be, the full earnings of labour; to secure work for all, and leisure for all, and abundance for all; to enable all to enjoy the advantages and blessings of an advancing civilisation–we must break down all monopolies and destroy all special privileges.

The rejection of protection and the abolition of the tariff will not of itself accomplish this, but it will be a long step towards it–a step that must necessarily be taken if labour is to be emancipated and industrial slavery abolished. Until the workingmen of the United States get over the degrading superstition of protection they must be divided and helpless. But when they once realise the true dignity of labour, once they see that the good of all can only be gained by securing the equal rights of each, then they can unite, and then they will be irresistible.

And this is the question that you will be asked this year to answer by your votes. Are you for restriction or are you for freedom? Are you in favour of taxing the whole people for the benefit of a few capitalists, in the hope that they will give their workmen some of the crumbs? or are you against all special privileges and in favour of equal rights to all?

To the man who thinks the matter over there can be no question as to what answer best accords with the interests of workingmen. It is possible for the few to become rich by taxing the many. But it is not possible for the many to become rich by taxing themselves to put the proceeds in the hands of the few.

Labor cannot be hurt by freedom. The only thing that can be hurt by freedom is monopoly. And monopoly means the robbery of labour. What labour needs is freedom, not protection; justice, not charity; equal rights for all, not special privileges for some.

# "Thy Kingdom Come"

W e have just joined in the most solemn, the most sacred, the most catholic of all prayers: "Our Father which art in Heaven!" To all of us who have learned it in our infancy, it oft calls up the sweetest and most tender emotions. Sometimes with feeling, sometimes as a matter of course, how often have we repeated it! For centuries, daily, hourly, has that prayer gone up. "Thy kingdom come!" Has it come? Let this Christian city of Glasgow answer–Glasgow, that was to "Flourish by the preaching of the Word." "Thy kingdom come!" Day after day, Sunday after Sunday, week after week, century after century, has that prayer gone up; and to-day, in this so-called Christian city of Glasgow, 125,000 human beings–so your medical officer says–125,000 children of God are living whole families in a single room. "Thy kingdom come!" We have been praying for it and praying for it, yet it has not come. So long has it tarried that many think it never will come. Here is the vital point in which what we are accustomed to call the Christianity of the present day differs so much from that Christianity which overran the ancient world– that Christianity which, beneath a rotten old civilisation, planted the seeds of a newer and a higher. We have become accustomed to think that God's kingdom is not intended for this world; that, virtually, this is the devil's world, and that God's kingdom is in some other sphere, to which He is to take good people when they die–as good Americans are said when they die to go to Paris. If that be so, what is the use of praying for the coming of the kingdom? Is God–the Christian's God, the Almighty, the loving Father of whom Christ told–is He such a monster as a god of that kind would be; a god who looks on this world, sees its sufferings and its miseries, sees high faculties aborted, lives stunted, innocence turned to vice and crime, and heart-strings strained and broken, yet,

---

*A sermon delivered in the City Hall, Glasgow, Scotland, Sunday, April 28, 1889, under the auspices of the Henry George Institute, and afterwards circulated extensively in tract form by the Scottish Land Restoration League.*[1]

having it in his power, will not bring that kingdom of peace, and love, and plenty, and happiness? Is God, indeed, a self-willed despot, whom we must coax to do the good He might?

But, think of it. The Almighty—and I say it with reverence—the Almighty could not bring that kingdom of Himself. For, what is the kingdom of God; the kingdom that Christ taught us to pray for? Is it not in the doing of God's will, not by automata, not by animals who are compelled, but by intelligent beings made in His image; intelligent beings clothed with free will, intelligent beings knowing good from evil. Swedenborg never said a deeper nor a truer thing, nor a thing more compatible with the philosophy of Christianity, than when he said God had never put any one into hell; that the devils went to hell because they would rather go to hell than go to heaven.[2] The spirits of evil would be unhappy in a place where the spirit of good reigned: wedded to injustice, and loving injustice, they would be miserable where justice was the law. And, correlatively, God could not put intelligent beings having free will into conditions where they *must* do right without destroying that free will. Nay! Nay! "Thy kingdom come!"—when Christ taught that prayer He meant, not merely that men must idly phrase these words, but that for the coming of that kingdom they must work as well as pray!

Prayer! Consider what prayer is. How true is the old fable! The wagoner, whose wagon was stuck in the rut, knelt down and prayed to Jove to get it out. He might have prayed till the crack of doom, and the wagon would have stood there. This world—God's world—is not that kind of a world in which the repeating of words will get wagons out of mire or poverty out of slums. He who would pray with effect must work!

"Our [F]ather which art in Heaven." Not a despot, ruling by his arbitrary fiats, but a father, a loving father, *our* [F]ather; a [F]ather for us all—that was Christ's message. He is our Father and we are His children. But there are men, who, looking around on the suffering and injustice with which, even in so-called Christian countries, human life is full, say there is no Father in heaven, there can be no God, or He would not permit this. How superficial is that thought! What would we as fathers do for our children? Is there any man, who, having a knowledge of the world and the laws of human life, would so surround his boy with safeguards that he could do no evil and could suffer no pain? What could he make by that course of education? A pampered animal, not a self-reliant man! We are, indeed, His children. Yet let one of God's children fall into the water, and if he has not learned to swim he will drown. And if he is a good distance from land and near no boat or anything on which he may get, he will drown anyhow, whether he can swim or not. God the Creator *might* have made men so that they could swim like the fishes, but how could He have made them so that they could swim like the fishes and yet have adapted this wonderful frame of ours to all the purposes which the intelligence that is lodged within it requires to use it for? God can make a fish; He can make a bird; but could He, His laws being what they are, make an animal that might at once swim as well as a fish and fly as well as a bird? That the intelligence which we must recognise behind nature is almighty does not mean that it can contradict itself and stultify its own laws. No; we are the children of God. What God is, who shall say? But every man is conscious of this, that behind what he sees there must have been a Power to bring that forth; that behind what he knows there is an intelligence far greater than that which is lodged in the human mind, but which human intelligence does in some infinitely less degree resemble.

Yes; we are His children. We in some sort have that power of adapting things which we know must have been exerted to bring this universe into being. Consider those great ships for which this port of Glasgow is famous all over the world; consider one of those great ocean steamers, such as the *Umbria,* or the *Etruria,* or the *City of New York,* or the *City of Paris.* There, in the ocean which such ships cleave, are the porpoises, there are the whales, there are the dolphins, there are all manner of fish. They are to-day just as they were when Cæsar crossed to this island, just as they were before the first ancient Briton launched his leather-covered boat.[3] Man to-day can swim no better than man could swim then, but consider how by his intelligence he has advanced higher and higher, how his power of making things has developed, until now he crosses the great ocean quicker than any fish. Consider one of those great steamers forcing her way across the Atlantic Ocean, four hundred miles a day, against a living gale. Is she not in some sort a product of a godlike power—a machine in some sort like the very fishes that swim underneath? Here is the distinguishing thing between man and the animals; here is the broad and impassable gulf. Man among all the animals is the only maker. Man among all the animals is the only one that possesses that godlike power of adapting means to ends. And is it possible that man possesses the power of so adapting means to ends that he can cross the Atlantic in six days, and yet does not possess the power of abolishing the conditions that crowd thousands of families into one room? When we consider the achievements of man and then look upon the misery that exists to-day in the very centres of wealth, upon the ignorance, the weakness, the injustice, that characterise our highest civilisation, we may know of a surety that it is not the fault of God; it is the fault of man. May we not know that in that very power God has given to His children here, in that power of rising higher, there is involved–and necessarily involved–the power of falling lower?

"Our Father!" "*Our* Father!" *Whose?* Not *my* Father–that is not the prayer. "Our Father"–not the father of any sect, of any class, but the Father of all men. The All-Father, the equal Father, the loving Father. He it is we ask to bring the kingdom. Aye, we ask it with our lips! We call him "Our Father," the All, the Universal Father, when we kneel down to pray to Him. But that He is the All-Father–that He is all men's Father– we deny by our institutions. The All-Father who made the world, the All-Father who created man in His image, and put him upon the earth to draw his subsistence from its bosom; to find in the earth all the materials that satisfy his wants, waiting only to be worked up by his labour! If He is the All-Father, then are not all human beings, all children of the Creator, equally entitled to the use of His bounty? And, yet, our laws say that this God's earth is not here for the use of all His children, but only for the use of a privileged few! There was a little dialogue published in the United States, in the West, some time ago. Possibly you may have seen it. It is between a boy and his father, when visiting a brick-yard. The boy looks at the men making bricks, and he asks who those dirty men are, why they are making up the clay, and what they are doing it for. He learns, and then he asks about the owner of the brick-yard. "He does not make any bricks; he gets his income from letting the other men make bricks." Then the boy asks about what title there is to the bricks, and is told that it comes from the men having made them. Then he wants to know how the man who owns the brick-yard gets his title to the brick-yard–whether he made it? "No, he did not make it," the father replies, "God made it." The boy asks, "Did God make it for him?" Whereat his father tells him that he must not ask questions such as that, but that anyhow it is all right, and it is all in accordance with God's law. Then the boy, who of course was a Sunday-school boy, and had been to church, goes off mumbling to himself that God so loved the world that He gave His only begotten Son to die for all men; but that He so loved the owner of this brick-yard that he gave him not merely his only begotten Son but the brick-yard too.

This has a blasphemous sound. But I do not refer to it lightly. I do not like to speak lightly of sacred subjects. Yet it is well sometimes that we should be fairly shocked into thinking. Think of what Christianity teaches us; think of the life and death of Him who came to die for men! Think of His teachings, that we are all the equal children of an Almighty Father, who is no respecter of persons, and then think of this legalised injustice–this denial of the most important, most fundamental rights of the children of God, which so many of the very men who teach Christianity uphold; nay, which they blasphemously assert is the design and the intent of the Creator himself. Better to me, higher to me, is the atheist, who says there is no God, than the professed Christian, who, prating of the goodness and the Fatherhood of God, tells us in words as some do, or tells us indirectly as others do, that millions and millions of human creatures–[at this point a child was heard crying]–don't take the little thing out–that millions and millions of human beings, like that little baby, are being brought into the world daily by the creative fiat, and no place in this world provided for them. Aye! tells us that, by the laws of God, the poor are created in order that the rich may have the unctuous satisfaction of dealing out charity to them–tells us that a state of things like that which exists in this city of Glasgow, as in other great cities on both sides of the Atlantic, where little children are dying every day, dying by hundreds of thousands, because, having come into this world–those children of God, with His fiat, by His decree–they find that there is not space on the earth sufficient for them to live; and are driven out of God's world because they cannot get room enough, cannot get air enough, cannot get sustenance enough. I believe in no such god. If I did, though I might bend before him in fear, I would hate him in my heart. Not room enough for the little children here! Look around any country in the civilised world; is there not room enough and to spare? Not food enough? Look at the unemployed labour, look at the idle acres, look through every country and see natural opportunities going to waste. Aye! that Christianity that puts on the Creator the evil, the injustice, the suffering, the degradation that are due to man's injustice, is worse, far worse, than atheism. That is *the* blasphemy, and if there be a sin against the Holy Ghost, *that* is the unpardonable sin!

Why, consider–"Give us this day our daily bread." I stopped in a hotel last week–a hydropathic establishment.[4] A hundred or more guests sat down to table together. Before they ate anything, a man stood up, and, thanking God, asked Him to make us all grateful for His bounty. So at every meal-time such an acknowledgment is made over well-filled boards. What do men mean by it? Is it mockery, or what?

If Adam, when he got out of Eden, had sat down and commenced to pray, he might have prayed till this time without getting anything to eat unless he went to work for it. Yet food *is* God's bounty. He does not bring meat all cooked, nor vegetables all prepared, nor lay the plates, nor spread the cloth. What He gives are the opportunities of producing these things—of bringing them forth by labour. His mandate is—it is written in the Holy Word, it is graven on every fact in nature—that by labour we shall bring forth these things. Nature gives to labour and to nothing else. What God gives are the natural elements that are indispensable to labour. He gives them, not to one, not to some, not to one generation, but to *all*. They are His gifts, His bounty to the whole human race. And yet in all our civilised countries what do we see? That a few men have appropriated these bounties, claiming them as theirs alone, while the great majority have no legal right to apply their labour to the reservoirs of nature and draw from the Creator's bounty. And thus it comes that all over the civilised world that class that is called peculiarly the "labouring class" is the poor class, and that men who do no labour, who pride themselves on never having done honest labour and on being descended from fathers and grandfathers who never did a stroke of honest labour in their lives, revel in a superabundance of all the things that labour brings forth.

Mr. Abner Thomas, of New York, a strict orthodox Presbyterian—and the son of that Dr. Thomas, famous in America if not here, the pastor of a Presbyterian church in Philadelphia, and the author of a commentary on the Bible that is still a standard work—wrote a little while ago an allegory, called "A Dream." Dozing off in his chair, he imagined that he was ferried over the River of Death, and, taking the straight and narrow way, came at last within sight of the Golden City.[5] A fine-looking old-gentleman angel opened the wicket, inquired his name, and let him in; warning him at the same time, that it would be better if he chose his company in heaven, and did not associate with disreputable angels.

"What!" said the new-comer, "is not this heaven?"

"Yes," said the warden, "but there are a lot of tramp angels here now."

"How can that be?" said Mr. Thomas, in his dream. "I thought everybody had plenty in heaven."

"It used to be that way some time ago," said the warden; "and if you wanted to get your harp polished or your wings combed, you had to do it yourself. But matters have changed since we adopted the same kind of property regulations in heaven as you have in civilised countries on earth, and we find it a great improvement, at least for the better class."

Then the warden told the new-comer that he had better decide where he was going to board.

"I don't want to board anywhere," said Thomas; "I would much rather go over to that beautiful green knoll and lie down."

"I would not advise you to do so," said the warden; "the angel who owns that knoll does not like to encourage trespassing. Some centuries ago, as I told you, we introduced the system of private property in the soil of heaven. So we divided the land up. It is all private property now."

"I hope I was considered in that division?" said Thomas.

"No," said the warden, "you were not; but if you go to work, and are saving, you can easily earn enough in a couple of centuries to buy yourself a nice piece. You get a pair of wings free as you come in, and you will have no difficulty in hypothecating them for a few days' board until you find work.[6] But I would advise you to be quick about it, as our population is constantly increasing, and there is a great surplus of labour. Tramp angels are, in fact, becoming quite a nuisance."

"What shall I go to work at?" said Thomas.

"Our principal industries," responded the warden, "are the making of harps and crowns and the growing of flowers; but there are many opportunities for employment in personal service."

"I love flowers," said Thomas, "and I will go to work growing them. There is a beautiful piece of land over there that nobody seems to be using. I will go to work on that."

"You can't do that," said the warden. "That property belongs to one of our most far-sighted angels, who has got very rich by the advance of land values, and who is holding that piece for a rise. You will have to buy it or feu it before you can work on it, and you can't do that yet."

And so the story goes on to describe how the roads of heaven, the streets of the New Jerusalem, were filled with disconsolate tramp angels, who had pawned their wings, and were outcasts in heaven itself.

You laugh, and it *is* ridiculous. But there is a moral in it that is worth serious thought. Is not the ridiculousness in our imagining the application to God's heaven of the same rules of division that we apply to God's earth, even while we pray that His will may be done on earth as it is done in heaven?

Really, if you come to think of it, it is impossible to imagine heaven treated as we treat this earth, without seeing that, no matter how salubrious were its air, no matter how bright the light that filled it, no matter how magnificent its vegetable growth, there would be poverty, and suffering, and a division of classes in heaven itself, if heaven were parcelled out as we have parcelled out the earth. And, conversely, if men in this life were to act towards each other as we must suppose the inhabitants of heaven to do, would not this earth be a very heaven? "Thy kingdom come." No one can think of the kingdom for which the prayer asks without feeling that it must be a kingdom of justice and equality–not necessarily of equality in condition, but of equality in opportunity. And no one can think of it without seeing that a very kingdom of God might be brought on this earth if men would but seek to do justice–if men would but acknowledge the essential principle of Christianity, that of doing to others as we would have others do to us, and of recognising that we are all here equally the children of the one Father, equally entitled to share His bounty, equally entitled to live our lives and develop our faculties, and to apply our labour to the raw material that He has provided. Aye! and when a man sees that, then there arises that hope of the coming of the kingdom that carried the Gospel through the streets of Rome, that carried it into pagan lands, that made it, against the most ferocious persecution, the dominant religion of the world. Early Christianity did not mean, in its prayer for the coming of Christ's kingdom, a kingdom in heaven, but a kingdom on earth. If Christ had simply preached of the other world, the high priests and the Pharisees would not have persecuted Him, the Roman soldiery would not have nailed His hands to the cross. Why was Christianity persecuted? Why were its first professors thrown to wild beasts, burned to light a tyrant's gardens, hounded, tortured, put to death, by all the cruel devices that a devilish ingenuity could suggest? Not that it was a new religion, referring only to the future. Rome was tolerant of all religions. It was the boast of Rome that all gods were sheltered in her Pantheon; it was the boast of Rome that she made no interference with the religions of peoples she conquered. What was persecuted was a great movement for social reform–the Gospel of Justice–heard by common fishermen with gladness, carried by labourers and slaves into the Imperial City. The Christian revelation was the doctrine of human equality, of the [F]atherhood of God, of the brotherhood of man. It struck at the very basis of that monstrous tyranny that then oppressed the civilised world; it struck at the fetters of the captive, at the bonds of the slave, at that monstrous injustice which allowed a class to revel on the proceeds of labour, while those who did the labour fared scantily. That is the reason why early Christianity was persecuted. And when they could no longer hold it down, then the privileged classes adopted and perverted the new faith, and it became, in its very triumph, not the pure Christianity of the early days, but a Christianity that, to a very great extent, was the servitor of the privileged classes.[7] And, instead of preaching the essential [F]atherhood of God, the essential brotherhood of man, its high priests engrafted on the pure truths of the Gospel the blasphemous doctrine that the All-Father is a respecter of persons, and that by His will and on His mandate is founded that monstrous injustice which condemns the great mass of humanity to unrequited hard toil. There has been no failure of Christianity. The failure has been in the sort of Christianity that has been preached.

Nothing is clearer than that if we are all children of the universal Father, we are all entitled to the use of His bounty. No one dare deny that proposition. But the men who set their faces against its carrying out say, virtually: "Oh, yes! that is true; but it is impracticable to carry it into effect!" Just think of what this means: This is God's world, and yet such men say that it is a world in which God's justice, God's will, cannot be carried into effect. What a monstrous absurdity, what a monstrous blasphemy! If the loving God does reign, if His laws are the laws not merely of the physical but of the moral universe, there must be a way of carrying His will into effect, there must be a way of doing equal justice to all His creatures.

And so there is. The men who deny that there is any practical way of carrying into effect the perception that all human beings are equally children of the Creator, shut their eyes to the plain and obvious way. It is of course impossible in a civilisation like this of ours to divide land up into equal pieces. Such a system might have done in a primitive state of society, among a people such as that for whom the Mosaic [C]ode was framed. It would not do in this state of society. We have progressed in civilisation beyond such rude devices, but we have not, nor can we, progress beyond God's providence. There is a way of securing the equal rights of all, not by dividing land up into equal pieces, but by taking for the use of all that value which attaches to land, not as the result of individual labour upon it, but as the result of the increase of population, and the improvement of society. In that way everyone would be equally interested in the land of his native country. If he used a more valuable piece than his neighbour he would pay a heavier tax. If he made no direct use of any land he would still be an equal sharer in the revenue. Here is the simple way. Aye! and it is a way that impresses the man who really sees its beauty with a more vivid idea of the beneficence of the providence of the All-Father than it seems to me anything else. One cannot look, it seems to me, through nature; whether he look at the stars through a telescope, or have the microscope reveal to him those worlds that we find in drops of water, whether he consider the human frame, the adjustments of the animal kingdom, or of any department of physical nature, he must see that there has been a contriver and adjuster, that there has been an intent. So strong is that feeling, so natural is it to our minds, that even men who deny the creative intelligence are forced, in spite of themselves, to talk of intent. The claws of one animal were *intended*, we say, to climb with; the fins of another to propel it through the water. Yet, while in looking through the laws of physical nature, we find intelligence, we do not so clearly find beneficence. But in the great social fact that as population increases, and improvements are made, and men progress in civilisation, the one thing that rises everywhere in value is land, we may see a proof of the beneficence of the Creator.

Why, consider what it means! It means that the social laws are adapted to progressive man! In a rude state of society where there is no need for common expenditure, there is no value attaching to land. The only value which attaches there is to things produced by labour. But as civilisation goes on, as a division of labour takes place, as men come into centres, so do the common wants increase and so does the necessity for public revenue arise. And so in that value which attaches to land, not by reason of anything the individual does, but by reason of the growth of the community, is a provision, intended—we may safely say *intended*–to meet that social want. Just as society grows, so do the common needs grow, and so grows this value attaching to land–the provided fund from which they can be supplied. Here is a value that may be taken, without impairing the right of property, without taking anything from the producer, without lessening the natural rewards of industry and thrift. Nay, here is a value that must be taken if we would prevent the most monstrous of all monopolies. What does all this mean? It means that in the creative plan, the natural advance in civilisation is an advance to a greater and greater equality instead of to a more and more monstrous inequality.

"Thy kingdom come!" It may be that we shall never see it. But to the man who realises that it may come, to the man who realises that it is given to him to work for the coming of God's kingdom on earth, there is for him, though he never see that kingdom here, an exceeding great reward—the reward of feeling that he, little and insignificant though he may be, is doing something to help the coming of that kingdom, doing something on the side of that good power that shows all through the universe, doing something to tear this world from the devil's grasp, and make it the kingdom of righteousness. Aye, and though it should never come, yet those who struggle for it know in the depths of their hearts that it must exist somewhere—they know that somewhere, some time, those who strive their best for the coming of the kingdom, will be welcomed into the kingdom, and that to them, even to them, some time, somewhere, the King shall say: "Well done, thou good and faithful servant, enter thou into the joy of thy Lord."

# JUSTICE THE OBJECT—TAXATION
# THE MEANS

*Ladies and Gentlemen, Friends and Fellow-Citizens:*

A s I rise on this stage the past comes back to me. Twelve years ago—
it seems so far and yet so near—twelve years ago, when I was halt of
speech, when to face an audience, it seemed to me, required as much
courage as it would to face a battery–I stood on this platform to speak
my first word in the cause for which I stand now.[2] I stood on this platform to see, instead of the audience that greets me to-night, a beggarly
array of empty benches. It is a long time. Many times, in this country
and in the dear old world, I have stood before far greater audiences than
this; I have been greeted by thousands who never saw me before, as
they would greet a friend long known and well loved; but I don't think
it ever gave me such pleasure to stand before an audience as it does
here to-night.

For years and years I have been promising myself to come back to
San Francisco. I have crossed the Atlantic five times before I could fulfil that desire. I am here now to go in a few days to the antipodes; perhaps I may never return–who knows?[3] If I live I shall try to. But San
Francisco, though I never again can be a citizen of California–though
my path in life seems away so far that California seems but a ridge on
the horizon–my heart has always turned, and always will turn, to the
home of my youth, to the city in which I grew up, to the city in which I
have found so many warm friends–to the country in which I married,
and in which my children were born. Always it will seem to me home;
and it is sweet to the man long absent to be welcomed home.

Aye, and you men, old friends tried and true–you men who rallied in
the early times to our movement, when we could count each other
almost upon one's fingers–I come back to you to say that at last our tri-

*Address in Metropolitan Hall, San Francisco, February 4, 1890, on the way to the
Australian lecture tour.[1]*

umph is but a matter of time; to say that never in the history of thought has a movement come forward so fast and so well.

Ten years ago, when I left, I was anything but hopeful; ten years ago I would not have dared to say that in any time to which I might live, we should see the beginning of this great struggle. Nor have I cared. My part (and I think I can speak for every man who is enlisted in this movement)—my part has never been to predict results. Our feeling is the feeling of the great [S]toic emperor, "that is the business of Jupiter; not ours."[4] Ours to do the work as we may; ours to plant the seed which is to give the results. But now, so well forward is this cause, so many strong advocates has it in every land, so far has it won its way, that now it makes no difference who lives or who dies, who goes forward or who hangs back. Now the currents of the time are setting in our favour. At last—at last we can say with certainty that it will only be in a little while before all over the English speaking world, and then, not long after, over the rest of the civilised world, the great truth will be acknowledged that no human child comes into this world without coming into his equal right to all.

I am talking to-night to my friends; I am talking to-night to those who are as earnest and well informed in this cause as I am; but I am also probably talking to many who have but vague ideas concerning it. Let me, since I am in San Francisco, speak of the genesis of my own thought. I came out here at an early age, and knew nothing whatever of political economy. I had never thought upon any social problem. The first time I ever recollect talking on such a subject was one day, when I was about eighteen, after I had first come to this country, sitting on the deck of a topsail schooner with a lot of miners on the way to the Frazer River;[5] and we got talking about the Chinese, and I ventured to say—ventured to ask what harm the Chinese were doing here, if, as these miners said, they were only working the cheap diggings? And one old miner turned to me, and said, "No harm now; but it will not be always that wages are as high as they are to-day in California. As the country grows, as people come in, wages will go down, and some day or other white men will be glad to get these diggings that the Chinamen are now working." And I well remember how it impressed me, the idea that as the country grew in all that we are hoping that it might grow, the condition of those who had to work for their living must grow, not better, but worse.

And I remember, after having come down from the country, sitting one Christmas eve in the gallery of the old American Theatre, among the gods, when a new drop curtain fell, and we all sprang to our feet, for on that curtain was painted what was then a dream of the far future, the overland train coming to San Francisco; and after we had shouted ourselves hoarse, I began to think what good is it going to be to men like me? those who have nothing but their labour? I saw that thought grow and grow; we were all–all of us, rich and poor–hoping for the development of California, proud of her future greatness, looking forward to the time when San Francisco was to be one of the great capitals of the world; looking forward to the time when this great empire of the West was to count her population by millions, and underneath it all came to me what that miner told. What about the masses of the people?

When, after growing up here, I went across the continent, before the continental railway was completed, and in the streets of New York for the first time realised the contrasts of wealth and want that are to be found in a great city; saw those sights that, to the man who comes from the West, affright and appal, the problem grew upon me.[6] I said to myself there must be some reason for this; there must be some remedy for this, and I will not rest until I have found the one and discovered the other. At last it came clear as the stars of a bright midnight. I saw what was the cause; I saw what was the cure. I saw nothing that was new. Truth is never new.

When I lectured for the first time in Oxford, a professor of political economy in that great university met and opposed me, and he said, "I have read Mr. George's book from one end to the other; what I have to say is this: there is nothing in it both new and true; what is true is not new, and what is new is not true."[7] I answered him: "I accept your statement. It is a correct criticism; social truth never is, never can be new; and the truth for which we stand is an old truth; a truth seen by men everywhere, recognised by the first perceptions of all men; only over-clouded, only obscured in our modern times by force and fraud."

So it is. I notice that one of our papers gives to me the character of an apostle and speaks of my comrades as my disciples. It is not so. I have done no more to any man than point out God's stars. They were there for him to see. Millions and millions of years have seen them precisely as I saw them; every man may see them who will look.

When I first went to Ireland I got a note from the most venerable of the Irish bishops, Dr. Dougan, bishop of Waterford, asking me to come and have a private talk with him.[8] I went, and the old man–white haired, ruddy cheeked, like Willegis, Wagner's son[9]–the man who under the mitre of the bishop still keeps the fresh true heart of the Irish peasant—commenced, with the privilege of age, catechising me. He said: "What is this new doctrine that your name is associated with? You say that all men have equal rights to land; but all men can't use land; how do you propose to divide up?" And then he went on from one question to another, bringing all the arguments, all the objections that spring up in the minds of men, just as they probably sprung up in the minds of many who are here—just as they spring up in the mind of any man—all the objections that are so current; and I answered them all. Finally rising, without saying anything, the old man stretched out his hand. "God bless you, my son; I have asked you to come here and answer my questions, because I wanted to see if you could defend your faith. Go on; go on. What you say to me is nothing new; it is the old truth that through persecution and against force, though trodden down, our people have always held. What you say is not new to me. When a little boy, sitting by the peat fire in the west of Ireland, I have heard the same truths from the lips of men who could not speak a word of English. Go on; the time has come; I, an old man, tell you that there is no earthly power that can stop this movement." And the years have shown that the venerable bishop was right.

What is the cause of this dark shadow that seems to accompany modern civilisation—of this existence of bitter want in the very centres of life—of the failure of all our modern advances—of all the wonderful discoveries and inventions that have made this wonderful nineteenth century, now drawing to a close, so prominent among all the centuries? What is the reason, that as we add to productive power—that is, invention after invention—multiplying by the hundredfold and the thousandfold the power of human hands to supply human wants; that all over the civilised world, and especially in this great country, pauperism is increasing, and insanity is increasing, and criminality is increasing; that marriages are decreasing; that the struggle for existence seems not less, but more and more intense—what is the reason? There must be but one of two answers. Either it is in accordance with the will of God, either it is the result of natural law, or it is because of our ignorance and selfishness of our faith that we evade the natural law. We single taxers point to the one sufficient cause. Wherever these phenomena are to be seen the natural element on which and from which all men must live, if they are to live at all, is the property, not of the whole people, but of the few. We point to the adequate cure; the restoration to all men of their natural rights in the soil—the assurance to every child, as it comes into the world, of the enjoyment of its natural heritage—the right to live, the right to work, the right to enjoy the fruits of its work; rights necessarily conditioned upon the equal right to that element which is the basis of production; that element which is indispensable to human life; that element which is the standing place, the storehouse, the reservoir of men; that element from which all that is physical in man is drawn. For our bodies, themselves, they come from the land, and to the land they return again; we, ourselves, are as much children of the soil as are the flowers or the trees.

We call ourselves to-day single-tax men.[10] It is only recently, within a few years, that we have adopted that title. It is not a new title; over a hundred years ago there arose in France a school of philosophers and patriots—Quesnay, Turgot, Condorcet, Dupont—the most illustrious men of their time, who advocated, as the cure for all social ills the *impôt unique*, the single tax.[11]

We here, on this [W]estern [C]ontinent, as the nineteenth century draws to a close, have revived the same name, and we find enormous advantages in it.

We used to be confronted constantly by the question: "Well, after you have divided the land up, how do you propose to keep it divided?" We don't meet that question now. The single tax has, at least, this great merit: it suggests our method; it shows the way we would travel—the simple way of abolishing all taxes, save one tax upon land values.

Now mark, one tax upon land values. We do not propose a tax upon land, as people who misapprehend us constantly say. We do not propose a tax upon land; we propose a tax upon land values, or what in the terminology of political economy is termed rent; that is to say, the value which attaches to land irrespective of any improvements in or on it; that value which attaches to land, not by reason of anything that the user or improver of land does—not by reason of any individual exertion of labour, but by reason of the growth and improvement of the community. A tax that will take up what John Stuart Mill called the unearned increment; that is to say, that increment of wealth which comes to the owner of land, not as a user; that comes whether he be a resident or an absentee; whether he be engaged in the active business of life; whether he be an idiot and whether he be a child; that growth of value that we have seen in our own times so astonishingly great in this city; that has made sand lots, lying in the same condition that they were thousands of years ago, worth enormous sums, without any one putting any exertion of labour or any expenditure of capital upon them. Now, the distinction between a tax on land and a tax on land values may at first seem an idle one, but it is a most important one. A tax on land–that is to say, a tax upon all land– would ultimately become a condition to the use of land; would therefore fall upon labour, would increase prices, and be borne by the general community. But a tax on land values cannot fall on all land, because all land is not of value; it can only fall on valuable land, and on valuable land in proportion to its value; therefore, it can no more become a tax on labour than can a tax upon income or a tax upon the value of special privileges of any kind. It can merely take from the individual, not the earnings of the individual, but that premium which, as society grows and improves, attaches to the use of land of superior quality.

Now see, take it in its lowest aspect–take it as a mere fiscal change, and see how in accord with every dictate of expediency, with every principle of justice, is the single tax. We have invented and invented, improved and improved, yet the great fact is, that to-day we have not wealth enough. There are in the United States some few men richer than it is wholesome for men to be. But the great masses of our people are not rich as civilised Americans at the close of the nineteenth century ought to be. The great mass of our people only manage by hard work to live. The great mass of our people don't get the comforts, the refinements, the luxuries that in the present age of the world everyone ought to have. All over this country there is a fierce struggle for exis- tence. Only as I came to the door of this building, a beggar stopped me on the street–a young man; he said he could not find work. I don't know, perhaps he lied. I do know that when a man once commences upon that course there is rapid demoralisation. I do know that indis- criminate charity is apt to injure far more than it can help; yet I gave him something, for I did not know but that his story might be true.

This is the shore of the Pacific. This is the Golden Gate. The westward march of our race is terminated by the ocean, which has the ancient East on its further shore; no further can we go. And yet here, in this new country, in this golden State, there are men ready to work, anxious to work, and yet who, for longer or shorter periods, cannot get the oppor- tunity to work. The further east you go, the worse it grows. To the man from San Francisco, who has never realised it before, there are sights in New York that are appalling. Cross the ocean to the greater city–the metropolis of the civilised world[12]–and there poverty is deeper and darker yet. What is the reason? If there were more wealth wanted, why don't they get more? We cannot cure this evil of poverty by dividing up wealth, monstrous as are some of the fortunes that have arisen; and fortunes are concentrating in this country faster than ever before in the history of the world. But divide them and still there would not be enough. But if men want more wealth, why don't they get more wealth? If we, as people, want more wealth (and certainly ninety-nine out of every hundred Americans do want more wealth), why are some suffering for the opportunities of employment? Others are at work without making a living. But ninety-nine out of a hundred have some legitimate desire that they would like to gratify. Well, in the first place, if we want more wealth—if we call that country prosperous which is increasing in wealth—is it not a piece of stupidity that we should tax men for producing wealth?

Yet that is what we are doing to-day. Bring almost any article of wealth to this country from a foreign country, and you are confronted at once with a tax. Is it not from a common-sense standpoint a stupid thing, if we want more wealth—if the prosperous country is the country that increases in wealth, why in Heaven's name should we put up a barrier against the men who want to bring wealth into this country? We want more dry-goods (if you don't know, your wives surely will tell you). We want more clothing; more sugar; more of all sorts of the good things that are called "goods"; and yet by this system of taxation we virtually put up a high fence around the country to keep out these very things. We tax that convenient man who brings any goods into the country.

If wealth be a good thing; if the country be a prosperous country—that is, increasing in wealth—well, surely, if we propose to restrict trade at all, the wise thing would be to put the taxes on the men who are taking goods out of the country, not upon those who are bringing goods into the country. We single-tax men would sweep away all these barriers. We would try to keep out small-pox and cholera and vermin and plagues. But we would welcome all the goods that anybody wanted to send us, that anybody wanted to bring home. We say it is stupid, if we want more wealth, to prevent people from bringing wealth to the country. We say, also, that it is just as stupid to tax the men who produce wealth within the country.

Here we say we want more manufactures. The American people submit to enormous taxes for the purpose of building up factories; yet when a man builds a factory, what do we do? Why, we come down and tax him for it. We certainly want more houses. There are a few people who have bigger houses than any one reasonable family can occupy; but the great mass of the American people are underhoused. There, in the city of New York, the plight to which all American cities are tending, you will find that sixty-five per cent. of the population are living two families or more to the single floor. Yet let a man put up a house in any part of the United States, and down comes the tax-gatherer to demand a fine for having put up a house.

We say that industry is a good thing, and that thrift is a good thing; and there are some people who say that if a man be industrious, and if a man is thrifty, he can easily accumulate wealth. Whether that be true or not, industry is certainly a good thing, and thrift is certainly a good thing. But what do we do if a man be industrious? If he produces wealth enough and by thrift accumulates wealth at all, down comes the tax-gatherer to demand a part of it. We say that that is stupid; that we ought not by our taxes repress the production of wealth; that when a farmer reclaims a strip of the desert and turns it into an orchard and a vineyard, or on the prairie produces crops and feeds fine cattle, that, so far from being taxed and fined for having done these things, we ought to be glad that he has done it; that we ought to welcome all energy; that no man can produce wealth for himself without augmenting the general stock, without making the whole country richer.

We impose some taxes for the purpose of getting rid of things, for the purpose of having fewer of the things that we tax. In most of our counties and States when dogs become too numerous, there is imposed a dog tax to get rid of dogs. Well, we impose a dog tax to get rid of dogs, and why should we impose a house tax unless we want to get rid of houses? Why should we impose a farm tax unless we want fewer farms? Why should we tax any man for having exerted industry or energy in the production of wealth? Tax houses and there will certainly be fewer houses.

If you go east to the city of Brooklyn, you may see that demonstrated to the eye.[13] What first surprised me in the ["]city of churches["] was to see long rows of buildings, of brown-stone houses, two stories in front and three stories behind; or three stories in front and four stories behind; and I thought for a moment what foolish idea ever entered the brains of those men, to have left out half an upper story in that way? I found out by inquiring that it was all on account of the tax. In the city of Brooklyn, the assessor is only supposed to look in front, and so by making the house in that way, you can get a three-story building behind with only a two-story front.

So in England, in the old houses, there you may see the result of the window tax. The window tax is in force in France to-day, and in France there are two hundred thousand houses, according to the census, that have no window at all in order to escape the tax.

So if you tax ships there will be fewer ships. What old San Franciscan cannot remember the day when in this harbour might be seen the graceful forms and lofty spars of so many American ships, the fleetest and best in the world? I well remember the day that no American, who crossed to Europe, thought of crossing on any other than an American ship. To-day, if you wish to cross the Atlantic, you must cross on a British steamer, unless you choose to cross on a German or French steamer. On the high seas of the world the American ship is becoming almost as rare as a Chinese junk. Why? Simply because we have taxed our ships out of existence. There is the proof. Tax buildings, and you will have fewer or poorer buildings; tax farms, and you will have fewer farms and more wilderness; tax ships, there will be fewer and poorer ships; and tax capital, and there will be less capital; but you may tax land values all you please and there will not be a square inch the less land. Tax land values all you please up to the point of taking the full annual value—up to the point of making mere ownership in land utterly unprofitable, so that no one will want merely to own land—what will be the result? Simply that land will be the easier had by the user. Simply that the land will become valueless to the mere speculator—to the ["]dog in the manger["], who wants merely to hold and not to use; to the forestaller, who wants merely to reap where others have sown, to gather to himself the products of labour, without doing labour. Tax land values, and you leave to production its full rewards, and you open to producers natural opportunities.

Take it from any aspect you please, take it on its political side (and surely that is a side that we ought to consider clearly and plainly), while we boast of our democratic republicanism, democratic republicanism is passing away. I need not say that to you, men of San Francisco—San Francisco ruled by a boss; to you men of California, where you send to the Senate the citizen who dominates the State as no duke could rule.[14] Look at the corruption that is tearing the heart out of our institutions; where does it come from? Whence this demoralisation? Largely from our system of taxation. What does our present system of taxation do?

Why, it is a tax upon conscience; a tax upon truth; a tax upon respect to law; it offers a premium for lying and perjury and evasion; it fosters and stimulates bribery and corruption.

Go over to Europe; travel around for a while among the effete monarchies of the [O]ld [W]orld, and what you see will make you appreciate democracy; then come home. At length you take a pilot. There is the low-lying land upon the horizon–the land of the free and the home of the brave–and if you are entering the port of New York, as most Americans do, finally you will see that great statue, presented by a citizen of the French [R]epublic–the [S]tatue of Liberty holding aloft a light that talks to the world.[15] Just as you get to see that statue clearly, Liberty [E]nlightening the [W]orld, you will be called down by a custom-house officer to form in line, men and women, and to call on God Almighty, Maker of heaven and earth, to bear witness that you have nothing dutiable in your trunks or in your carpet sacks, or rolled up in your shawl straps; and you take that oath; the United States of America compels you to. But the United States of America don't leave you there; the very next thing, another official steps up to demand your keys and to open your box or package and to look through it for things dutiable, unless, as may be, his eyes are stopped by a greenback.[16] Well, now, everyone who has made that visit does know that most passengers have things dutiable; and I notice that the protectionists have them fully as often as the free traders. I have never yet seen a consistent protectionist. There may be protectionists who would not smuggle when they get a chance; but I think they must be very, very few. Go right through that daily stream–from the very institution of laws–down to the very lobby that gathers at Washington when it is proposed to repeal a tax, bullying, bragging, stealing to keep that particular tax on the American people, so patriotic are they; very much interested in protecting the poor workingman.

See the private interests that are enlisted in merely the petty evasions of law that go on by passengers; but the gigantic smuggling, the under-valuation frauds of all kinds; the private interests that are enlisted in class; that enter the primaries; that surround our national legislature with lobbyists that in every presidential election put their millions into the corruption fund. Does not the whole system reek with fraud and corruption? Is it not a discrimination against honesty, against conscience, a premium on evasion and fraud? Come into our States and look at their taxes, or look, if you please, by the way, on the internal revenue. You remember how, when it was proposed to abolish that stamp

tax on matches, that was in force during the war, how the match combination fought hard and fought long against the repeal of that tax. You
remember how the whiskey ring spent its money to prevent the reduction of the whiskey tax; how to-day it stands ready to spend money to
keep up the present tax. Go then into our States; take our system of
direct taxation; what do you find? We pretend to tax all property; many
of our taxes are especially framed to get at rich men; what is the result?
Why, all over the United States the very rich men simply walk from
under those taxes. All over the United States the attempt to tax men
upon their wealth is a farce and a fraud. If there were no other reason,
this would be a sufficient reason why all such taxes should be abolished. In their very nature they permit evasion, law breaking, perjury,
bribery and corruption; but the tax on land values, it has at least this
advantage: land cannot be hid; it cannot be carried off; it always
remains, so to speak, out of doors. If you don't see the land you know
that it is there; and of all values the value which attaches to land is the
most definite, the most easily ascertained. Why, I may go into San
Francisco, into Denver, into New York, into Boston, into any city where
I am totally unacquainted, and if one offers to sell me a lot, I can go to
any real-estate dealer and say: "Here is a lot of such a frontage and such
a depth, and on such a street; what is it worth?" He will tell me closely.
How can he tell me the value of the house that is upon it? Not without
a close examination; still less, how can any one tell me, without the
examination of experts, what is the value of the things contained in that
house, if it be a large and fine house; and still less, how can any one tell
me the value of the various things that the man who lives in that house
may own. But land–there it is. You can put up a simple little sign on
every lot, or upon every piece of agricultural land, saying that this tract
is of such a frontage and of such a depth, having such an area, and it
belongs to such a person, and is assessed at so much, and you have published information checking the assessment; you have the assessment
on a value that can be ascertained more definitely, more certainly than
any other value; substitute that tax for all the many taxes that we now
impose. See the gain in morals; see the gain in economy! With what a
horde of tax-gathering and tax-assessing officials could we dispense;
what swearing and examination and nosing around to find out what
men have or what they are worth!

Now take the matter of justice. We single-tax men are not deniers of
the rights of property; but, on the contrary, we are the upholders and

defenders of the rights of property. We say that the great French
[C]onvention was right when it asserted the sacred right of property;[17]
that there is a right of property, that comes from no human law, which
antedates all human enactments; that is a clear genesis; that which a
man produces, that which by his exertion he brings from the reservoir
of nature and adapts to forms suited to gratify the wants of man—that is
his; his as against all the world. If I by my labour catch a fish, that fish
is and ought to be mine; if I make a machine, that machine belongs to
me; that is the sacred right of property. There is a clear title from the
producer, resting upon the right of the individual to himself, to the use
of his own powers, to the enjoyment of the results of his exertion; the
right that he may give, that he may sell, that he may bequeath.

What do we do when we tax a building? When a man puts up a building by his own exertion, or it comes to him through the transfer of the
right that others have to their exertion down comes the community and
says, virtually, you must give us a portion of that building. For where a
man honestly earns and accumulates wealth, down come the tax-gatherers and demand every year a portion of those earnings. Now, is it not
as much an impairment of the right of property to take a lamb as to take
a sheep? To take five per cent. or twenty per cent., as to take a hundred
per cent.? We should leave the whole of the value produced by individual exertion to the individual. We should respect the rights of property
not to any limited extent, but fully. We should leave to him who produces wealth, to him to whom the title of the producer passed, all that
wealth. No matter what be its form, it belongs to the individual. We
should take for the uses of the community the value of land for the same
reason. It belongs to the community because the growth of the community produces it.

What is the reason that land in San Francisco to-day is worth so
much more than it was in 1860 or 1850? Why is it that barren sand,
then worth nothing, has now become so enormously valuable? On
account of what the owners have done? No. It is because of the growth
of the whole people. It is because San Francisco is a larger city; it is
because you all are here. Every child that is born; every family that
comes and settles; every man that does anything to improve the city,
adds to the value of land. It is a value that springs from the growth of
the community. Therefore, for the very same reason of justice, the very
same respect for the rights of property which induces us to leave to the
individual all that individual effort produces, we should take for the

community that value which arises by the growth and improvement of the community.

What would be the direct result? Take this city, this State or the whole country; abolish all taxes on the production of wealth; let every man be free to plough, to sow, to build, in any way add to the common stock without being fined one penny. Say to every man who would improve, who would in any way add to the production of wealth: ["]Go ahead, go ahead; produce, accumulate all you please; add to the common stock in any way you choose; you shall have it all; we shall not fine or tax you one penny.["] What would be the result of abolishing all these taxes that now depress industry; that now fall on labour; that now lessen the profits of those who are adding to the general wealth? Evidently to stimulate production; to increase wealth; to bring new life into every vocation of industry. And mark the results.

On the other side what would be the effect when abolishing all these taxes that now fall on labour or the products of labour, if we were to resort for public revenue to a tax upon land values; a tax that would fall on the owner of a vacant lot just as heavily as upon the man who has improved a lot by putting up a house; that would fall on the speculator who is holding 160 acres of agricultural land idle, waiting for a tenant or a purchaser, as heavily as it would fall upon the farmer who had made the 160 acres bloom? Why, the result would be everywhere that the ["]dog in the manger["] would be checked; the result everywhere would be that the men who are holding natural opportunities, not for use but simply for profit, by demanding a price of those who must use them, would have either to use their land or give way to somebody who would.

Everywhere from the Atlantic to the Pacific, from the [L]akes to the [G]ulf, opportunities would be opened to labour; there would come into the labour market that demand for the products of labour that never can be satisfied–the demands of labour itself. We should cease to hear of the labour question. The notion of a man ready to work, anxious to work, and yet not able to find work, would be forgotten, would be a story of the misty past.

Why, look at it here to-day, in this new country, where there are as yet only sixty-five millions of us scattered over a territory that in the present stage of the arts is sufficient to support in comfort a thousand millions; yet we are actually thinking and talking as if there were too many people in the country. We want more wealth. Why don't we get it?

Is any factor of production short? What are the factors of production? Labour, capital, and land; but to put them in the order of their importance: land, labour, capital. We want more wealth; what is the result? Is it in labour; is there not enough labour? No. From all parts of the United States we hear of what seems like a surplus of labour. We have actually got to thinking that the man who gives another employment is giving him a boon. Is there any scarcity of capital? Why, so abundant is capital to-day that United States bonds, bought at the current rate, will only yield a fraction over two per cent. per annum. So abundant is capital that there can be no doubt that a government loan could be floated to-day at two per cent., and little doubt but that it would soon command a premium. So abundant is capital that all over the country it is pressing for remunerative employment. If the limitation is not in labour and not in capital, it must be in land.

But there is no scarcity of land from the Atlantic to the Pacific, for there you will find unused or only half-used land. Aye, even where population is densest. Have you not land enough in San Francisco? Go to that great city of New York, where people are crowded together so closely, the great majority of them, that physical health and moral health are in many cases alike impossible; where, in spite of the fact that the rich men of the whole country gravitate there, only four per cent. of the families live in separate houses of their own, and sixty-five per cent. of the families are crowded two or more to the single floor—crowded together layer on layer, in many places, like sardines in a box. Yet, why are there not more houses there? Not because there is not enough capital to build more houses, and yet not because there is not land enough on which to build more houses. To-day one half of the area of New York City is unbuilt upon—is absolutely unused. When there is such a pressure, why don't people go to these vacant lots and build there? Because, though unused, the land is owned; because, speculating upon the future growth of the city, the owners of those vacant lots demand thousands of dollars before they will permit any one to put a house upon them.

What you see in New York, you may see everywhere. Come into the coal fields of Pennsylvania; there you will frequently find thousands and thousands of miners unable to work, either locked out by their employers, or striking as a last resource against their pitiful wages being cut down a little more.

Why should there be such a struggle? Why don't these men go to work and take coal for themselves? Not because there is not coal land enough in those mining districts. The parts that are worked are small as compared to her whole coal deposits. The land is not all used, but it is all owned, and before the men who would like to go to work can get the opportunity to work the raw material, they must pay thousands of dollars per acre for land that is only nominally taxed to its owner.

Go [W]est, find people filing along, crowding around every Indian reservation that is about to be opened; travelling through unused and half-used land in order to get an opportunity to settle—like men swimming a river in order to get a drink. Come to this State, ride through your great valleys, see those vast expanses, only dotted here and there by a house, without a tree; those great ranches, cultivated as they are cultivated by blanket men, who have a little work in ploughing time, and some more work in reaping time, and who then, after being fed almost like animals, and sheltered worse than valuable animals are sheltered, are enforced to tramp through the State.[18] It is the artificial scarcity of natural opportunities.

Is there any wonder that under this treatment of the land all over the civilised world there should be want and destitution? Aye, and suffering—degradation worse in many cases than anything known among savages, among the great masses of the people?

How could it be otherwise in a world like this world, tenanted by land animals, such as men are? How could the Creator, so long as our laws are what they are—how could He Himself relieve it? Suppose that in answer to the prayers that ascend for the relief of poverty, the Almighty were to rain down wealth from heaven or cause it to spout up from the bowels of the earth, who, under our system, would own it? The landowner. There would be no benefit to labour. Consider, conceive any kind of a world your imagination will permit. Conceive of heaven itself, which, from the very necessities of our minds, we cannot otherwise think of than as having an expansion of space—what would be the result in heaven itself, if the people who should first get to heaven were to parcel it out in big tracts among themselves? Oh, the wickedness of it; oh, the blasphemy of it! Worse than atheists are those so-called Christians, who by implication, if not by direct statement, attribute to the God they call on us to worship, the God that they say with their lips is all love and mercy, this bitter suffering which to-day exists in the very centres of our civilisation. Good heavens! When I was last in London, the first morning that I spent there, I rose early and walked out, as I always like to walk when I go to London, through streets whose names I do not know; I came to a sign—a great big brass plate, "Office of the Missionary Society for Central Africa."[19] I walked half a block, and right by the side of the Horse Guards, where you may see the pomp and glare of the colour mounting, there went a man and a woman and two little children that seemed the very embodiment of hard and hopeless despair.

A while ago I was in Edinburgh, the modern Athens, the glorious capital (for such it is in some parts)—the glorious capital of Scotland;[20] aye, and I went into those tall houses, monstrous they seemed, those relics of the old time, and there, right in the shadow, in the centre of such intellectual activity, such wealth, such patriotism, such public spirit, were sights that would appal the veriest savage. I saw there the hardest thing a man can look at. They took me to an institution where little children are taken in and cared for, whose mothers are at work, and here I saw the bitterest of all sights—little children shrunken and sickly from want of food; and the superintendent told me a story. He pointed out a little girl, and said that little thing was brought in there almost starving, and when they set food before her, before she touched it or tasted it, she folded her hands and raised her eyes, and thanked her heavenly Father for His bounty. Good God! Men and women, think of the blasphemy of it! To say that the bounty of that little child's heavenly Father was conceded so. No, no, no. He has given enough and to spare for all that His providence brings into this world. It is the injustice that disinherits God's children; it is the wrong that takes from those children their heritage, not the Almighty.

Aye, years ago, I said on this platform that the seed had been set.[21] Now the grand truth is beginning to appear. From one end of Great Britain to the other, all through this country, into the antipodes to which I am going—wherever our English tongue is spoken—aye, and beyond, on the continent of Europe—the truths for which we stand are making their way. The giant Want is doomed. But I tell you, and I call upon my comrades to bear me witness, whether there is not a reward in this belief, in this work, which is utterly independent of results.

In London, on one of my visits, a clergyman of the Established Church asked a private interview with me. He said: "I want to talk with you frankly. Something I have seen of your sayings has made me think that you could give me an answer. Let me tell you my story. I was educated for the [C]hurch; graduated at one of the universities; took orders; was sent to a foreign country as a missionary. After a while I became a chaplain in the navy; finally, a few years since, I took a curacy in London, and settled here. I have been, up till recently, a believing Christian. I have believed the Bible to be the word of God, and I have rested implicitly on its promises; and one promise I have often thought of: 'Once I was young, and now I am old, yet never have I seen the righteous forsaken, nor his seed begging their bread.' I believed that till I came to my own country. I believed that until I undertook the ministerial work in London. I believed it was true. Now I know it is not true; I have seen the righteous forsaken and his seed begging their bread." He said: "My faith is gone; and I am holding on here, but I feel like a hypocrite. I want to ask you how it seems to you." And I told him in my poor way, as I have been trying to tell you to-night, how it is, simply because of our violation of natural justice; how it is, simply because we will not take the appointed way.

Aye, in our own hearts we all know. To the man who appreciates this truth, to the man who enters this work, it makes little difference—this thing of results. This at least he knows, that it is not because of the power that created this world and brought men upon it that these dark shades exist in our civilisation to-day; that it is not because of the niggardliness of the Creator.

And there arises in me a feeling of what the world might be. The prayer that the Master taught His disciples: "Thy kingdom come, Thy will be done on earth as it is in heaven," was no mere form of words. It is given to men to struggle for the kingdom of justice and righteousness. It is given to men to work and to hope for and to bring on that day of which the prophets have told and the seers have dreamed; that day in which involuntary poverty shall be utterly abolished; that day in which there shall be work for all, leisure for all, abundance for all; that day in which even the humblest shall have his share, not merely of the necessities and comforts, but of the reasonable luxuries of life; that day in which every child born among us may hope to develop all that is highest and noblest in its nature; that day in which in the midst of abundance the fear of want shall be gone. This greed for wealth that leads men to turn their backs upon every thing that is just and true, and to trample upon their fellows lest they be trampled upon; to search and to strive, and to strain every faculty of their natures to accumulate what they cannot take away, will be gone, and in that day the higher qualities of man shall have their opportunity and claim their reward.

We cannot change human nature; we are not so foolish as to dream that human nature can be changed. What we mean to do is to give the good in human nature its opportunity to develop.

Try our remedy by any test. The test of justice, the test of expediency. Try it by any dictum of political economy; by any maxim of good morals, by any maxim of good government. It will stand every test. What I ask you to do is not to take what I or any other man may say, but to think for yourselves.

# CAUSES OF THE BUSINESS DEPRESSION

I am asked by "Once a Week" to state what, in my opinion, are the causes of the existing business depression.² It should be possible to do more. For the method that has fixed with certainty the causes of natural phenomena once left to varying opinion or wild fancy, ought to enable us to bring into the region of ascertained fact the causes of social phenomena so clearly marked and so entirely within observation.

To ascertain the cause of failure or abnormal action in that complex machine, the human body, the first effort of the surgeon is to locate the difficulty. So the first step towards determining the causes of business depression is to see what business depression really is.

By business depression we mean a lessening in rapidity and volume of the exchanges by which, in our highly specialised industrial system, commodities pass into the hands of consumers. This lessening of exchanges which, from the side of the merchant or manufacturer, we call business depression, is evidently not due to any scarcity of the things that merchants or manufacturers have to exchange. From that point of view there seems, indeed, a plethora of such things. Nor is it due to any lessening in the desire of consumers for them. On the contrary, seasons of business depression are seasons of bitter want on the part of large numbers–of want so intense and general that charity is called on to prevent actual starvation from need of things that manufacturers and merchants have to sell.

It may seem, on first view, as if this lessening of exchanges came from some impediment in the machinery of exchange. Since tariffs have for their object the checking of certain exchanges, there is a superficial plausibility in looking to them for the cause. While, as money is the common measure of value and a common medium of exchange, in terms of which most exchanges are made, it is, perhaps, even more plausible to look to monetary regulations. But however important any

*A contribution to "Once a Week," New York, March 6, 1894.*¹

tariff question or any money question may be, neither has sufficient importance to account for the phenomena. Protection carried to its furthest could only shut us off from the advantage of exchanging what we produce for what other countries produce; free trade carried to its furthest could only give us with the rest of the world that freedom of exchange that we already enjoy between our several States; while money, important as may be its office as a measure and flux of exchanges, is still but a mere counter. Seasons of business depression come and go without change in tariffs and monetary regulations, and exist in different countries under widely varying tariffs and monetary systems. The real cause must lie deeper.

That it does lie deeper is directly evident. The lessening of the exchanges by which commodities pass into the hands of consumers is clearly due, not so much to increased difficulty in transferring these commodities as to decreased ability to pay for them. Every business man sees that business depression comes from lack of purchasing power on the part of would-be consumers, or, as our colloquial phrase is, from their lack of money. But money is only an intermediary, performing in exchanges the same office that poker-chips do in a game. In the last analysis it is a labour certificate. The great mass of consumers obtain money by exchanging their labour, or the proceeds of their labour, for money, and with it purchasing commodities. Thus what they really pay for commodities with is labour. It is not merely true in the sense he meant it that, as Adam Smith says, *"Labour was the first price, the original purchase money that was paid for all things."* It is the final price that *is* paid for all things.

The lessening of "effective demand," which is the proximate cause of business depression, means, therefore, a lessening of the ability to convert labour into exchangeable forms—means what we call scarcity of employment. These two phrases are, in fact, but different names for different aspects of one thing. What from the side of the business man is "business depression," is, from the side of the workman, "scarcity of employment." The one always comes with the other and passes away with the other. They act on each other, and again react, as when the merchant or manufacturer discharges his employees on account of business depression, and thus adds to scarcity of employment. But in the primary causal relation scarcity of employment comes first. That is to say, scarcity of employment does not come from business depression, as is sometimes assumed, but business depression comes from the scarcity of employment. For it is the effective demand for consumption that determines the extent and direction in which labour will be expended in producing commodities—not the supply of commodities that determines the demand.

What is employment? It is the expenditure of exertion in the production of commodities or satisfactions. It is what, in a phrase having clearer connotations, we term work. For the term employment is, for economic use, somewhat confused by our habitual distinction between employers and employees. This distinction only arises from the division of labour, and disappears when we consider first principles. I employ a man to black my boots. He expends his labour to give me the satisfaction of polished boots. What is the five cents I give him in return? It is a counter or chip through which he may obtain at will the expenditure of labour to that equivalent in any of various forms—food, shelter, newspapers, a street-car ride, and so on. In final analysis the transaction is the same as if I had employed him to black my boots and he had employed me to render to him some of these other services; or as if I had blacked my own boots and he had performed these other services for himself. Even in a narrow view there are only three ways by which men can live—by work, by beggary and by theft; for the man who obtains work without giving work is, economically, only a beggar or a thief. But on a larger view these three come down to one, for beggars and thieves can only live on workers. It is human labour that supplies all the wants of human life—as truly now, in all the complexities of modern civilisation, as in the beginning, when the first man and first woman were the only human beings on the globe.

Now, employment, or work, is the expenditure of labour *in* the production of commodities or satisfactions. But *on* what? Manifestly on land, for land is to man the whole physical universe. Take any country as a whole, or the world as a whole. On what and from what does its whole population live? Despite our millions and our complex civilisation, our extensions of exchanges and our inventions of machines, are we not all living as the first man did and the last man must, by the application of labour to land? Try a mental experiment: Picture, in imagination, the farmer at the plough, the miner in the ore vein, the railroad train on its rushing way, the steamer crossing the ocean, the great factory with its whirring wheels and thousand operatives, builders erecting a house, linemen stringing a telegraph wire, a salesman selling goods, a bookkeeper casting up accounts, and a bootblack polishing the boots of a customer. Make any such picture in imagination, and then by mental exclusion withdraw from it, item by item, all that belongs to land. What will be left?

Land is the source of all employment, the natural element indispensable to all work. Land and labour—these are the two primary factors that, by their union, produce all wealth and bring about all material satisfactions. Given labour—that is to say, the ability to work and the willingness to work—and there never has and never can be any scarcity of employment so long as labour can obtain access to land. Were Adam and Eve bothered by "scarcity of employment"? Did the first settlers in this country or the men who afterwards settled those parts of the country where land was still easily had know anything of it? That the monopoly of land—the exclusion of labour from land by the high price demanded for it—is the cause of scarcity of employment and business depressions is as clear as the sun at noonday. Wherever you may be that scarcity of employment is felt—whether in city or village, or mining district or agricultural section—how far will you have to go to find land that labour is anxious to use (for land has no value until labour will pay a price for the privilege of using it), but from which labour is debarred by the high price demanded by some non-user? In the very heart of New York City, two minutes' walk from Union Square will bring you to three vacant lots. For permission to use the smallest and least valuable of these a rental of $40,000 a year has been offered and refused. This is but an example of what may everywhere be seen, from the heart of the metropolis to the Cherokee Strip.[3] Where labour is shut out from land it wastes. Desire may remain, but "effective demand" is gone. Is there any mystery in the cause of a business depression? Let the whole earth be treated as these lots are treated, and who of its teeming millions could find employment?

At the close of the last great depression I made "An Examination of the Cause of Industrial Depression" in a book better known by its main title, "Progress and Poverty," to which I would refer the reader who would see the genesis and course of business depressions fully explained.[4] But their cause is clear. Idle acres mean idle hands, and idle hands mean a lessening of purchasing power on the part of the great body of consumers that must bring depression to all business. Every great period of land speculation that has taken place in our history has been followed by a period of business depression, and it always must be so. Socialists, Populists and charity-mongers—the people who would apply little remedies for a great evil—are all "barking up the wrong tree." The upas of our civilisation is our treatment of land.[5] It is that which is converting even the march of invention into a blight.

Charity and the giving of "charity work" may do a little to alleviate suffering, but they cannot cure business depression. For they merely transfer existing purchasing power. They do not increase the sum of "effective demand." There is but one cure for recurring business depression. There is no other. That is the single tax—the abolition of all taxes on the employment and products of labour and the taking of economic or ground rent for the use of the community by taxes levied on the value of land, irrespective of improvement. For that would make land speculation unprofitable, land monopoly impossible, and so open to the possessors of the power to labour the ability of converting it by exertion into wealth or purchasing power that the very idea of a man able to work, and yet suffering from want of the things that work produces, would seem as preposterous on earth as it must seem in heaven.

# PEACE BY STANDING ARMY

*Mr. Chairman and Fellow-Citizens:*

I come here to-night at considerable personal inconvenience, to discharge what I believe to be a duty. I come here to talk to you, as I have always talked, frankly and plainly. In some things I do not agree with the men who have invited me to come here. In some things I probably differ from the majority of this audience. I do not believe in strikes.[2] (Hisses and faint cheers.) I am not disposed to denounce George M. Pullman. (Prolonged hisses and groans.) I come here as a citizen, as a Democrat—(Slight applause, followed by hisses and groans, continuing for several minutes.)

—I come as a Democrat who, from his great tariff message in 1887, has earnestly and with all his strength and ability supported Grover Cleveland (more hisses and groans), to protest against his action.[3] (Great cheers.)

—I come here to say what no daily paper in New York City has dared to say—that the action of Grover Cleveland (hisses and cries of "Order!") in throwing the standing army, without call from local authority, into the struggle between the railroads and their workmen, was in violation of the fundamental principles of our Government, and dangerous to the Republic. Governor Altgeld (loud cheering) has spoken the true Democratic doctrine.[4] (Renewed hisses.) You men who are hissing the name of Democracy know no more about that doctrine than do the so-called Democrats who rule and rob this city. The Democracy that I am talking about, the Democracy to which I belong and as a representative of which I stand here, is not that Democracy; it is the Democracy of

*Speech at the labour meeting, Cooper Union, New York, July 12, 1894, called to protest against President Cleveland's sending Federal troops to Chicago during the great railroad strike. Contrary to the rule of omission followed in the preceding addresses, the interruptions of the audience are here inserted, as being needed to show the full nature of the speech.[1]*

Thomas Jefferson! It is not the false Democracy of to-day, but it is the true Democracy; the Democracy that believes in equal rights to all and special privilege to none; the Democracy that would crush monopolies under its foot. (Cheers.) It is not the Democracy which now rules, but the Democracy that I trust soon will. (Long cheers.)

I am not a lawyer. I have had no time to make a special study of the matter from a legal standpoint. I cannot say how far, if at all, the President has violated the written law of the land. But this I do say positively: he has violated that law more important than the written law; he has violated the fundamental principles of our polity. (Cheers.)

The doctrine that the Federal power should be slow to interfere in that in which it is not directly concerned is a foundation stone of our Republic. Governor Altgeld and Governor Waite are right.[5] (Cheers.) If the standing army is to be sent into the States of this nation as it has been sent into the State of Illinois and other States, if the Federal Executive of its own motion is to undertake to keep the peace between citizens throughout the land, what shall the end be? We shall need a standing army of hundreds of thousands of men. The moment this principle is acknowledged, there is an end to local self-government, the Republic dies, and in all but name and hereditary succession the Empire has come. It is the lesson of the history of the world—peace kept by a standing army is incompatible with a true republic. (Loud cheering.)

This is a time for every sober man who loves his country and wishes to see it exist in peace and plenty to redeem its promise and fulfil its high destiny, to enter his protest against this Presidential action, temperately, firmly, unequivocally. (Cheers.)

But it is said that the President's action has been to maintain law and order. Let that be granted. Does the end always justify the means? I yield to nobody in my respect for law and order and my hatred of disorder, but there is something more important even than law and order, and that is the principle of [L]iberty. I yield to nobody in my respect for the rights of property, yet I would rather see every locomotive in this land ditched, every car and every depot burned and every rail torn up, than to have them preserved by means of a Federal standing army. That is the order that reigned in Warsaw.[6] (Long applause.) That is the order in the keeping of which every democratic republic before ours has fallen. I love the American Republic better than I love such order. (Long cheering.)

What is the pretence that is made a justification for the action of the President? It is that the running of the mail trains of United States has been interfered with. Debs has been indicted and arrested, charged with conspiracy to interfere with the mails of the United States.[7] (Groans and hisses.) Is that charge a true or a fair one? (Shouts of "No!") I do not believe that there is an honest man to-day who will say that he believes in his heart that there is any basis for this charge. Debs from the first declared that he and those following him were anxious to carry the mail trains of the United States.

But the railroads used the United States mail as a tool to crush labour organisation. (Cheers.) The railroads were the real conspirators so far as conspiracy to interfere with the transportation of the mails is concerned. (Loud cheers.) They did not carry nor attempt to carry the mails on the regular mail trains as usual. If they had, Debs and his men would have seen to it that the mail cars went through. What they did do was to change the position of the mail cars, and to scatter the mails among all their trains, and demand then that all trains should be run through because there was mail matter on them. (Cries of "Shame!" and long hissing.)

The conspiracy was by the millionaire monopolists. They deliberately conspired to use the mails so as to call upon the Federal Government to send its troops to crush down their employees. (Cries of "That is right!")

Look at California, where this struggle has been fiercest. I know something of that State. Citizen of New York as I now am, yet the greater part of my life has been spent in California. The people of that State are an orderly and law-abiding people. Do you suppose that they would look easily upon any movement that contemplated an interference with the mail service, which means so much to them? I know that they would not. I have not been in California for years, yet to-night I would stake my life that the great majority of the people of that State are in sympathy with the employees as against the railroad monopolies. Can there be stronger proof that if law is on one side, justice and liberty are on the other side? When a law-loving people sympathise with violations of law, there must be injustice behind the law. (Applause.)

The masses of California hate the railroad power, and there is reason why they should. It has been the railroad power that has utterly demoralised California politics and debauched its public service. It is the railroad power that has given control of that great State into the hands of a few railroad magnates—such a control as no prince ever exercised over his principality.

I stood by when the first spadeful of earth was turned in Sacramento for the Pacific roads. The men who were then back of that enterprise were but moderately wealthy men—the richest of them worth perhaps $100,000. To-day those men, or those who have succeeded them, are multi-millionaires. How did they get their great fortunes? Not as C. P. Huntington says in a newspaper paragraph this evening—by industry and frugality. (Laughter.) They got those fortunes by robbery—by robbery that is worse than highway robbery because it has been coupled with the bribery of those whom the people elected to serve them in high office, even on the benches of their courts. (Cheers.)

These men have used what they got in trust from the Nation and the State, to corrupt the Government of Nation and State. They have bought their way from primary elections to the United States Senate; they have made the managers of both parties their henchmen, put their friends on the bench, controlled newspapers, and kept lawyers under fee to take no case against them; they have throttled enterprise and held the State in a bond of iron. Over and over the people of California have rebelled at the ballot only to find after election was over that the railroad was still in control. (Cheering.)

What is true of California is true of other Western States, and true in large degree all over the country. And this great corrupt power, not content with legislative control, has been looking forward to the use of the Federal courts and of the standing army. We have been building ships of war that are of no use unless for the purpose of furnishing some pleasant gentlemen with pleasure trips and of furnishing the Carnegies with money.[8] (Cheers and laughter.) We now have a standing army of 25,000 men, and there are demands that it shall be increased to 50,000 men. In the days when our Government was weaker, when we had hostile savages on our frontier lines, and had real fighting to do, we had an army of only 10,000 men and a navy in proportion.

What is the reason that we are building ships of war and increasing the size of our army? It is because the millionaire monopolists are becoming afraid of a poverty-stricken people which their oppressive trusts and combinations are creating. It is because great wealth, unjustly acquired, always wants the security of standing armies and navies. (Long cheering.)

I want to speak with the utmost respect of Mr. Cleveland. (Prolonged hissing and groaning.) No man has been given such high honour from the American people. They made him President once, and then after a four years lapse showed their confidence in him by making him President again, a compliment never paid to any man before. He has received higher honour from the American people than even did George Washington, Thomas Jefferson, Abraham Lincoln, or Ulysses S. Grant.

(A voice, "Why did you support him?")

Why I supported him—why against politicians and powers he was elected—was because I believed, and the people believed, he had sounded the key-note against monopoly. I am slow to attribute to Mr. Cleveland anything but the best motives, but the facts are plain. Not only has he left undone that which he had asked the warrant and received the command of the people to do, but from the very first, I am sorry to say, he seems to have taken the side, wantonly taken the side, of those very monstrous monopolies that have oppressed the people and which they believed he would begin to break down. (Loud cheering.)

It is at least the fact that his Federal appointments in California have been such as the railroad magnates themselves would have dictated had they been allowed to dictate, and I am not so sure that they were not. To the most important Federal office in California Mr. Cleveland appointed a man who was denounced at a Democratic State Convention as a traitor to his party because he had sold out to the railroad companies. Mr. Cleveland did this in spite of the fact that these things were formally presented to him by representative men of California. (Hisses.) And his other California appointments, so far as I have learned, are of the same character.

With Democratic lawyers of national reputation to choose from, one of Mr. Cleveland's first steps was to take as his Attorney-General a corporation attorney, a man whom I, and I think most of you, never had heard of. I refer to Mr. Olney.[9] (Groans.)

It is from such capturing by great corporate interests of the legal machinery and law courts of the Federal Government that we get injunctions that look to the punishing of a man for not going to work when he did not choose to go to work, and I fear it is from the same power that the order comes which sends the standing army into States where the State authority has not asked for it, and even protests against its presence. (Groans.)

You have heard of the Senate sugar investigation, an investigation designed to do anything except to find out facts.[10] (Laughter.) When in Washington, before that investigation was ordered, or the newspaper charges which compelled it had been made, I was told by reliable authority that a Democratic United States [S]enator, who has been once, and if I mistake not, twice, Chairman of the National Democratic Executive Committee and consequently in a position to know, was declaring that the Sugar Trust interests must be taken care of in the tariff revision because it had contributed $200,000 to Mr. Cleveland's election. Whether the railroads made any such contributions I do not know. (Laughter and cries of "Certainly they did!" "Sure!" and "You bet!")

I said in beginning that I came here to say what our daily papers in New York dared not say. That is true as far as my knowledge goes. But it has only been true since last Saturday. On last Friday, the 6th, the greatest of our Democratic papers, the "New York World," came out in a long and ringing article denouncing the use by President Cleveland of the standing army. On Saturday it ate its words of the day before and applauded the President, and has continued to do so ever since. What brought about such a change? If telegrams could be dragged out as the telegrams of the strike managers have been, we might find out; but it certainly was not a change of heart, a change of conviction. It is ominous to find the entire press applauding action which violates so grossly American principles and American tradition; but it is even more ominous still, it seems to me, to see the ease with which a power that has bent courts and executive to its will can between sunrise and sunset wheel around a great paper–a paper that in so many things has stood as the exponent of true Democratic principles. (Great applause.)

But I must stop. (Cries of "No, no; go on!" from all parts of the hall.) I would, indeed, like to go on, but I have exceeded my time, and others are to follow. Still, something yet I must say, but I must be brief. The purpose of this meeting is not only to express opinion on the action of the President, but to consider the industrial situation.

Well, what are we going to do about it? (Cries of "Impeach Cleveland!" "We have the ballot!" "Let us have political action!")

There is no royal road to relief. It cannot be found in electing this man or that man, or in merely changing from this party to that party. Political action amounts to nothing unless it is the expression of thought, not impulse. This is a time which calls for our best and most sober thought. Consider what is proposed. On the one side there are calls for a general strike. Can anything be accomplished by a general strike? A strike unaccompanied by violence is simply a test of endurance–a trial of who can live longest when the exertion of labour is stopped. Now, as a matter of fact, who can live longest when the earnings of labour are stopped–the men who have wealth in store or the men who are dependent on their daily earnings for their daily bread? the rich man or the poor man? (Applause, and cries of "The rich!) Yes; the rich man every time." (Continued applause.)

Again, we are told that arbitration is the sovereign remedy–that we must have compulsory arbitration. This is as idle and more dangerous than the cry we used to hear for bureaus of labour statistics. Compulsory arbitration! That must mean, if it means anything, that behind the arbitrators there must be power to enforce their decree. Have you considered what compulsory arbitration means? Arbitrators must be appointed. In the long run who will get the arbitrators, the rich men or the poor men? (Cries of "The rich!" "The rich every time!") Yes; judging from experience, the rich. Are you willing, then, to submit your wrongs to arbitration? (Cries of "No!") To call for the establishment of courts which, if they amount to anything at all, are to have power to compel you to work when you do not want to work? ("No, no!" and applause.)

Then there is a third proposition. The "Morning Journal" of this city is the proposer. It concedes and declares the impolicy and weakness of strikes. It proposes instead of striking that the men in sympathy with the Pullman strikers should keep at work, save their money, and raise a fund which should enable every Pullman striker to leave Pullman! Well, supposing you did. Where are you to take them? (Laughter.) Is there a city, a town, a hamlet in this country where their trades are carried on, that there are not to-day three idle men in those trades for one at work? (Applause.) Suppose you did raise money to take these Pullman strikers out of Pullman, could anything better please Mr. Pullman? Poor as are the wages he pays, would he have any difficulty in filling his works were the strikers removed? (Applause.)

I speak of this proposition because it brings us to the heart of the labour question. Strikes, labour troubles, low wages, all the bitter injustice which the masses are feeling, come at bottom from the fact that there are more men seeking work than can find opportunities to work. (Applause and cries of "That is it!") Yet the country abounds in opportunities. Its natural resources are so great as to seem without limit. The trouble is that the natural resources have been monopolised. (Much applause.)

Let me tell you what I have told you many times before. It is something I must tell you, or I should be dishonest. This whole great organised labour movement is on a wrong line—a line on which no large and permanent success can possibly be won. Trades-unions, with their necessary weapon, the strike, have accomplished something and may accomplish something, but it is very little and at great cost. The necessary endeavour of the strike to induce or compel others to stop work is in its nature war, and furthermore it is war that must necessarily deny a fundamental principle of personal liberty—the right of every man to work when, where, for whom and for what he pleases. Those who denounce labour organisations and their works use this moral principle against you. Stated alone, it is their strength and your weakness. ("That is true!")

But above the wrongs which strikes involve, there is a deeper, wider wrong, which must be recognised and asserted if the labour movement is to obtain the moral strength that is its due. It is the great denial of liberty to work which provokes these small denials of liberty to work. It is the shutting up by monopolisation of the natural, God-given opportunities for work that compels men to struggle and fight for the opportunity to work, as though the very chance of employment were a prize and a boon. (Applause.)

The key to the labour question is the land question. The giant of monopolies is the monopoly of the land. That which no man made, that which the Almighty Father gives us, that which must be used in all production, that which is the first material essential to life itself, must be made free to all. In the single tax alone can labour find relief. (Great and long continued applause.)

# EDITOR'S NOTES

## PREFACE

1. The reader is encouraged to consult the appropriate pages in Henry George, Jr., *Henry George*, ed. Paul M. Gaston (1900; reprint, New York, Chelsea House, 1981) and Charles A. Barker, *Henry George* (New York: Robert Schalkenbach Foundation, 1992) for more detailed information and short synopses of *Our Land and Land Policy*.

2. Henry George, *The Science of Political Economy* (1898; reprint, Robert Schalkenbach Foundation, 1992), 163.

3. George, Jr., *Henry George*, 210.

4. Ibid., 219–20.

5. Henry George, Jr., "A Visit to Tolstoy," *The Public*, Nov. 26, 1909, 1145, Henry George School of Social Sciences, New York [hereafter cited as HGS]. This article was a reprint from *The New York World*, Nov. 14, 1909. For more details about Henry George and Leo Nikolaevich Tolstoy, see *An Anthology of Tolstoy's Spiritual Economics*, vol. 2 of *The Henry George Centennial Trilogy* published by the University of Rochester Press.

6. Tolstoy to Henry George, Jr., June 2, 1909, *Polnoe sobranie sochinenii* [Complete works] (Moscow: Gosudarstvennoe izdatel'stvo khudozhestvennoi literatury, 1928–64), 79:214.

7. Henry George, Jr., "Tolstoy in the Twilight," *Land Values*, March 1910, 208 and 210, HGS. Bracketed passages added from "Tolstoy's Latest Word on George," in *The Public*, July 23, 1909, 714, HGS. The entire text of this letter is found in *Polnoe sobranie sochinenii*, 38:70–71.

8. Since the early nineteenth century members of the intelligentsia had waged war with the tsarist government either for liberal reforms, radical changes, or a complete transformation of society–the Bolshevik coup d'état was the result.

9. Here Tolstoy is referring to the land reforms of Prime Minister Peter A. Stolypin (1862–1911), who sought to convert communal landholdings into privatized individual parcels.

10. To be more precise, the Russian Orthodox Church, which is an independent part of the Orthodox Eastern Church. "Greek Church" is a term used in the West to refer collectively to the latter.

11. Sergei D. Nikolaev (1861–1920) translated these Georgist works (with dates of publication): *Progress and Poverty* (1896), *A Perplexed Philosopher* (1902), *Protection or Free Trade* (1903), *The Land Question* (1907), and *Social Problems* (1907), as well as many articles and speeches.

## OUR LAND AND LAND POLICY

### *I. The Lands of the United States*

1. Henry George was thirty-one years old and living in San Francisco when he began writing *Our Land and Land Policy* on March 26, 1871. He finished it four months later on July 29. Originally it was titled *Our Land and Land Policy, National and State* and was published as a forty-eight-page pamphlet selling for twenty-five cents.
2. If only George could have foreseen the potential of Alaska! Known as Seward's Folly, it was purchased in 1867 for $7,200,000 and became a state in 1959.
3. E. T. Peters was a Treasury official, economist, and statistician. William M. Stewart (1827–1909) was a lawyer and senator from Nevada who wrote the fifteenth amendment to the Constitution (1870), which guaranteed the right to vote for any man irrespective of background.
4. In fact the population for 1900 was 75,994,575 with a 20.7 percent increase from the previous census of 1890, and for 1920 it was 105,710,620 with a corresponding 14.9 percent increase.
5. "Government" refers to the federal government.
6. The Dakota Territory was organized in 1861, and in 1889 North Dakota and South Dakota were admitted as states.
7. In France, the farmers-general were men appointed by the king (originally in 1681). They received a lease to collect certain revenues. These posts were much sought after because they were quite lucrative since these tax collectors only had to pay the state a fixed amount of money. There was much corruption in this system.
8. The Homestead Laws: a collective designation for a series of laws to enable American citizens to acquire land. The Homestead Act was passed by Congress in 1862. It gave, for a nominal fee, up to a quarter section (160 acres) of unoccupied government land to anyone over twenty-one who would reside on it for five years.
9. Congress passed the Morrill Land-Grant College Act in 1862. This bill provided thirty thousand acres of federal land to the states (for each representative and senator it had in Congress) to induce them to finance the establishment of coeducational agricultural colleges. Sixty-nine land-grant colleges were established

for the promotion of research and more advanced agricultural methods. Justin S. Morrill (1810–98) was a Republican representative and senator from Vermont.

10. For the Act of 1866, see endnote 8 on page 236.

11. The federal government granted 131 million acres and the states 49 million acres (equivalent to the size of Texas!) to the railroads to foster their construction, and to stimulate the economy and the settlement of the West. With the laying of about 240,000 miles of rail between 1865 and 1910, the railroads greatly contributed to the creation of a national market.

12. In the Hebrew Bible, Esau, the son of Isaac, was fooled out of his inheritance by his twin and rival Jacob. See Gen. 25:23. The story of these two is purportedly reflected in the history of the Edomites (represented by Esau) and the Israelites (represented by Jacob).

13. Joshua was the successor of Moses who led the Hebrews into the Promised Land and divided it among the tribes.

14. The Washington Territory was organized in 1853 and admitted as a state in 1889.

## II. The Lands of California

15. "Department" possibly refers to the General Land Office mentioned in the first paragraph of this essay.

16. "Color" is used here in the legal sense meaning an apparent or prima-facie right or basis.

17. A "league" can range between 2.4 and 4.6 statute miles.

18. "Commission" is probably a reference to the United States Commission.

19. Mariposa was a boom town in the "Mother Lode" during the gold rush of 1848. The Mariposa region was claimed by Fremont. See next endnote.

20. John C. Fremont (1813–90), known as the Pathfinder, was an explorer and soldier who was prominent in the taking of California from Mexico. He became a governor and later senator of this state and was the unsuccessful Republican candidate for the presidency, losing to Buchanan in 1856. He was also governor of the Arizona Territory from 1878 to 1882.

21. During the late 1860s and early 1870s, W. S. Chapman was the most rapacious land speculator. He amassed more than a million acres, but later lost his fortune in a canal project.

   "Sioux warrant" is probably an expression referring to a specious land-grant claim, since Indian rights were looked upon as a joke. This attitude is but a small part of the sad story of Indians forced to leave their native grounds for more restricted areas.

22. James Stuart was a noted criminal condemned to death and hanged in 1851 by "The Committee of Vigilance of San Francisco."

23. Thomas A. Scott (1824–1881) was the assistant secretary of war under Lincoln and organized the railroad system during the Civil War. Later on, he was president of the Pennsylvania Railroad and other lines.

24. A "quitclaim deed" is the release, relinquishment, or transfer of one's right, title, or interest, such as in a parcel of land, without any guarantee or warranty.

25. A "pueblo" is the communal house or group of houses built of adobe or stone by certain southwestern Indian tribes, or in this use of the Spanish term, a town or village.

26. A "vaquero" is a cowboy.

27. The "evil" is a reference to Leland Stanford (1824–1893), Collis P. Huntington (1821–1900), and other railroad barons in the West who engaged in a number of unethical dealings to enrich themselves.

28. "Placer" is a superficial alluvial or glacial deposit containing valuable minerals, as distinguished from a lode.

29. A "greenback" was a legal tender note first printed by the U.S. government in 1862 (usually in green on the back) and was issued against the credit of the country rather than against gold or silver on deposit. With the hard times after the Panic of 1873 a hot debate ensued over the increase of its issuance contracted during previous times of higher prices. The Greenback Party favored this expansion in order to wipe out farm debts, stop declining farm prices, and foster general prosperity. Greenbacks became legally redeemable in specie and a permanent part of the currency in 1879.

30. James W. Nye (1814–76) was territorial governor of Nevada from 1861 to 1864 and Republican senator from 1864 to 1873.

31. California was admitted as the thirty-first state in 1850.

32. It is possible that a "Green [L]aw" is legislation named after William S. Green, a newspaper editor, who is mentioned on page 43.

33. Henry H. Haight (1825–1878) was the Democratic governor from 1868 to 1872.

34. John A. Sutter (1803–80), born in Germany of Swiss parents, made his way west as a trader. He received a land grant of 49,000 acres from Mexico and became a citizen of Mexico and an official for its government. He aided the U.S. in the seizure of California and welcomed settlers, but with the discovery of gold in 1848 a flood of prospectors came. Some of them successfully challenged the validity of his ownership of the lands up to the Supreme Court. Within five years of the discovery, $285,000,000 in gold was produced, twenty-one times more than the value of the entire previous amount in the U.S.

35. Aaron S. Sargent (1827–1887) was a congressman (1861–1863 and 1869–1873) and Republican senator from California (1873–1879) who was quite amenable to railroad interests. He was the author of the first Pacific railroad bill passed by Congress.

36. "Grain King" was a derisive and generic name for the monopolistic control of different aspects of farming and the grain market. The American farmer was vulnerable to economic problems since he primarily relied on a single cash crop and became more susceptible to international market fluctuations. Because of the opening up of farmlands in other countries the value of crops dwindled and tenancy and indebtedness increased by 1900. He was thus beholden to financiers. In addition, many articles and equipment he needed were controlled by trusts (such as McCormick Harvester). There were also conglomerates that controlled grain storage, monopolistic railroads that transported the farm products, and myriads of middlemen. No wonder there was discontent and insurgency in the countryside in the nineteenth century.

37. More than 300,000 Chinese came to the U.S. between 1849 and 1880. Initially attracted by the "gold rush" of 1848, most of them settled on the West Coast. Because of their racial and cultural differences and willingness to work for less pay, much disdain and resentment was created. Since they desired to earn money to help their families back home or to return and buy farms it was also thought that they would drain money away from the U.S. Henry George was among these Americans who shared this anti-Chinese sentiment.

## III. Land and Labor

38. The law of diminishing returns states that when any factor in production, such as capital or labor, is increased the output per unit factor will decrease beyond a certain point.

39. The English slave trade was abolished in 1807 and slavery in the British West Indies in 1833.

40. Royal and parliamentary commissions were methods used in Great Britain to investigate various abuses and problems, and to suggest methods of amelioration including the passage of laws. George's *Progress and Poverty* (1879) had an enormous impact there in the 1880s. His influence helped undermine the doctrine of laissez-faire and his insistence that poverty is manmade and could be eradicated helped foster social action.

41. Simon Legree was the cruel slaveowner in Harriet B. Stowe's (1811–1896) *Uncle Tom's Cabin; or, Life among the Lowly,* which first appeared serially in 1851. This novel was immensely popular and influential.

42. "Fee" (or feu) has a number of definitions: a) an estate or territory held by a feudal lord on condition of service; b) full ownership in land; c) an inherited estate of land limited to a class of heirs (fee tail), or in this usage (fee simple), without limitation to any particular class of heirs.

## IV. The Tendency of Our Present Land Policy

43. Thomas Carlyle (1795–1881), was an eminent British author, critic, historian, and translator.

44. In England (beginning in the 1100s and reaching its height in the late seventeenth century), enclosure was the growing practice of fencing off lands formerly considered to be under common rights. This activity was part of the shift from the feudal system to free cultivation, and caused a population shift of the poor from the countryside to the cities. It did foster more efficient husbandry, stock raising, and agricultural methods.

45. The Industrial Revolution primarily refers to the years 1750 to 1850 in English history. Great changes in the economic and then political and social structures transpired, resulting from a transition from a predominantly agricultural (rural) to an industrial (urban) base. This change was fostered by new inventions in manufacturing, communications, and transportation. The Industrial Revolution in the U.S. took off after the Civil War with much the same patterns of change, although these elements appeared earlier.

46. James Watt (1736–1819) was the Scottish inventor who in 1769 improved on Newcomen's steam engine. George Stephenson (1781–1848) was the English inventor of the steam locomotive in 1815; however, it was his *Rocket* constructed in 1829 which made railroading feasible.

## V. What Our Present Land Policy Should Be

47. A much older definition of "usury" equates the term with any interest charged for the use of money, but today, as in George's time, it refers to exorbitant interest, or interest beyond the legal rate.

48. Henry VIII (1491–1547) was famous for his six wives, his antipapal policy, and the establishment of the Anglican Church.

49. George's first mention of the idea of the single tax without using the term. Thomas G. Shearman (1834–1900), who was a well-known lawyer and friend of George, coined the term "single tax" in 1887.

50. John Stuart Mill (1806–1873) was a proponent of utilitarianism. It is a system of ethics that claims that good actions are morally right and justified if they produce the greatest happiness and utility for the greatest number of people. Happiness can therefore be measured in economic terms. Liberalism developed among the commercial and industrial classes in their struggle with the monarchy, the church, and feudal landowners. It sought (albeit more restrictively than now) greater freedoms, representative government, and state protection of the individual. Economically it was associated with laissez-faire and international free trade.

51. The Slough of Despond and Pilgrim are references to John Bunyan's (1628–1688) *The Pilgrim Progress from This World to That Which Is to Come.* The first part was published in 1678 and the second part in 1684. The Slough of Despond (a place of doubt and fear for the sinner who has awakened to his condition) represents one of the numerous travails the protagonist Christian must travel to reach the Celestial City.

52. Catherine II, frequently called Catherine the Great (1729–96), who ruled from 1762 until her death, was quite generous in giving serfs away to her favorites. Despite espousal of enlightened thought, serfdom reached its height during her reign and her policies aggravated unrest in the countryside, most notably Pugachev's rebellion in 1773, which was ruthlessly suppressed.

It was Pope Alexander VI who issued a number of bulls dividing the discoveries of the New World in half between Spain and Portugal. The Treaty of Tordisillas in 1494 negotiated between Spain and Portugal themselves, however, finalized the demarcation. The former received all possessions west of and the latter east of a line from north to south 360 leagues west of the Cape Verde Islands. It was not confirmed by the papacy until 1506.

53. In Greek mythology the sphinx was a winged lion with a woman's head who asked all passing travelers a riddle ("What is it which has four feet in the morning, two at noon, and three at night?) and killed all who failed to do so. It was Oedipus who solved it ("Man") and then the sphinx threw herself over a cliff. This story is presented in Sophocles' *Oedipus Rex.*

54. Reformers tried to ameliorate the condition of children in Great Britain as early as 1802. Succeeding legislation passed Parliament in 1819, 1825, 1833, 1844, and 1878. At first these laws were ineffective but they were gradually broadened and strengthened. Some provisions included factory inspection, shorter hours, and the raising of the working age. The first effective law was passed in 1878.

55. The First International (International Workingmen's Association) was established in London in 1864 by Karl Marx (1818–1883) and, due to much internal disunity, primarily from Michael Bakunin (1814–1876), it dissolved in New York in 1874.

56. Thomas Babington Macaulay (1800–59) was a noted English historian, author, poet, and Whig parliamentarian. His most famous work was *The History of England from the Accession of James the Second.* Edward Gibbon (1737–1794) was the English historian who wrote the monumental *Decline and Fall of the Roman Empire,* which appeared in six volumes between 1776 and 1783.

Attila (ca. 433–53), king of the Huns, known as the Scourge of God, invaded Italy in 452. Legend has it that he abandoned the taking of Rome when Pope Leo I pleaded for the city, but it was probably due to a lack of supplies. Genseric (ca.390–477), king of the Vandals, invaded North Africa and took Carthage in 439, and then sacked Rome in 455.

57. For "northern possessions," see endnote no. 6 on page 236. The "great river" is probably a reference to the Yukon River.

58. Rome was purportedly founded in 753 B.C. by Romulus. Henry II (1133–89) was the first Plantagenet who ruled England from 1154 until his death. The "Bastard" refers to the Norman William I (ca.1027–87), known as William the Conqueror, who reigned in England from 1066 (Battle of Hastings).

59. Augustus (63 B.C.–14 A.D.), originally named Gaius Octavius, became the first emperor of Rome in 31 B.C. It was during his reign that Rome reached her apex of glory. He imposed the Pax Romana on "the known world." Rome experienced the longest period of relative peace and prosperity during the reigns of Trajan, Hadrian, Antoninus Pius, and Marcus Aurelius between 98 and 180 A.D. The last three named were the Antonines.

60. The words "Great estates ruined Italy!" were written by Pliny the Elder (ca. 23–79 A.D.) in his great encyclopedia of thirty-seven books titled *Historia Naturalis* (17:7). The first ten books were published in 77 A.D. and the remainder posthumously.

61. Cincinnatus (5th c. B.C.) was a semi-legendary Roman hero who left his farm to become dictator during a successful war against the Aequi and the Volsci in 458 B.C. Immediately thereafter he returned to his work on the soil. Marcus Atilius Regulus (d. 250 B.C.) was a Roman general during the First Punic War who inflicted staggering initial successes against the Carthaginians but was defeated and captured in 255 B.C. He was released on parole and was sent to Rome with a Carthaginian delegation to plead for peace but urged the senate to wage war. Thereafter he returned to Carthage even though he could have escaped, but endured death by torture. He became a national hero, but some scholars believe this story was fabricated as propaganda to justify Roman actions.

## THE STUDY OF POLITICAL ECONOMY

1. In this speech George rails against the classical economists for not keeping up with the times. Political economy, "the dismal science," can not only be understandable but should be a tool for the improvement of the laboring man rather than his enemy. He also calls for a change in people's economic thinking, for: "Where wealth most abounds, there poverty is deepest; where luxury is most profuse, the gauntest want jostles it." This theme permeates *Progress and Poverty*.

2. The quote, "No, I cannot play the fiddle. . . ." was declared by Themistocles (ca. 525–ca. 460 B.C.). He was an Athenian statesman who persuaded his people to build a navy to fight the Persians (King Xerxes I). The navy defeated them at Salamis in 480 B.C. By this means a strong city-state was forged. He died in exile. The fiddle George refers to was a lyre.

3. Adam Smith (1723–90) was the noted Scottish economist who had a tremendous impact on later economic theory, primarily from his work *An Inquiry into the Nature and Causes of the Wealth of Nations*, published in 1776.

David Ricardo (1772–1823) was an English economist. His theory of rent stipulates that the interests of those who own land were opposed to those of society, since the proprietor wanted a continuous increase in population so that the land of poorer quality would have to be brought into use. The landowner does not produce rent but merely takes it. This argument formed part of the basis of George's land-value taxation. Ricardo also propounded the theory that wages cannot rise above the minimal level of subsistence. The value and not the price of goods is the gauge by how much labor was put into their production. His *Principles of Political Economy and Taxation* of 1817 was quite influential.

4. In Australia, "pocket-nerve" is the fear of reaching for one's wallet.

5. Ephesus was a major port on the west coast of Asia Minor and in which was situated the temple of Artemis (Diana), known as the Artemisian, one of the Seven Wonders of the World. This asylum and site of pilgrimage, built ca. 550 B.C., was burned down a number of times and finally destroyed in 262 A.D.

6. "An idea of political economy" and the ensuing passage refer to Social Darwinism linked with laissez-faire.

7. In Genesis 8, 9, and 10 of the Hebrew Bible, Ham was the second of Noah's three sons who repopulated the earth through his four sons after the flood. It is here that some people believe that racial distinctions began.

8. For Mill, see endnote 50 on page 240.

9. Herod the Great (ca. 73–4 B.C.) was the founder of the dynasty that ruled Palestine, or parts of it, under Roman suzerainty beginning in 37 B.C. and lasted to about 100 A.D. Although he gave Palestine a period of relative peace his internal policies were ruthless and punctuated by violence. St. Vincent de Paul (ca. 1581–1660), an escaped galley slave who was captured by corsairs, was the founder of the Lazarist missionary order and the Sisters of Charity. He devoted his life to works of charity. He was canonized in 1737.

10. A reference to George's youth; he grew up in Philadelphia.

11. The Tierra del Fuego (Land of Fire) is an archipelago and the southernmost part of South America with an extremely harsh climate. The Indians were quite poor and their lifestyle was primitive, as it was difficult to eke out a living.

## THE AMERICAN REPUBLIC: ITS DANGER AND POSSIBILITIES

1. George was chosen as the main orator for this major San Franciscan event. Henry George, Jr., considers this speech along with the previous lecture as warm-ups for *Progress and Poverty*. Part of it became the famed "Ode to Liberty"

in the concluding section of *Progress and Poverty*, which he was to begin in two months. He warns people that the extremes between poor and rich and avariciousness perpetuate slavery and will destroy the United States. It is America's mission, George declares, to renew the world for a reassertion of the rights and liberties of man in a worldwide federation.

2. Reconstruction was the name given to the years after the Civil War and to the policy by which the federal government imposed certain restrictive conditions on the former Confederate states. The South was divided into five military districts and many governments were controlled by Northerners known as carpetbaggers and their Southern allies were referred to as scalawags. Many areas suffered from a breakdown of authority and a growth in crime.

Francis Marion (ca. 1732–95), known as the Swamp Fox, was a guerrilla leader in South Carolina during the War of Independence. The noted American naval commander John Paul Jones was born in Scotland in 1747 and died in 1792. Marie Joseph Paul Yves Roch Gilbert du Motier, Marquis de Lafayette (1757–1834) served as a major general in the Continental Army and was also active in the French Revolution and the July Revolution of 1830. He was a staunch advocate of democratic principles.

3. John Adams (1735–1826) served in both Continental Congresses, signed the Declaration of Independence, was vice-president under Washington, and the second president from 1797 to 1801. Thomas Jefferson (1743–1826) was the author of the Declaration of Independence, was secretary of state under Washington, and was the third president from 1801 to 1809. John Rutledge (1739–1800) was a member of both Continental Congresses and associate justice of the Supreme Court from 1789 to 1791. The Livingstons were a prominent family who contributed a number of distinguished men to the War of Independence and the early Republic. The reference is probably to Robert Livingston (1746–1813), who was a member of both Continental Congresses, helped draw up the Declaration of Independence, and held a number of prestigious posts thereafter.

4. "Eternal vigilance is the pirce of liberty" is attributed to Thomas Jefferson; however, it was written by John P. Curran (1750–1817) in a speech given in 1790.

5. The "syrens" (sirens) refers to one of the travails of Ulysses who had himself tied to the mast while his crew plugged their ears to row by these dangerous women who could lure men into a shipwreck on a rocky coast with their enchanted voices.

6. Originally the Senate was a council of patricians who advised the Roman monarch, then over time it became the main ruling body and held broad legislative, administrative, and diplomatic powers under the Roman Republic. Under the empire it maintained high prestige, for it held the theoretical formal

basis of power for the emperors and was also a consultative body. It gradually lost its independence, declined in power, and became subordinated to the ruler.

7. Prior to the adoption of divine right by Western monarchs, it is possible that Germanic tribes had elected their kings. Tribal chieftains had exercised little power during times of peace, for affairs were decided by a vote of all free men. In time of war, however, royal authority was invested in this leader.

8. Caligula ("little boots," 12–41 A.D.) was the nickname of Caius Caesar Germanicus. He was the emperor of the Roman Empire from 37 A.D. until his death. Known for his aberrant behavior, cruelty, and harsh rule, he was assassinated. Nero (Claudius Caesar, 37–68 A.D.) ruled Rome for the last fourteen years of his life. He was also known for his cruelty, brutality, and use of murder. He blamed the burning of Rome (64 A.D.) on the Christians, which led to their first persecution.

9. The Praetorians were bodyguards to the Roman emperors, who, after time, became corrupt and amassed such power that they could depose and enthrone them.

10. The French Academy was founded in 1635 by Cardinal Richilieu (1585-1642) to govern literature, grammar, rhetoric, and orthography with a mandate to award prizes. Its members are known as the Forty Immortals. It is one of the five academies comprising the French Institute.

Solon (ca. 639– ca. 559 B.C.) was called upon as *archon* (chief magistrate) of Athens in 594 B.C. to alter the growing oppressive conditions created by a strong oligarchy and a debt-ridden society. He cancelled debts and mortgages, limited land accumulation, reformed the monetary standard, promulgated constitutional reforms based on class structure, and created a new series of moderate laws and other regulations touching on all aspects of life.

11. "Rack rent" has two definitions: Rent equal to or nearly equal to the full annual rent of a property or, in this instance, the practice of exacting the highest possible rent.

12. The "crime that filled Italy" refers to the breakdown of individual Roman land-holdings and the development of large estates known as *latifundias* on which labored people in slave-like circumstances in return for protection.

13. The first lines are a reference to industrialization; see endnote no. 45 on page 240.

14. In Europe during the Middle Ages, feudalism, a system based on agricultural uses of the land and mutual obligations in a hierarchal society of vassalage, was sanctioned by the Western Christian Church. So ingrained was this way of life, and given the Christian world view, it seemed that the celestial spheres, the saints, the universe, and the trinity would be organized in the same manner.

15. Richard Neville, the earl of Warwick and Salisbury (1428–71), was known as the Kingmaker. A successful leader for the Yorkists during the War of the Roses, he was virtual ruler of England from 1461 to 1464 during the first years of Edward IV's reign. Displeased with this monarch's rule, he bolted and then supported Henry VI, and again amassed power. But Edward returned and defeated him in 1471.

16. The Magna Carta (1215) issued by King John (1167?–1216) after his loss at Runnymede ensured feudal rights for the aristocracy and protection from encroachment of their privileges and royal arbitrariness. There were other provisions regarding assessment without consent, the rights of churches, towns, and other subjects. It has been considered a starting point of the supremacy of the British constitution over the monarch with due process of law, and hence the beginnings of democracy.

17. A "muniment" is evidence or a document (title, deed, or charter) which maintains or defends a claim to rights, privileges, or an estate.

18. Stephen Langton (ca. 1150–ca. 1228) was cardinal and archbishop of Canterbury. He was an advocate of baronial rights in the aristocratic feud with King John and a signed witness to the Magna Carta. John Hampden (1594–1643) was part of the antiroyalist faction in the House of Commons who opposed the raising of loans by Charles I without parliamentary sanction and monarchical usurpation of this body's prerogatives. When this king tried to arrest him and others the Great Rebellion began in 1642. Hampden died in battle against the royalists. Wat Tyler (d. 1381) was an English rebel leader of a popular movement protesting fixed wages and increased taxes. Although Richard II promised him concessions, Tyler was murdered by the mayor of London. The Mad Priest of Kent could possibly be Father James Quigley, who was arrested in Kent and executed in 1798 for treasonous activity.

19. A "villein" has three definitions: 1) A free peasant villager lower in rank than a thane; 2) a free peasant lower than a sokeman but higher than a cotter, and 3) an unfree peasant who in respect to his lord is a slave, but legally free in relation to others. George is probably using the third definition.

20. Charles III (879–929) of France, known as Charles the Simple, ceded Normandy in 911. Eleven years later his subjects rebelled and he was then deposed and imprisoned by a group of nobles.

22. References to the following fallen states: the Great Sphinx of Gizeh in Egypt; Nineveh was the royal capital of the Assyrian Kingdom; Persepolis was the capital of the Persian Empire; the advanced pre-Columbian civilization of the Mayas in the Yucatan; and Carthage, which was destroyed by the Romans in 146 B.C.

23. A Queen Anne musket was a military issue during the reign of the last Stuart Queen Anne (1702–14) to the British army. It was similar to a flintlock and

featured a dog-latch mechanism as a safety. Various pistols of the time also bore her name.

24. In the Hebrew Bible Saul was the first king of the Jews (ca. 1025 B.C.). Although heroic in warfare, as a king he was less successful, especially in terms of his relations with David. He lost his life in battle with the Philistines.

25. By the mid-13th century B.C. the Phoenicians had settled on the east coast of the Mediterranean and established themselves as sailors, traders, and craftsmen. They were organized into city-states and founded colonies, most notably Carthage. Their most important legacy was the alphabet. "Great King" is a reference to the Persian King Darius I (549–485? B.C.), who led two unsuccessful expeditions against the Greek city-states. "Augustus wept his legions" is a reference to the defeat of Augustus's (63 B.C.–14 A.D.) Roman legions commanded by Varus by the German tribes under Arminus in 9 A.D.

26. "A new world unveiled": With the disintegration of imperial authority in western Europe and no powerful feudal noblility in the Holy Roman Empire, there arose a number of states in northern Italy which developed from the territorial expansion of wealthy towns beginning in the mid-thirteenth century. By the fifteenth century a new class of nobility or oligarchy wielded power based on aggressive commercial, banking, and trade activity. In this atmosphere of growing wealth, although punctuated by violence, the Renaissance came into being.

27. Crecy (1346) was a major victory for the English over the French during the Hundred Years War. The English longbow was the major factor. Agincourt (1415) was also another battle between the victorious English and the French. Tudors refers to the autocratic Henry VII (1457–1509), his son, the despotic, but well-loved Henry VIII (1491–1547), his granddaughter Mary I (1516–58), who was called Bloody Mary because of the religious persecutions during her reign, and the other granddaughter, the imperious Elizabeth I (1533–1603). The Tudors ruled England from 1485 to 1603 and were characterized as opportunistic, cunning, and brutal but practical.

"Crowned tyrant": Charles I (1600–49) was the Stuart king of England whose Catholic sympathies and bitter struggle with Parliament led to the Puritan Revolution. He was convicted of treason and beheaded by Cromwell's government.

The Golden Age of Spain was in the sixteenth century under three Habsburgs who ruled as Holy Roman Emperors: Charles V (1516–56), Philip II (1556–98), and Philip III (1598–1621). Its possessions stretched around the globe and made Spain the most powerful and richest European power. The seeds of decline, due to the exhaustion of mines, costly foreign adventures, and agricultural problems, among others, had already begun during this period.

The reference to seventeeth-century tyranny in France is to Louis XIV (1638–1715). The Sun King was the consummate absolute monarch who broke the power of the nobility, waged incessant wars, persecuted the Huguenots, and built Versailles.

28. The "crazy king" was George III (1738–1820) who had his first bout of dementia in 1765. His condition became progressively worse, and he went insane in 1811. His ministers were known for their severity. The Reform Bill of 1832 eliminated fifty-six "rotten boroughs," which were sparsely populated parliamentary districts.

29. "Citizen whom we have twice deemed worthy" refers to Ulysses S. Grant (1822–85) who was elected to the presidency twice (1868 and 1872).

30. William Pitt (1708–78), the elder, was the earl of Chatham. His eloquence and popularity earned him the nickname "the Great Commoner," for he was a champion of constitutional liberties. He was secretary of state in the cabinet and advocated reconciliation with the American colonies but did not favor their independence. Pitt sought a peaceful solution to the subsequent rebellion, which broke out in 1776.

31. The Place Vendôme is located in Paris. A column made from the melted bronze of 1,200 cannons captured by Napoleon in 1805 at the Battle of Austerlitz was erected there. The defeat of the Prussians at the Battle of Valmy in 1792 was an important boost for the French Revolutionary forces.

32. "Those who dream of bringing back the middle ages" refers to the Romantics who looked to a golden past as a source of inspiration and to the radicals who looked to a golden future through revolution. In 1861, Victor Emmanuel II (1820–1878) was proclaimed the king of a united Italy and nine years later the papal states were annexed. In 1871, William I (1797-1888) of Prussia was declared Emperor of Germany at the end of the Franco-Prussian War. "Russia moves" refers either to the more liberal reforms of Tsar Alexander II, who reigned from 1855 to 1881 and who freed the serfs in 1861, or to the radical intelligentsia who desired more radical policies. Most likely it refers to the former.

## THE CRIME OF POVERTY

1. Henry George rails against the cause of poverty-land monopoly, for the earth lies at the basis of all social questions and the unjust distribution of wealth which he claims it creates. There should be an equitable use of Nature's resources. No man should want, since there is abundance for all.

2. Ira D. Sankey (1840–1908) was an evangelist engaged in revival work who compiled and composed devotional music.

3. Henry Hallam (1777–1859) was an English historian. Although he wrote with a Whig bias, he was noted for accurate research and he opened new doors of historical inquiry. Thorold Rogers (1823–90) was a historian and economist who

taught at Oxford. Two of his works were *Six Centuries of Work and Wages* and *History of Agriculture and Prices.*

4. The first eight-hour day established by law in the United States was for railroadmen in 1916 under threat of a general strike. By the end of World War I the eight-hour day became common practice in most industries as a result of collective bargaining between labor unions and employers, not by legislation in both the U.S. and Great Britain.

5. Child labor was widespread during the Industrial Revolution. Children aged five and up were compelled to work up to sixteen hours a day. The first legislation to limit child labor in the United States appeared in 1813, but it was not until the first decade of the twentieth century that a number of states enacted legal measures that led to sharp reductions in the number of children employed. It was not until 1916 and later in 1933 that federal laws mandated the minimum age of employment, but both were ruled unconstitutional in 1918 and 1935, respectively, by the Supreme Court. There was also a failed Constitutional amendment passed by both houses of Congress in 1924. Subsequent federal and state laws have been passed.

6. For the enclosure movement, see endnote no. 44 on page 240.

7. It was not an uncommon practice for parents, especially those in straitened circumstances, to take out insurance on their children with themselves as beneficiaries and then report their deaths, many times, according to authorities, "under suspicious circumstances."

8. Daniel DeFoe (1660–1731) was an English author most famous for *The Life and Adventures of Robinson Crusoe,* published in 1719. He was a political pamphleteer who at times was blessed with royal support but was also jailed and pilloried for his dissent against the High Church.

9. "God set manna down" refers to Exodus 16:14–36 in the Hebrew Bible.

10. Hugh Miller was a self-educated Scottish geologist, stone mason, and bank accountant. Thomas Chalmers (1780–1847) was a theologian, professor of moral philosophy, and a popular preacher known for his social work. He led a group of prelates in a secession from the Scottish Church, which became the Free Church of Scotland and declared an independent position from civil authority in spiritual matters.

11. James II (1633–1701), who reigned England from 1685 to 1688, was an unpopular ruler because of his severe methods and his Catholicism (especially regarded negatively when his son was born). His issuing of the Declaration of Indulgence in 1687, allowing for liberty of conscience, also antagonized the Established Church. He fled to France after his army deserted him, and he unsuccessfully tried to regain the throne.

12. Peter Stuyvesant (1592–1672) was the Dutch governor of New Netherland from 1647 until he surrendered this colony to the English in 1664. George is probably referring to one of his descendants.

13. James Lick (1796–1876) was an industrialist and philanthropist who donated funds to the University of California for the building of an observatory completed in 1888.

14. Ground was broken for Philadelphia's city hall in 1871. It was occupied in 1881 and officially completed in 1901.

## LAND AND TAXATION: A CONVERSATION BETWEEN DAVID DUDLEY FIELD AND HENRY GEORGE

1. David Dudley Field (1805–94) was an eminent American law reformer whose ideas pertaining to criminal law and civil law procedures were adopted by many states and England. He was also influential in international law, especially with the arbitration of war. By this time the famous forty-eight-year-old George, now living in New York and writing *Protection or Free Trade*, was able to arouse public opinion and attract attention from noteworthy people. Here the jurist debates George on the single tax and its benefits.

2. "The Democratic Party of the last generation": The Jeffersonian Republicans, often perceived as forerunners of the Democrats, had opposed the growth of federal power. Later Jeffersonians became relatively friendly to the federal government on such issues as a national bank and internal improvements. The Democratic Party that achieved formal structure under the leadership of Jackson was hostile to both a national bank and a protective tariff. Although it would use military and diplomatic powers to extend territory, they opposed federal restrictions on slavery in these new areas. In the years after the Civil War the Democrats resisted the extensive imposition of federal power over the conquered Confederacy and the party continued to advocate free trade even into the twentieth century.

## "THOU SHALT NOT STEAL"

1. Henry George had lost his first mayoral bid the previous year but this defeat did not slow down the social reformer. The Anti-Poverty Society was beginning to form as early as March 1887, and this speech was presented one week after its first public meeting. George was an important contributor to this group, which only lasted for one year. Both George and Edward McGlynn (see subsequent endnote) brought thousands to tears with the language of hope. George speaks about God's bounty: since there is enough for all people there should be no

poverty; the root cause of our evils is that we do not do unto others as we expect them to do unto us, especially by the denial of access to the soil. He extols the right of property as a product of labor, but this right does not apply to God's creation–the land.

2. Reverend Edward McGlynn (1837–1900), an eloquent orator who was the president of the Anti-Poverty Society and one of George's most ardent disciples. Later on, their political views grew apart, which led to a break in their relations. The excommunication of McGlynn became a cause célèbre. The struggle between this priest and Archbishop Corrigan of New York was a watershed in the development of the Roman Catholic Church in the United States and in the world. It represented two distinct viewpoints (free speech, civil and political freedom, and social justice versus hierarchal control) fighting for ascendancy. It also signifies the concern of the Vatican over the Georgist assault on private property in land. Some scholars regard Leo XIII's *Rerum Novarum* of 1891 as a direct attack on his political economy. (George also suspected this.)

3. Giuseppe Mazzini (1805–72) was a freedom fighter instrumental in the Italian unification *(Risorgimento)* and a writer known for revolutionary political idealism.

4. John J. Astor (1763–1848) was born in Germany but made a fortune in the United States as a merchant and fur trader. When he died he was the richest man in the country. Some of his descendants were prominent in public affairs and were known for a lifestyle well above the norm here and in Great Britain. The Rhinelanders, a very wealthy family, controlled large tracts of real estate.

5. The parable refers to Matthew 25.

6. Thomas Nulty, the Bishop of Meath in Ireland, irritated the Vatican by his pastoral letter affirming common rights in land.

7. James Redpath (1833–91) was a correspondent, journalist, and editor born in Scotland who championed the causes of abolition and Irish independence. He founded the Lyceum Bureau, which promoted lectures, and was also a committed supporter of George.

## TO WORKINGMEN

1. At the time this article appeared, Henry George was forty-eight years old. He was a seasoned journalist at the helm of *The Standard* and a celebrity. Here he discusses free trade and protection. He attacks the latter in the most disparaging terms, especially for its deleterious affects on the laborer and the enrichment of the few.

2. "Presidential campaign this year" refers to the upcoming 1888 campaign between Democrat Grover Cleveland and Republican Benjamin Harrison. Harrison won.

3. *Protection or Free Trade: An Examination of the Tariff Question, with Especial Regard to the Interests of Labor* was first published in 1886.
4. James G. Blaine (1830–93) was a representative from Maine and speaker of the house, senator, and secretary of state under Garfield and Harrison. Nominated by the Republicans for president in 1884, he lost to Cleveland in a close election. He also organized the first Pan-American Congress.

## "THY KINGDOM COME"

1. After "Moses" this selection is probably Henry George's best-known speech. It was delivered to a standing-room-only audience and was enthusiastically received. This example of his oratory is infused with religiosity. We are the children of God, George declares, and we must live accordingly. We must be self-sufficient and work to earn our keep, but we should have a just opportunity to do so. Although man has subdued Nature we are still plagued with injustice and degradation-not a part of the divine plan. The word of God is not just of the spirit but is also one of social justice, and we should arrange our lives in a manner commensurate with His will. This new order would be based on the taking of revenue from the "value attaching to land" for the benefit of the community and will forestall the monopolistic aggrandizement of the soil.
2. Emmanuel Swedenborg (1688–1772) was a Swedish religious thinker and mystic. Followers founded the Church of the New Jerusalem.
3. Julius Caesar (102?–44 B.C.) landed with his Roman legions in Great Britain in 55 B.C.
4. Hydropathy was also known as "the water cure." The patient undergoes daily baths wrapped in wet sheets for over an hour.
5. "Ferried over the River of Death" refers to the ferryman Charon, who transported dead souls on the River Styx (one of the five rivers of the underworld) to Hades.
6. "Hypothecate": a pledge to a creditor as security.
7. Christians were granted freedom of worship with Constantine's (280–337 A.D.) Edict of Milan in 313. Christianity became the official state religion of the Roman Empire in 380 A.D. by Theodsius the Great (ca. 346–395), who reigned from 379 until his death. He actively suppressed heresies.

## JUSTICE THE OBJECT –TAXATION THE MEANS

1. Henry George was greeted with wild applause before delivering this speech. The audience was not disappointed, for here the former San Franciscan evinces an incredible amount of exuberance and belief in his own cause. A succinct

description of the single tax, its benefits, and the shortcomings of other taxes are presented.

2. "To speak my first word in the cause": George is referring to a speech ("Why Work Is Scarce, Wages Low, and Labor Restless") he gave on March 26, 1878 under the auspices of the Land Reform League of California. One of his biographers, Charles Barker, calls it George's "first success," and his son writes that here "he had made a start to preach that faith which came from his heart's core; and that counted for more than all else to him."

3. "Antipodes" refers to Australia and New Zealand.

4. "The great [S]toic emperor" refers to the Roman Emperor Marcus Aurelius (121–180 A.D.), who ruled from 161 to 180 and is most famous for his Stoic work *Meditations.* Stoicism was a school of philosophy founded by Zeno of Citium (ca. 200 B.C.). The putting aside of emotions was paramount in this philosophy.

5. Gold was discovered in 1859 on this main river of British Columbia.

6. The driving of the golden spike in 1869 at Promontory Point, Utah, symbolized the completion of the transcontinental railroad.

7. It was in 1884 that George's lecture at Oxford caused quite a furor.

8. George first visited Ireland in 1881–82.

9. St. Willegis (d. 1011) was archbishop of Mainz from 975 until his death. He was a noted scholar and the chief regent of Otto III (980–1002), the Holy Roman Emperor from 991 to 996. He was canonized in 1011.

10. For the single tax, see endnote no. 49 on page 240.

11. The Physiocrats were French eighteenth-century economic thinkers, led by François Quesnay (1694–1774). They believed that all wealth originated from the land, therefore taxation *(impôt unique)* should be levied only the land. A laissez-faire approach was essential for a prosperous economy. For an outstanding essay on the Physiocrats, see François Velde's essay "The Physiocrats and the Single Tax," in *An Anthology of Single Land Tax Thought,* ed. Kenneth C. Wenzer, vol. 3 of *The Henry George Centennial Trilogy,* published by the University of Rochester Press.

12. "The metropolis of the civilized world" refers to London.

13. Brooklyn was first settled in 1636 by Dutch and Walloons and became a borough of New York City in 1898.

14. "The boss" and "the citizen": The San Francisco mayor at the time of this speech was Edward Pond (1887–91) and the Republican senator was Leland Stanford (1885–93). Politics in San Francisco and California were plagued by boss rule and corruption.

15. The Statue of Liberty (also called Liberty Enlightening the World) was designed by F. A. Bartholdi (1834–1904) and was presented to the U.S. by the Franco-American Union to commemorate both the American War of Independence and

the French Revolution. It was unveiled in 1886 and declared a national monument in 1924.

16. For greenback, see endnote no. 29 on page 238.

17. The French Convention was the third assembly of deputies chosen by the people after 1789 and which assumed governmental power with the end of the Bourbon monarchy in 1792. Its first resolution was to declare the end of royal power and proclaim the French Republic. The Jacobins became increasingly predominant until the republic was controlled by the dictatorial powers of Robespierre and the Committee of Public Safety. After Robespierre's overthrow the convention disbanded itself in 1795 after issuing a new constitution. Power then devolved upon the directory.

18. "Blanket men" was a term for Indians who remained in a "savage" state.

19. The last time George visited London was in 1889.

20. His last time in Edinburgh was also in 1889.

21. For "Years ago, I said on this platform," see endnote no. 2 on page 253.

## Causes of the Business Depression

1. The fifty-five-year-old Henry George wrote this piece during a time of economic depression characterized by misery and violent labor disturbances. He analyzes the causes of and explains the nature of depressions. The root evil of this problem, he reiterates, is land monopolization. This article appeared the day before he first began his unfinished *The Science of Political Economy.*

2. A severe panic swept the nation in early 1893, which brought about a five-year depression. It was characterized by profound economic stagnation and other problems.

3. The Cherokee Strip was also known as the Cherokee Outlet. It was part of the Cherokee Nation's western territory in Oklahoma and sold to the federal government in 1892 so it could be opened up for settlement.

4. "At the close of the last great depression" probably refers to the major business slump from 1884 to 1886.

5. The poisonous sap of the upas tree is used on arrow tips.

## Peace By Standing Army

1. Henry George, Jr., reports that 10,000 people listened to this speech regarding the Pullman strike of 1894. It displays Henry George's indignation with President Cleveland's callousness, and the use of the military is likened to the feared tsarist Cossacks. George calls for an end to strikes, because they weaken the workers and strengthen the rich. The core of this problem is his oft-

repeated call for an end to land monopolization with its denial of the bounties of God.

2. George was a critic of labor strikes. He thought that although they would gain some short-term benefits, in the long run they would detract from a total reform of society based on the single tax. For more details, see pages 192 to 194 in *An Anthology of Henry George's Thought*, ed. Kenneth C. Wenzer, vol. I of *The Henry George Centennial Trilogy*. George M. Pullman (1831–97) who invented the sleeping car and introduced the dining car, also founded the Pullman Palace Car Company in 1867.

3. (Stephen) Grover Cleveland (1837–1908) served two terms as Democratic president, 1885–89 and 1893–97. In his annual message to Congress in December 1887, among other things, he called for a cautious change in the tariffs on certain manufactured goods and for the admission of some raw materials duty-free. The tariff issue became quite lively during the 1888 election; he lost to Harrison although he garnered more popular votes. During Cleveland's second term, high-tariff measures were included in the Wilson-Gorman Tariff Act; it became law in 1894 without his signature.

4. Although born in Germany, John P. Altgeld (1847–1902) served as governor of Illinois from 1892 to 1896. An ardent champion of human rights, he pardoned the surviving men convicted for the Haymarket Riot (1886) and opposed the use of federal troops at the Pullman strike in 1894.

5. Davis H. Waite (1825–1901) was governor of Colorado from 1893 to 1895, running on the People's Party ticket.

6. "That is the order that reigned in Warsaw" probably refers to the riots there and in other cities that spread across Poland (part of the Russian Empire at this time) from 1863 to 1864. Tsarist troops put it down in a most brutal fashion, and extreme measures of Russification with the enforcement of more restrictions ensued.

7. Eugene V. Debs (1855–1926) was head of the American Railway Union which participated at the Pullman strike, and was imprisoned for violating an injunction. He was arrested in 1918 under the Espionage Act for espousal of pacificism and ran for president five times on the Socialist Party ticket. While in jail he received almost one million votes.

8. Andrew Carnegie (1835–1919) had the consummate rags-to-riches story. Starting off as a poor émigré from Scotland, he founded the Carnegie Steel Company. By 1900 it produced one-quarter of the steel in the United States. He also engaged in a number of philanthropic activitities.

9. Richard Olney (1835–1917) was the U.S. attorney general from 1893 to 1895 who advocated sending federal troops to Pullman, Illinois. He was also secretary of state from 1895 to 1897 during Cleveland's administration.

10. Beginning in 1887, the American Sugar Refining Company (the "sugar trust"), owned by the Havemeyer family, made a number of successful attempts to monopolize this product, and by 1891 it controlled ninety-five percent of American sugar production. There were also collusive arrangements with customs officials. In the famous E. C. Knight decision of the Supreme Court (1895), it was declared that this monopoly could not be broken up under the Sherman Antitrust Act for it did not hinder interstate commerce. This decision served as a signal to business that there would be no effective federal interference.